Junior Certificate
Higher Level Paper 2

Mathematics

Michelle Kelly and Gillian Russell

The Educational Company of Ireland

Edco

Published 2017

The Educational Company of Ireland
Ballymount Road
Walkinstown
Dublin 12
www.edco.ie
A member of the Smurfit Kappa Group plc

ISBN: 978-1-84536-758-9

Book design: Liz White Designs

Cover design: Identikit

Layout: Compuscript

Editor: Stephen Cashmore

Illustrations: Compuscript, Shutterstock

Proofreaders: Stephen Cashmore, Eric Pradel

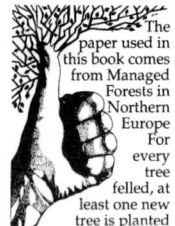

The paper used in this book comes from Managed Forests in Northern Europe For every tree felled, at least one new tree is planted

While every care has been taken to trace and acknowledge copyright, the publishers tender their apologies for any accidental infringement where copyright has proved untraceable. They would be pleased to come to a suitable arrangement with the rightful owner in each case.

Web references in this book are intended as a guide for teachers. At the time of going to press, all web addresses were active and contained information relevant to the topics in this book. However, The Educational Company of Ireland and the authors do not accept responsibility for the views or information contained on these websites. Content and addresses may change beyond our control and students should be supervised when investigating websites.

01J20

CONTENTS

Introduction

This book covers the material required for Paper 2 of the Junior Certificate Higher Level Mathematics examination.

Each chapter contains the essential key information required for that given topic. There are detailed revision notes and well explained examples throughout each chapter. Along with this, we provide a comprehensive Exercise section complete with detailed Solutions in each chapter. These questions range from simple to exam-style questions.

It is extremely important to note that any topic covered on the Junior Certificate syllabus can appear on either Paper 1 or Paper 2 of the exam. This is why we have, where appropriate, indicated any links between chapters within the same book, but also chapters which are linked across both books.

Study tips

- When studying maths, we need to just roll up our sleeves and actually solve some maths problems. Practise, practise, practise!

- After you make a mistake, which we all do, it is important to review and understand where you went wrong in the problem. This is why we have included complete detailed solutions to all our exercises.

- *Understanding* the mathematical process is more important than memorising the process.

- Getting the most from your study sessions will require concentration. This is why we suggest a distraction-free zone.

- We recommend that you create a bank of notes with key points such as terminology, definitions and the basic concepts. You will see these throughout our chapters in coloured boxes.

- It is important to study all topics – not just the topics you like.

We would like to wish you every success in your study of Mathematics.

Michelle Kelly & Gillian Russell

Fundamental Principles of Counting

1

Learning objectives

In this chapter you will learn:

- About the key terminology associated with the fundamental principles of counting
- How to apply the fundamental principles of counting
- How to list all possible outcomes of an experiment
- How to list outcomes of experiments using a sample space.

Key terminology and information

Key Terminology

Word	Meaning
Trial	An experiment involving probability or chance which gives a set of repeatable outcomes. For example, rolling a die, tossing a coin, selecting one card from a deck of cards, etc.
Outcome	The result of a single trial of an experiment. For example, when rolling a die the possible outcomes are: 1, 2, 3, 4, 5, 6.
Sample space	The set of all the possible outcomes of a trial. A sample space can be represented using a list of outcomes, a two-way table or a tree diagram.
Event	A subset of the sample space.
Probability	The measure of how likely an event is to happen.
Fundamental principle of counting	There are two fundamental principles of counting, as described below.

Fundamental principles of counting

Example

David wishes to buy a new car. He wishes to buy an SUV or saloon car body shape. He can choose between a diesel or petrol model. He can choose either black or silver.

(a) How many different choices of car does David have?

(b) List all the possible outcomes.

Solution

(a) As David needs to choose a car body shape **and** a fuel type **and** a colour, we use the fundamental principle of counting 1 rule.

Number of different choices of car

= (car body shape) **and** (fuel type) **and** (colour)

= 2 × 2 × 2

= 8

> **Remember**
>
> The first fundamental principle of counting states that 'and' means 'multiply'.

(b) The 8 possible outcomes are:

SUV, Diesel and Black

SUV, Diesel and Silver

Saloon, Diesel and Black

Saloon, Diesel and Silver

SUV, Petrol and Black

SUV, Petrol and Silver

Saloon, Petrol and Black

Saloon, Petrol and Silver

Example

Eileen is going on holiday. She goes into a shop to buy a pair of shorts **or** a dress. She likes four pairs of shorts and three dresses. How many possible outcomes are there for the item of clothing she buys?

Solution

As Eileen needs to buy a pair of shorts **or** a dress, we use the fundamental principle of counting 2 rule.

Total number of outcomes
= (number of pairs of shorts) **or** (number of dresses)

$= 4 + 3$

$= 7$

Remember

The second fundamental principle of counting states that '**or**' means '**add**'.

Example

A restaurant offers a set menu for special events. The menu offers three starters, six main courses, seven desserts and a choice of coffee or tea. In how many different ways can you order a four course meal?

Solution

As with the first example, remember that '**and**' means '**multiply**'.

So the number of different meal options
= (starters) **and** (mains) **and** (desserts) **and** (drinks)

$= 3 \times 6 \times 7 \times 2$

$= 252$

Example

A coin is tossed **and** a die is rolled.

(a) How many outcomes are possible?

(b) List all the possible outcomes.

Solution

(a) Let n = the number of possible outcomes when a coin is tossed.

∴ $n = 2$

Let m = the number of possible outcomes when a die is rolled.

∴ $m = 6$

Using the first fundamental principle of counting the number of possible outcomes = $n \times m$

So the number of possible outcomes

= (number of coin outcomes) **and** (number of die outcomes)

= (number of coin outcomes) × (number of die outcomes)

= 6×2

= 12

(b) The three methods which can be used to list the outcomes are:

1 making a straightforward list,

2 drawing up a two-way table, or

3 drawing a tree diagram.

Method 1: List of outcomes (sample space).

A coin has two possible outcomes = {Head, Tail} = {H, T}

A die has six possible outcomes = {1, 2, 3, 4, 5, 6}

The possible outcomes can be written in pairs as:

(H, 1), (T, 1), (H, 2), (T, 2), (H, 3), (T, 3), (H, 4), (T, 4), (H, 5), (T, 5), (H, 6), (T, 6).

Method 2: A two-way table (sample space).

One set of outcomes is listed across the top of a table, and the other set down the side. Then each box in the table represents one of the possible pairs of outcomes.

		Die					
		1	2	3	4	5	6
Coin	H	(H, 1)	(H, 2)	(H, 3)	(H, 4)	(H, 5)	(H, 6)
	T	(T, 1)	(T, 2)	(T, 3)	(T, 4)	(T, 5)	(T, 6)

Method 3: A tree diagram (sample space).

From a starting point, one set of outcomes branches out, and then the second set of outcomes branches out from each of the first branches.

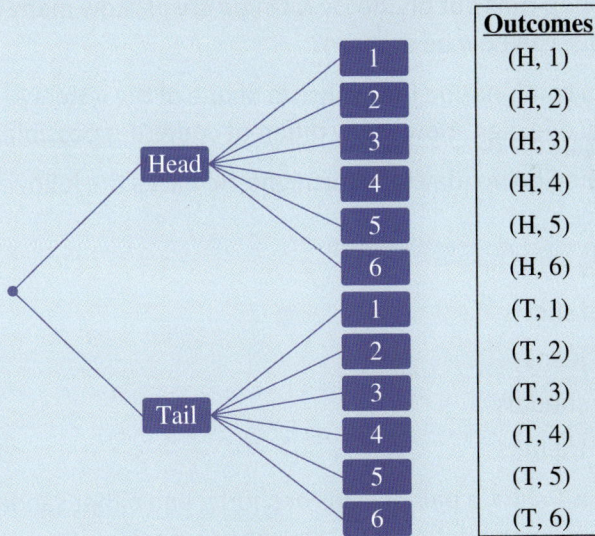

Outcomes
(H, 1)
(H, 2)
(H, 3)
(H, 4)
(H, 5)
(H, 6)
(T, 1)
(T, 2)
(T, 3)
(T, 4)
(T, 5)
(T, 6)

Exercise

Q1 Jack goes into an electrical shop to buy either a laptop or a smartphone. The shop has four laptops and three smartphones that he likes. How many possible purchase options does Jack have?

Q2 A local shop offers the 'Student Lunch Special' shown in the table.

Student Lunch Special		
Any sandwich, packet of crisps and drink for €4		
Sandwich	**Crisps**	**Drink**
Ham	Salt & Vinegar	Water
Chicken	Cheese & Onion	Cola
Tuna	Ready Salted	Orange
Cheese		
Egg Mayonnaise		

(a) Calculate the number of different 'Lunch Specials' that can be ordered.

(b) If the shop runs out of Cheese & Onion crisps, how many 'Lunch Specials' can now be ordered?

Q3 A code for a combination lock consists of one of the letters A, B, C or D followed by one digit. How many different codes are possible?

Q4 Conor is going on holiday for a fortnight. He packs the following items in his suitcase:

5 T-shirts

4 pairs of shorts

1 pair of jeans

1 pair of sandals

1 pair of trainers

If he wears a T-shirt, a pair of jeans or shorts, and either sandals or trainers each day, how many different outfits can he wear?

Q5 Joanne prints off her holiday photographs on her home printer. She can choose from the print options shown in the table.

Size	Colour	Quality	Finish
10 × 15 cm	Black and white	Best	Matt
13 × 18 cm	Colour	Better	Glossy
A4		Draft	

(a) In how many different ways can she print off her photographs?

(b) Joanne decides that she **does not** want her photos printed in draft quality or with a matt finish. How many ways can she now print off her photos?

Q6 A game consists of spinning a fair spinner and tossing a coin.

Spinner

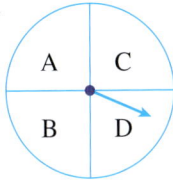

(a) How many possible outcomes are there?

(b) List all possible outcomes of the game using:

   (i) the list method

   (ii) a two-way table

   (iii) a tree diagram.

(SEC 2012)

Q7 A game consists of spinning a fair spinner and rolling a die.

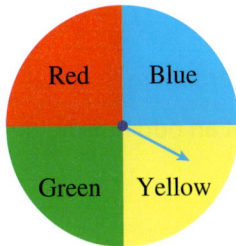

(a) How many possible outcomes are there?

(b) List all possible outcomes of the game using:

   (i) the list method

   (ii) a two-way table.

(SEC 2014)

Q8 A football strip consists of a shirt, shorts and socks. Aspen United has two shirts, one blue and one green, from which to select. They can also select from three different colours of shorts and five different colours of socks, including red in each case.

(a) Calculate how many different strips Aspen United can have.

(b) Willow Celtic plays in an all-red strip. When Aspen United plays Willow Celtic, Aspen United are not allowed to use their red shorts or their red socks. Calculate how many different strips Aspen United can have when they play Willow Celtic.

(SEC 2013)

Q9 Jack rolls a fair die and spins a fair spinner as shown.

Die   Spinner

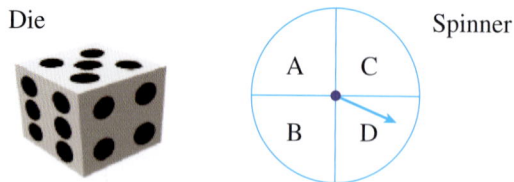

(a) Complete the table below showing all possible outcomes.

		Spinner			
		A	B	C	D
Die	1	(1, A)			
	2				
	3				
	4				
	5				
	6				(6, D)

(b) How many possible outcomes are there?

(c) How many outcomes consist of an odd number and B?

(SEC 2012)

Solutions

Q1 As 'or' is in the question we use the fundamental principle of counting 2 rule.

Total number of outcomes

= (number of laptops) **or** (number of smartphones)

= 4 + 3

= 7

Q2 (a) Number of possible different 'Lunch Specials'

= (sandwich choices) **and** (crisp choices) **and** (drink choices)

= (no. of sandwich choices) × (no. of crisp choices) × (no. of drink choices)

= 5 × 3 × 3

= 45

(b) Number of possible different 'Lunch Specials' without Cheese and Onion crisps

= (sandwich choices) **and** (crisp choices – Cheese and Onion) **and** (drink choices)

= (no. of sandwich choices) × (no. of crisp choices – 1) × (no. of drink choices)

= 5 × 2 × 3

= 30

Remember

Don't forget: '**or**' means '**add**', and '**and**' means '**multiply**'.

Q3 The combination lock can use the following letters and numbers:

Letters = {A, B, C, D}   Digits = {0, 1, 2, 3, 4, 5, 6, 7, 8, 9}

Number of letters = 4   Number of digits = 10

So the number of possible codes for the combination lock

= (letter choices) **and** (digit choices)

= (number of letter choices) × (number of digit choices)

= 4 × 10

= 40

Q4 Number of possible outfits Conor can wear on holiday

= (T-shirts) **and** (shorts or jeans) **and** (sandals or trainers)

= (no. of T-shirts) × (no. of shorts or jeans) × (no. of sandals or trainers)

= 5 × (4 + 1) × 2

= 5 × 5 × 2

= 50

Q5 (a) Number of possible ways Joanne can print off her holiday photographs

= (size choices) **and** (colour choices) **and** (quality choices) **and** (finish choices)

= (number of size choices) × (number of colour choices) × (number of quality choices) × (number of finish choices)

= 3 × 2 × 3 × 2

= 36

(b) Number of possible ways Joanne can print off her holiday photographs if she **does not** want draft quality or a matt finish

= (size choices) **and** (colour choices) **and** (quality choices – draft) **and** (finish choices – matt)

= (number of size choices) × (number of colour choices) × (number of quality choices – 1) × (number of finish choices – 1)

= 3 × 2 × 2 × 1

= 12

Q6 (a) The options for the spinner = {A, B, C, D}   The options for the coin = {H, T}

Number of spinner options = 4   Number of coin options = 2

Number of possible outcomes for the game

= (spinner options) **and** (coin options)

= 4 × 2

= 8

(b) (i) Method 1

List of outcomes:

(H, A), (H, B), (H, C), (H, D)

(T, A), (T, B), (T, C), (T, D)

(ii) Method 2

Using a two-way table:

		Spinner			
		A	B	C	D
Coin	H	(H, A)	(H, B)	(H, C)	(H, D)
	T	(T, A)	(T, B)	(T, C)	(T, D)

(iii) Method 3

Using a tree diagram:

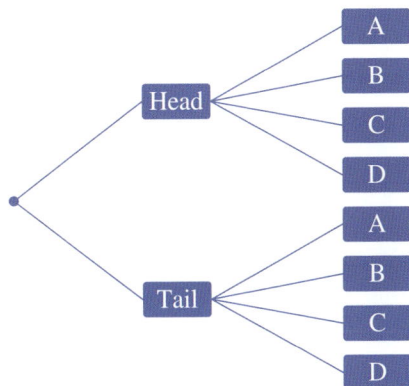

Q7 (a) Spinner options = {Red, Blue, Yellow, Green}   Die options = {1, 2, 3, 4, 5, 6}

Number of spinner options = 4   Number of die options = 6

Number of possible outcomes for the game

= (spinner options) **and** (die options)

= 4 × 6

= 24

(b) (i) Method 1

List of outcomes:

(Red, 1), (Red, 2), (Red, 3), (Red, 4), (Red, 5), (Red, 6)

(Blue, 1), (Blue, 2), (Blue, 3), (Blue, 4), (Blue, 5), (Blue, 6)

(Yellow, 1), (Yellow, 2), (Yellow, 3), (Yellow, 4), (Yellow, 5), (Yellow, 6)

(Green, 1), (Green, 2), (Green, 3), (Green, 4), (Green, 5), (Green, 6)

(ii) Method 2

Using a two-way table:

		Die					
		1	2	3	4	5	6
Spinner	Red	(Red, 1)	(Red, 2)	(Red, 3)	(Red, 4)	(Red, 5)	(Red, 6)
	Blue	(Blue, 1)	(Blue, 2)	(Blue, 3)	(Blue, 4)	(Blue, 5)	(Blue, 6)
	Yellow	(Yellow, 1)	(Yellow, 2)	(Yellow, 3)	(Yellow, 4)	(Yellow, 5)	(Yellow, 6)
	Green	(Green, 1)	(Green, 2)	(Green, 3)	(Green, 4)	(Green, 5)	(Green, 6)

Q8 (a) Number of different football strips

= (number of shirts) **and** (number of shorts) **and** (number of pairs of socks)

= 2 × 3 × 5

= 30 possible strips

(b) Number of different football strips

= (shirts) **and** (shorts – red shorts) **and** (pairs of socks – red socks)

= 2 × 2 × 4

= 16 possible strips

Q9 (a)

		Spinner			
		A	B	C	D
Die	1	(1, A)	(1, B)	(1, C)	(1, D)
	2	(2, A)	(2, B)	(2, C)	(2, D)
	3	(3, A)	(3, B)	(3, C)	(3, D)
	4	(4, A)	(4, B)	(4, C)	(4, D)
	5	(5, A)	(5, B)	(5, C)	(5, D)
	6	(6, A)	(6, B)	(6, C)	(6, D)

(b) Number of possible outcomes = (die options) **and** (spinner options)

= 6 × 4

= 24

(c) Outcomes consisting of an odd number and B are (1, B) and (3, B) and (5, B). So, the number of outcomes containing an odd number and B = 3.

Probability

2

Learning objectives

In this chapter you will learn about:

- Key terminology and information associated with probability
- The probability scale
- How to calculate probabilities for equally likely outcomes
- Relative frequency/experimental probability
- Using relative frequency to predict expected frequency
- Relative frequency versus theoretical probability
- Using two-way tables, tree diagrams and Venn diagrams to find probability.

Key terminology and information

Key Terminology

Word	Meaning
Trial	An **experiment** involving probability or chance which gives a set of repeatable outcomes. For example, rolling a die, tossing a coin, selecting one card from a deck of cards, etc.
Outcome	The result of a single trial of an experiment. For example, when rolling a die, the possible outcomes are: 1, 2, 3, 4, 5, 6.
Sample space	The set of all the possible outcomes of a trial. A **sample space** can be represented using a list of outcomes, a two-way table, a tree diagram or a Venn diagram.
Event (E)	A subset of the sample space. It is a **specific outcome**.

Probability $P(E)$	The chance or likelihood that an event will happen. $$P(E) = \frac{\text{number of favourable outcomes}}{\text{total number of possible outcomes}}$$
Fair	Each outcome has an equal chance of occurring. For example, a fair die is one where each number has an equal chance of occurring.
Biased	Each outcome does not have an equal chance of occurring.
Certain	100% chance of an event happening: $P(E) = 1$.
Impossible	0% chance of an event happening: $P(E) = 0$.
Evens 50/50	50% chance of an event happening: $P(E) = 0.5$ or 50% or $\frac{1}{2}$.
Likely	Greater than 50% chance of an event happening: $P(E) > 0.5$
Unlikely	Less than 50% chance of an event happenning: $P(E) < 0.5$
The probability scale	The **probability scale** goes from 0 to 1. **The Probability Scale** 0 1 Probability can be written as a fraction, decimal or percentage.
Favourable outcome	To calculate the probability of a particular event occurring.
Relative frequency	The likelihood of an event happening from carrying out an experiment or trial and recording the results. $$\text{Relative frequency} = \frac{\text{number of favourable outcomes (frequency)}}{\text{total number of trials}}$$ $$\text{Relative frequency} = \frac{\text{total number of times an event occurs}}{\text{total number of times an experiment is carried out}}$$ Note: Increasing the number of trials of an experiment leads to better estimates of probability. When the number of trials is big enough the relative frequency tends to the theoretical probability.
Expected frequency	**Expected frequency** = relative frequency × the number of trials
Theoretical probability	The relative frequency approaches the **theoretical probability** when there are a very large number of trials. $$\text{Theoretical probability} = \frac{\text{number of favourable outcomes that exist}}{\text{total number of possible outcomes}},$$ provided that all outcomes are equally likely to happen.

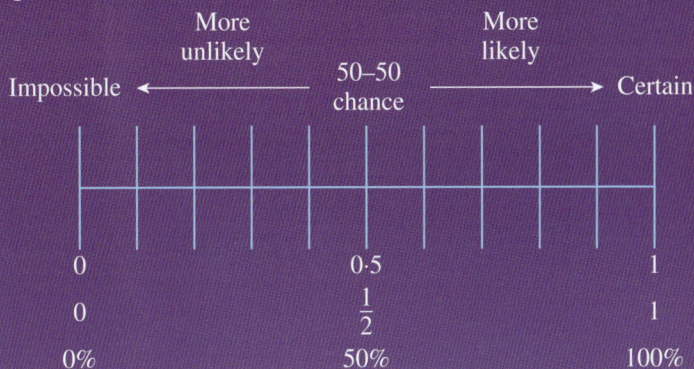

Example

From the probability scale shown, choose the words which best describe the probability of each of the statements below:

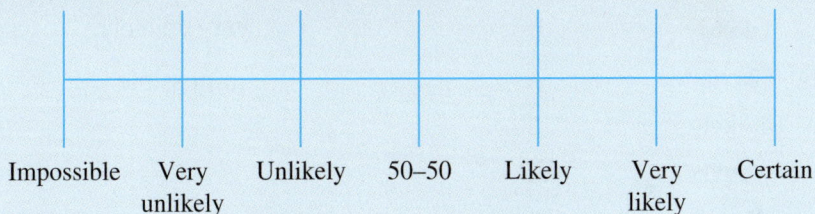

Impossible	Very unlikely	Unlikely	50–50	Likely	Very likely	Certain

(a) A pregnant woman will give birth to a baby boy.

(b) A rolled die will show a 6.

(c) It will rain in Ireland tomorrow.

(d) A student will do their Mathematics homework.

(e) Night will follow day.

(f) You are able to turn back time.

(g) You will pick a spade from a standard deck of cards.

Solution

(a) A woman can give birth to a baby boy or girl, so there is a **50–50 chance** that she will give birth to a baby boy.

(b) As there are six numbers on a die: 1, 2, 3, 4, 5 and 6, there is a 1 in 6 chance that the die will show a 6. So this event is possible, but **very unlikely**.

(c) There are approximately 225 days of rain in the wettest part of Ireland per year (Valencia Island). So there is a $\frac{225}{365}$ chance of rain in Ireland tomorrow. So, this event is **likely** to happen.

(d) A student is **very likely** to do their Mathematics homework.

(e) Night always follows day. So, this event is **certain** to happen.

(f) It is not possible to turn back time. So, this event is **impossible**.

(g) As there are 13 spades in a deck of cards, there is a $\frac{13}{52} = \frac{1}{4}$ chance of picking a spade. So this event is **unlikely** to happen.

Example

Match the letter with the probability.

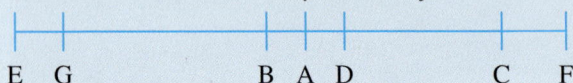

Probability	Letter
Certain	
Extremely likely	
Likely	
50–50 chance	
Unlikely	
Very unlikely	
Impossible	

Solution

Probability	Letter
Certain	F
Extremely likely	C
Likely	D
50–50 chance	A
Unlikely	B
Very unlikely	G
Impossible	E

How to calculate probabilities for equally likely outcomes

Points to note

For equally likely outcomes:

Probability of an event, $P(E) = \dfrac{\text{number of favourable outcomes}}{\text{total number of possible outcomes}}$

Probability of an event not happening = 1 − probability of an event happening

It is important to remember to always write your answer in its simplest form, for example: $\dfrac{12}{15} = \dfrac{4}{5}$.

Example

A pencil case contains four red pens, six black pens and
two blue pens. A pen is selected at random from the pencil case.

(a) What is the probability of selecting a blue pen?

(b) What is the probability of selecting a red pen?

(c) What is the probability of not selecting a red pen?

Solution

(a) $P(\text{blue pen}) = \dfrac{\text{number of favourable outomes}}{\text{number of possible outcomes}} = \dfrac{\text{number of blue pens}}{\text{total number of pens}} = \dfrac{2}{12} = \dfrac{1}{6}$

(b) $P(\text{red pen}) = \dfrac{\text{number of red pens}}{\text{total number of pens}} = \dfrac{4}{12} = \dfrac{1}{3}$

(c) **Method 1**

$P(\text{not a red pen}) = \dfrac{\text{number of pens which are not red}}{\text{total number of pens}} = \dfrac{8}{12} = \dfrac{2}{3}$

Method 2

$P(\text{not a red pen}) = 1 - P(\text{red pen}) = 1 - \dfrac{1}{3} = \dfrac{2}{3}$

Relative frequency (experimental probability)

Points to note

- **Relative frequency** is also known as **experimental probability** as it is found from carrying out an experiment.

- Relative frequency or experimental probability

$$= \frac{\text{number of favourable outcomes (frequency)}}{\text{total number of trials}}$$

$$= \frac{\text{total number of times an event occurs}}{\text{total number of times an experiment is carried out}}$$

- Relative frequency can give an estimate of the actual probability. The more trials, the more accurate it will be.

Example

A bag contains red discs, blue discs and white discs. In an experiment, each student in a class of 24 takes out a disc, records the colour and replaces it. This is repeated ten times. The results from the class are recorded in the table below.

Colour	Red	Blue	White	Total
Frequency	123	78	39	
Relative frequency				
% of total (relative frequency × 100)				

(a) In your opinion, why is the number of red discs selected greater than the number of blue or white discs?

(b) Complete the table above.

(c) Use the results from the table to estimate the probability of getting each colour when a disc is taken from the bag, and record your answers in the table below.

Colour	Red	Blue	White	Total
Probability				

(d) What do you notice about the sum of the relative frequencies?

Solution

(a) It is likely that there are more red discs in the bag than blue or white. This would explain why the red discs were selected more often than the others.

(b)

Colour	Red	Blue	White	Total
Frequency	123	78	39	240
Relative frequency	$\frac{123}{240} = 0.5125$	$\frac{78}{240} = 0.325$	$\frac{39}{240} = 0.1625$	1
% of total (relative frequency × 100)	51·25	32·5	16·25	100

(c)

Colour	Red	Blue	White	Total
Probability	0·5125	0·325	0·1625	1

(d) The sum of the relative frequencies is 1.

(SEC 2014)

Example

Sean, Sarah and Tom toss a Euro coin. Sean threw 109 heads from 200 tosses. Sarah threw 245 heads from 400 tosses. Tom threw 348 heads from 600 tosses. Sean, Sarah and Tom think that the coin may be biased.

(a) Complete the table below.

Number of heads thrown	Sean	Sarah	Tom
Frequency	109	245	348
Number of trials	200		
Relative frequency			
% of total (relative frequency × 100)			

(b) What do you understand the word 'biased' to mean?

(c) Give a reason why they think that the coin may be biased.

Solution

(a)

Number of heads thrown	Sean	Sarah	Tom
Frequency	109	245	348
Number of trials	200	400	600
Relative frequency	$\frac{109}{200} = 0.545$	$\frac{245}{400} = 0.6125$	$\frac{348}{600} = 0.58$
% of total (relative frequency × 100)	54·5	61·25	58

(b) Bias occurs when each outcome does not have an equal chance of occuring.

(c) The coin may be biased as each player tosses more than 50% heads.

Using relative frequency to predict expected frequency

> **Points to note**
>
> **Expected frequency** = relative frequency × the number of trials
>
> Expected frequency is used to predict the frequency of an event happening for larger numbers of trials, when the relative frequency can be calculated. It is used in many situations, such as manufacturing and sporting events.

Example

A soccer player has scored in 12 of the last 15 'on target shots' he has taken. How many of the next 50 'on target shots' would he expect to score?

Solution

Relative frequency of scoring $= \dfrac{12}{15} = \dfrac{4}{5}$

To find out how many 'on target shots' he would expect to score from the next 50 'on target shots', we need to calculate the expected frequency.

Expected frequency = relative frequency × the number of trials

$$= \dfrac{4}{5} \times 50$$

$$= 40$$

He should score in 40 of his next 50 'on target shots'.

Relative frequency versus theoretical probability

Points to note

- The relative frequency approaches the **theoretical probability** when there are a very large number of trials.
- Theoretical probability $= \dfrac{\text{number of favourable outcomes that exist}}{\text{total number of possible outcomes}}$, provided all outcomes are equally likely

Example

A fair die is rolled 300 times. It lands on a 4 a total of 57 times.

(a) Calculate the relative frequency of rolling a 4.

(b) How many times would you expect this die to land on a 4, if the die were rolled 6000 times?

(c) What is the theoretical probability of a 4 being rolled?

(d) In your opinion, why are the relative frequency and the theoretical probability answers different?

(e) What could be changed to produce a relative frequency that is closer to the theoretical probability?

Solution

(a) Relative frequency of rolling a $4 = \dfrac{57}{300} = 0.19$

(b) Expected frequency = relative frequency × the number of trials

$$= 0.19 \times 6000$$

$$= 1140$$

The die should land on a 4 a total of 1140 times from 6000 trials.

(c) Theoretical probability $= \dfrac{\text{number of favourable outcomes that exist}}{\text{total number of possible outcomes}}$, so the theoretical probability of a 4 being rolled $= \dfrac{1}{6} = 0.1\dot{6}$.

(d) The relative frequency and the theoretical probability answers are different because relative frequency is based on experimental data. In this example the number of trials was small.

(e) Recall that the relative frequency approaches the theoretical probability when there are a very large number of trials. So to produce a relative frequency that is closer to the theoretical probability the number of trials carried out would need to be increased.

The use of two-way tables, tree diagrams and Venn diagrams to find probability

Remember

Venn diagrams and probability have been covered briefly in Revise Wise 1, Chapter 12, Sets. Two-way tables and tree diagrams have been covered in Revise Wise 2, Chapter 1, Fundamental Principles of Counting.

Example

A woman gave birth to non-identical twins. Assume that each child born has an equal chance of being either a boy or a girl.

(a) List all the possible outcomes to represent this situation.

(b) What is the probability that:

    (i) both children are boys?

    (ii) both children are girls?

    (iii) one child is a boy and the other is a girl?

Solution

(a) **Method 1**: List of outcomes

The possible outcomes can be written in pairs as:

(Boy, Boy), (Boy, Girl), (Girl, Boy) or (Girl, Girl).

Method 2: A two-way table

		2nd child	
		Boy	**Girl**
1st child	**Boy**	(Boy, Boy)	(Boy, Girl)
	Girl	(Girl, Boy)	(Girl, Girl)

Method 3: A tree diagram

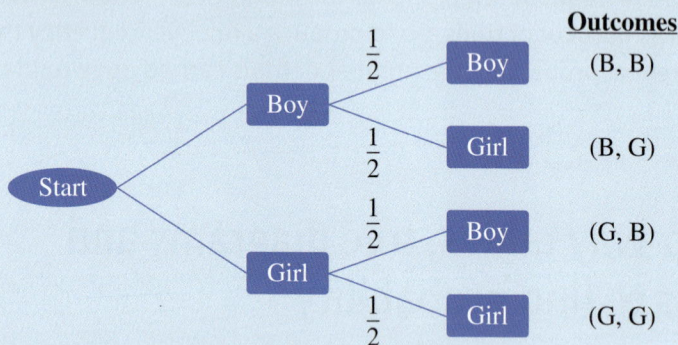

Outcomes

Boy → $\frac{1}{2}$ → Boy → (B, B)

$\frac{1}{2}$ → Girl → (B, G)

Girl → $\frac{1}{2}$ → Boy → (G, B)

$\frac{1}{2}$ → Girl → (G, G)

(b) (i) $P\,(\text{Boy and Boy}) = P(B \times B) = \dfrac{1}{2} \times \dfrac{1}{2} = \dfrac{1}{4}$

(ii) $P\,(\text{Girl and Girl}) = P(G \times G) = \dfrac{1}{2} \times \dfrac{1}{2} = \dfrac{1}{4}$

(iii) $P\,(\text{1 Boy and 1 Girl}) = \dfrac{2}{4} = \dfrac{1}{2}$

Remember

Note: Please revise Chapter 12 of *Revise Wise Mathematics for Junior Certificate Higher Level Paper 1* on sets and operations of sets – intersection, union, complement and set difference – before tackling this section!

Example

A 2-set problem

Nicola surveyed 175 transition year students to find which social media app they use. The results were as follows:

- 123 said they used Snapchat and Instagram
- 21 said they used Snapchat only
- 9 said they used Instagram only

(a) Represent the information on a Venn diagram.

(b) What is the probability that a randomly selected student uses neither app?

(c) What is the probability that a randomly selected student uses Snapchat only?

(d) What is the probability that a randomly selected student uses both social media apps?

Solution

(a)

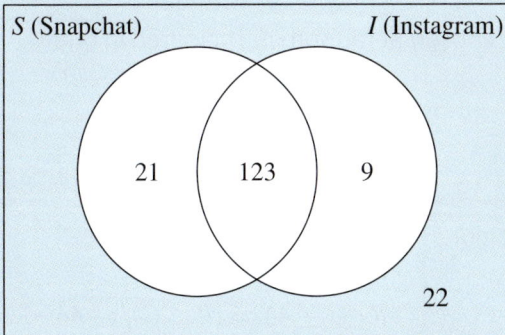

Venn diagram showing Snapchat and Instagram users

(b)

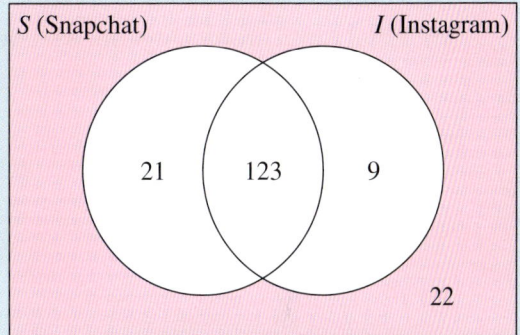

Probability (student uses neither app)

$$= P(S \cup I)' = \frac{22}{175}$$

(c)

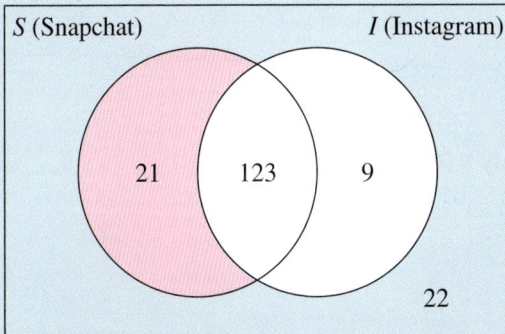

Probability (student uses snapchat only)

$$= P(S/I) = \frac{21}{175}$$

(d)

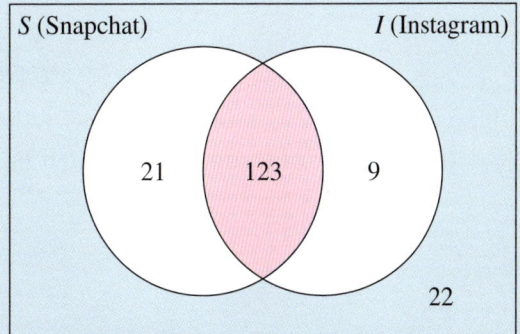

Probability (student uses both apps)

$$= P(S \cap I) = \frac{123}{175}$$

Example

A 3-set problem

A survey of the leisure activities of 90 students was carried out, and the the results were as follows:

- 60 students watch TV (T)
- 60 students read (R)
- 70 students go to the cinema (C)
- 26 students watch TV, read and go to the cinema
- 20 students watch TV and go to the cinema, but do not read
- 44 students read and go to the cinema
- 36 students read and watch TV

(a) Represent the information on a Venn diagram.

(b) Calculate how many students watch TV only.

(c) What is the probability of a student going to the cinema or reading?

(d) What is the probability that a student chosen at random participated in one activity only?

Solution

(a)

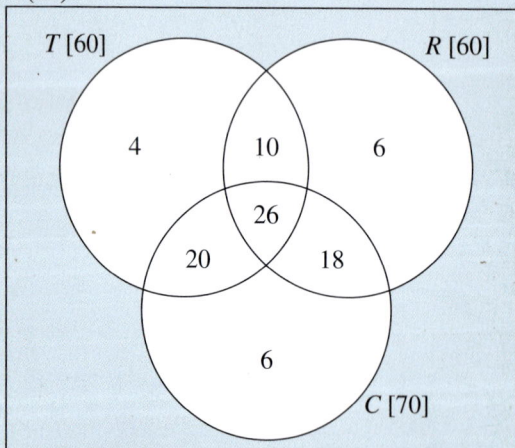

$\#S = 90$, $\#T = 60$, $\#R = 60$ and $\#C = 70$

$\#T \cap R \cap C = x = 26$

$\#(T \cap C)/R = 20$

$\#R \cap C = 44 \Rightarrow (R \cap C)/x = 44 - 26 = 18$

$\#R \cap T = 36 \Rightarrow (R \cap T)/x = 36 - 26 = 10$

$\#T$ only $= 60 - 10 - 26 - 20 = 60 - 56 = 4$

$\#C$ only $= 70 - 20 - 26 - 18 = 70 - 64 = 6$

$\#R$ only $= 60 - 10 - 26 - 18 = 60 - 54 = 6$

$\#(T \cup R \cup C)' = 90 - 4 - 10 - 26 - 20 - 6 - 18$

$= 90 - 90 = 0$

(b) Number of students that watch TV only $= 60 - 20 - 26 - 10 = 4$

(c) S (90)

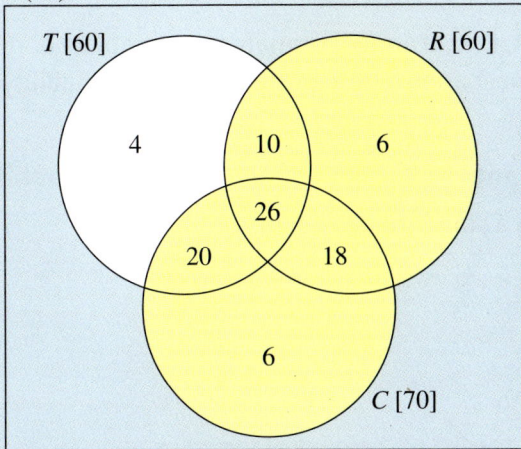

Probability (student goes to the cinema or reads)

$$= P(C \cup R) = \frac{90}{90} - \frac{4}{90} = \frac{86}{90} = \frac{43}{45}$$

(d) S (90)

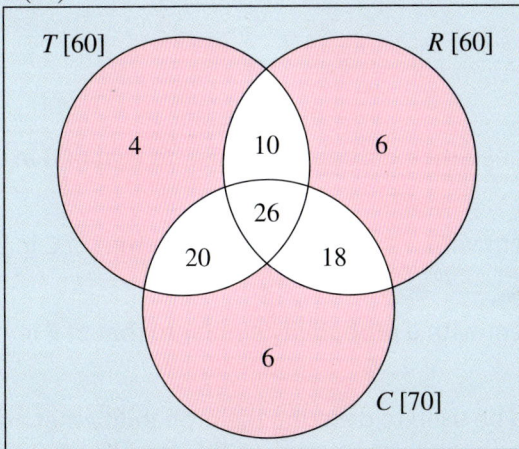

Probability (student partcipated in one activity only)

$$= \frac{4 + 6 + 6}{90} = \frac{16}{90} = \frac{8}{45}$$

Exercise

Q1 (a) For each of the events A, B, C, D and E, estimate its probability and place the letter at the most appropriate position on the probability scale.

Event	Probability
A card is picked at random from a standard deck of playing cards.	
A = Ace of hearts is picked.	
A fair coin is tossed.	
B = a tail is the outcome for the toss.	
A day is chosen at random from the list of the days of the week.	
C = the day contains the letter **a**.	
A month is chosen at random from the list of months of the year.	
D = the month contains the letter **r**.	
A letter is picked at random from the word ENORMOUS.	
E = the letter is **W**.	

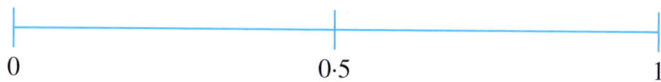

```
├──────────────────────┼──────────────────────┤
0                     0·5                      1
```

(b) Write down another event with a probability similar to that of B in the scale above.

(c) Write down another event with a probability similar to that of C in the scale above.

(d) Write down another event with a probability similar to that of E in the scale above.

Q2 (a) The following terms can be used to describe the probability that an event happens: Likely, Certain, Unlikely, Impossible, 50:50.

For each event in the table below, use one of these terms to describe the probability that it happens.

Event	Probability
When a fair coin is tossed you get a head.	
If you buy a lottery ticket for next Saturday's draw, you will win the Jackpot.	
The 1st of January will be New Year's Day.	

(b) Four events, A, B, C and D, are listed below.

A: You pick a red ball from a bag containing three black and seven red balls.

B: You get a natural number less than 7 when you roll a regular six-sided die.

C: You pick a red card from a standard deck of playing cards.

D: You pick a yellow ball from a bag containing four red balls and two white balls.

Write each of the letters A, B, C and D into the correct box on the probability scale below, to show the probability of each event.

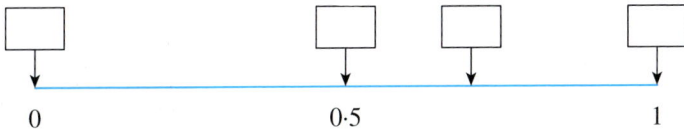

0   0·5   1

(SEC 2014)

Q3 Shirts in a clothes shop come in the following four sizes: Small (S), Medium (M), Large (L) and Extra Large (XL). Kristina makes the following list, showing the size of each of the shirts in the shop.

S	S	L	M	L	L	XL	M	XL
L	L	S	M	M	M	M	L	M

(a) Write down the total number of shirts in the shop.

(b) Use Kristina's list to fill in the frequency table below.

Shirt size	S	M	L	XL
Frequency				

Kristina picks one shirt at random.

(c) Find the probability that it is a large (L) shirt.

Kristina puts one of the large (L) shirts on display. She then picks another shirt at random from those that are left.

(d) Find the probability that it is a small (S) shirt.

(SEC 2016)

Q4 The songs on Gavin's phone are shown in the table below.

Singer	Number of songs
Usher	
Pharrell	15
Ed Sheeran	4
Hozier	3

Gavin has 30 songs on his phone, in total.

(a) Find how many songs by Usher are on Gavin's phone.

Gavin plays a song at random on his phone.

(b) Find the probability that this song is by Hozier.

(c) Find the probability that this song is by Ed Sheeran or Pharrell.

Gavin plays a song by Ed Sheeran, and then plays a song by Hozier.

(d) In how many different ways can he do this? Remember that he has four songs by Ed Sheeran and three songs by Hozier.

(SEC 2015)

Q5 A hurling match is played between Team A and Team B. A player on Team A, Fiachra, has the ball and attempts to score. The probability of Fiachra scoring a point is 0·6 and the probability of him scoring a goal is 0·1.

(a) Is Fiachra more likely to score a point or a goal?

(b) What is the probability that Fiachra will not score a point in this attempt?

A player on Team B, Peadar, has the ball and attempts to score. The probability of Peadar scoring a point is 0·7 and the probability of him scoring a goal is 0·2.

(c) Peadar is more likely to score than Fiachra. Give a reason why this is true.

(d) A spectator says, 'Peadar will always score more than Fiachra in a game between the two teams.' Do you agree with the spectator? Give a reason for your answer.

(e) A penalty is awarded to Team B. The goalkeeper for Team A has saved 12 penalties out of 20 this season. What is the probability that the goalkeeper will save the penalty based on his previous record?

(SEC 2013)

Q6 A group of 106 students returning from a day trip stopped at a food court on the way home. When they got back on the bus, a student carried out a survey to find out which food outlet they had eaten in. The results are recorded in the table shown.

	Burger outlet	Sandwich outlet	Chinese outlet
Boys	34	16	6
Girls	11	x	32

(a) If all students ate at one of the food outlets, find the value of x.

(b) What is the probability that the student chosen is a girl who ate at the Chinese outlet?

(c) If a student is chosen at random, what is the probability that the student is a boy?

(d) If a student is chosen at random, what is the probability that the student is a girl?

(e) If a student is chosen at random, what is the probability that the student ate in the burger outlet?

Q7 In a survey, 1500 people were asked which national radio station they normally listen to. The results of the survey are given in the table below.

	RTE 1	Today FM	Newstalk	Lyric FM	2FM	No national station
Frequency	375	195	120	45	165	
Relative frequency (as a fraction)	$\dfrac{375}{1500}$					
Relative frequency (as a decimal)			0·08			

(a) How many of the people surveyed do not listen to a national radio station?

(b) Complete the table above.

(c) Find the sum of the relative frequencies written as fractions.

(d) Find the sum of the relative frequencies written as decimals.

(e) Jackie wrote the relative frequencies as percentages. She found their sum to be 80%. Do you think her calculations are correct? Give a reason for your answer.

(f) Denis looked at the data and said, 'I can find out how many people in the survey normally listen to local radio.' Do you agree or disagree with Denis? Explain your answer.

(SEC 2012)

Q8 A machine part manufacturer finds that 4 out of 360 parts are faulty.

(a) What is the relative frequency of manufacturing a faulty part?

(b) How many faulty parts would you expect to find if:

(i) 500 parts were tested?

(ii) 1350 parts were tested?

(iii) 20 000 parts were tested?

Q9 A card is chosen from a deck of cards and then replaced. Each student in a class of 30 students selects a card and notes the card chosen. 17 students chose a red card.

   (a) Calculate the relative frequency of selecting a red card, correct to two decimal places.

   (b) What is the theoretical probability of a red card being selected?

   (c) In your opinion, why are the relative frequency and the theoretical probability answers different?

   (d) What could be changed to produce a relative frequency that is closer to the theoretical probability?

Q10 A game is played using the two spinners shown.

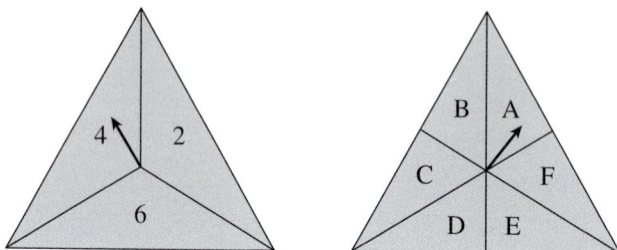

The first spinner has three segments labelled 2, 4 and 6.

The arrow has the same chance of stopping at each number.

The second spinner has six segments labelled A, B, C, D, E and F.

The arrow has the same chance of stopping at each letter.

Two possible outcomes are (2, A) and (6, D).

   (a) List all the possible outcomes in the table below.

		2nd spinner					
		A	B	C	D	E	F
1st spinner	**2**	(2, A)					
	4						
	6				(6, D)		

   (b) How many outcomes contain the letter E?

   (c) What is the probability that the outcome contains the letter E?

   (d) What is the probability that the outcome contains the number 6?

   (e) What is the probability that the outcome contains E, or 6, or both?

(SEC 2014)

Q11 In a survey, 500 students were asked what sporting activities they had participated in during the summer holidays. The results were as follows:

- 250 played cricket (C)
- 230 went swimming (S)
- 125 played tennis (T)
- 175 went swimming and played cricket
- 100 played cricket and tennis
- 50 went swimming and played tennis
- 30 participated in all three sports.

(a) Represent the information on a Venn diagram.

(b) Calculate how many students did not participate in any of the three sporting activities listed.

(c) What is the probability that a student did not participate in any of these activities?

(d) What is the probability that a student participated in at least one of the activities listed?

(e) What is the probability that a student participated in at least two of the activities listed?

Q12 An archer shoots arrows at a bullseye. The probability that an arrow hits the bullseye is 0·4. The archer shoots three arrows.

(a) Draw a tree diagram to represent this information.

(b) What is the probability that all arrows hit the bullseye?

(c) What is the probability that none of the arrows hit the bullseye?

(d) What is the probability that at least one arrow hits the bullseye?

Q13 The arrows represent the different routes that a skier can take when skiing down a mountain. The circles on the diagram represent different points on the routes.

(a) When leaving any particular point on the mountain a skier is equally likely to choose any of the available routes from that point. Fill in the boxes in the diagram which represent the probability that the skier will take that route.

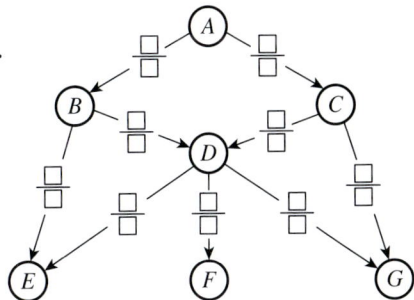

(b) (i) If the skier starts at point A, in how many different ways can the skier reach the point E?

(ii) If the skier starts at point A, find the probability that the skier will reach the point E.

(SEC 2013)

Q14 In a survey, 54 people were asked which political party they had voted for in the last three elections. The results are as follows:

- 30 had voted for the Conservatives

- 22 had voted for the Liberals

- 22 had voted for the Republicans

- 12 had voted for the Conservatives and for the Liberals

- 9 had voted for the Liberals and for the Republicans

- 8 had voted for the Conservatives and for the Republicans

- 5 had voted for all three parties.

(a) Represent the information on a Venn diagram.

(b) If one person is chosen at random, what is the probability that the person chosen did not vote in any of the three elections?

(c) If one person is chosen at random, what is the probability that the person chosen voted for at least two different parties?

(d) If one person is chosen at random, what is the probability that the person chosen voted for the same party in all three elections?

(SEC 2013)

Solutions

Q1 (a)

Event	Probability
A card is picked at random from a standard deck of playing cards. A = Ace of hearts is picked.	$\dfrac{1}{52}$
A fair coin is tossed. B = a tail is the outcome for the toss.	$\dfrac{1}{2}$
A day is chosen at random from the list of the days of the week. C = the day contains the letter **a**.	$\dfrac{7}{7} = 1$
A month is chosen at random from the list of months of the year. D = the month contains the letter **r**.	$\dfrac{9}{12} = \dfrac{3}{4}$
A letter is picked at random from the word ENORMOUS. E = the word contains the letter **W**.	$\dfrac{0}{8} = 0$

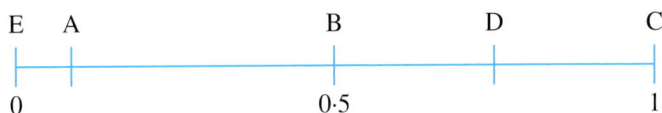

```
E  A                        B        D        C
├──┼────────────────────────┼────────┼────────┤
0                          0·5               1
```

(b) Rolling an odd number on a die.

(c) Selecting a positive number from the natural numbers.

(d) Selecting a black heart from a standard deck of cards.

Q2 (a)

Event	Probability
When a fair coin is tossed you get a head.	**50:50**
If you buy a lottery ticket for next Saturday's draw, you will win the Jackpot.	**Unlikely**
The 1st of January will be New Year's Day.	**Certain**

(b)

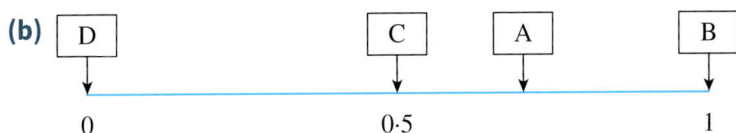

```
D                    C      A          B
│                    │      │          │
↓                    ↓      ↓          ↓
0                  0·5                 1
```

Q3 (a) The total number of shirts in the shop is 18.

(b)

Shirt size	S	M	L	XL
Frequency	3	7	6	2

(c) $P(\text{large shirt}) = \dfrac{\text{number of favourable outcomes}}{\text{number of possible outcomes}} = \dfrac{6}{18} = \dfrac{1}{3}$

(d) There are now 17 shirts to choose from.

$P(\text{small shirt}) = \dfrac{\text{number of favourable outcomes}}{\text{number of possible outcomes}} = \dfrac{3}{17}$

Q4 (a) Number of songs by Usher on Gavin's phone $= 30 - (15 + 4 + 3) = 30 - 22 = 8$

(b) $P(\text{song by Hozier}) = \dfrac{\text{number of favourable outcomes}}{\text{number of possible outcomes}} = \dfrac{3}{30} = \dfrac{1}{10}$

(c) $P(\text{song by Ed Sheeran or Pharrell}) = \dfrac{\text{number of favourable outcomes}}{\text{number of possible outcomes}}$
$= \dfrac{4 + 15}{30} = \dfrac{19}{30}$

(d) If Gavin has four songs by Ed Sheeran and three songs by Hozier, and he plays a song by Ed Sheeran, and then plays a song by Hozier, the number of different ways he can play a song $= 4 \times 3 = 12$, using the Fundamental Principle of Counting 1.

Q5 (a) $P(\text{Fiachra scoring a goal}) = 0·1$ and $P(\text{Fiachra scoring a point}) = 0·6$

$\therefore P(\text{scoring a point}) > P(\text{scoring a goal})$

Fiachra is more likely to score a point, as the probability is higher, by 0·5, i.e. 50%.

(b) P(Fiachra will not score a point) $= 1 - P$(Fiachra will score a point) $= 1 - 0 \cdot 6 = 0 \cdot 4$

(c) P(Fiachra scoring a goal) $= 0 \cdot 1$ and P(Peadar scoring a goal) $= 0 \cdot 2$
$\therefore P$(Peadar scoring a goal) $> P$(Fiachra scoring a goal) by $0 \cdot 1$, i.e. 10%.

P(Fiachra scoring a point) $= 0 \cdot 6$ and P(Peadar scoring a point) $= 0 \cdot 7$
$\therefore P$(Peadar scoring a point) $> P$(Fiachra scoring a point) by $0 \cdot 1$, i.e. 10%.
Overall, Peadar is more likely to score than Fiachra, as the probability of him scoring either a goal or point is $0 \cdot 1$ (10%) greater than Fiachra.

(d) The spectator is wrong. While the probability of Peadar scoring is higher, it does not mean that he will score (or score more) in any particular game. Hurling is a team game, and every player relies on their team mates.

(e) P(goalkeeper will save the penalty) $= \dfrac{12}{20} = \dfrac{3}{5} = 0 \cdot 6$

Q6 (a) $x = 106 - (34 + 16 + 6 + 11 + 32) = 106 - 99 = 7$

(b) P(girl who ate at the Chinese outlet) $= \dfrac{32}{106} = \dfrac{16}{53}$

(c) P(boy) $= \dfrac{56}{106} = \dfrac{28}{53}$

(d) P(girl) $= 1 - P$(boy) $= 1 - \dfrac{28}{53} = \dfrac{25}{53}$

(e) P(student ate in the burger outlet) $= \dfrac{\text{number of favourable outcomes}}{\text{number of possible outcomes}} = \dfrac{45}{106}$

Q7 (a) Number of the people surveyed who do not listen to a national radio station $= 1500 - (375 + 195 + 120 + 45 + 165) = 1500 - 900 = 600$

(b)

	RTE 1	Today FM	Newstalk	Lyric FM	2FM	No national station
Frequency	375	195	120	45	165	600
Relative frequency (as a fraction)	$\dfrac{375}{1500}$	$\dfrac{195}{1500}$	$\dfrac{120}{1500}$	$\dfrac{45}{1500}$	$\dfrac{165}{1500}$	$\dfrac{600}{1500}$
Relative frequency (as a decimal)	$0 \cdot 25$	$0 \cdot 13$	$0 \cdot 08$	$0 \cdot 03$	$0 \cdot 11$	$0 \cdot 4$

(c) Sum of the relative frequencies

$$= \dfrac{375}{1500} + \dfrac{195}{1500} + \dfrac{120}{1500} + \dfrac{45}{1500} + \dfrac{165}{1500} + \dfrac{600}{1500} = \dfrac{1500}{1500} = 1$$

(d) Sum of relative frequencies as decimals
$= 0{\cdot}25 + 0{\cdot}13 + 0{\cdot}08 + 0{\cdot}03 + 0{\cdot}11 + 0{\cdot}4 = 1$

(e) No. They should add up to 1.

(f) Disagree. Some people may not listen to the radio at all.

Q8 (a) Relative frequency of manufacturing a faulty part $= \dfrac{4}{360} = \dfrac{1}{90}$

   (b) (i) Expected frequency = relative frequency × the number of trials
$$= \frac{1}{90} \times 500 = 5{\cdot}\dot{5}$$
As we can only have whole numbers of products, the number of faulty parts expected is 6.

   (ii) Expected frequency = relative frequency × the number of trials
$$= \frac{1}{90} \times 1350 = 15$$
The number of faulty parts expected is 15.

   (iii) Expected frequency = relative frequency × the number of trials
$$= \frac{1}{90} \times 20\,000 = 222{\cdot}\dot{2}$$
As we can only have whole numbers of products, the number of faulty parts expected is 223.

Q9 (a) Relative frequency of selecting a red card $= \dfrac{17}{30} = 0{\cdot}57$

   (b) Theoretical probability of a red card being selected
$$= \frac{\text{number of favourable outcomes that exist}}{\text{total number of possible outcomes}} = \frac{26}{52} = 0{\cdot}5.$$

   (c) The answers are different as relative frequency is based on experimental data. In this situation the number of trials was small.

   (d) Recall that the relative frequency approaches the theoretical probability when there are a very large number of trials. So to produce a relative frequency that is closer to the theoretical probability the number of trials carried out would need to be increased.

Q10 (a)

		2nd spinner					
		A	**B**	**C**	**D**	**E**	**F**
1st spinner	**2**	(2, A)	(2, B)	(2, C)	(2, D)	(2, E)	(2, F)
	4	(4, A)	(4, B)	(4, C)	(4, D)	(4, E)	(4, F)
	6	(6, A)	(6, B)	(6, C)	(6, D)	(6, E)	(6, F)

(b) There are three outcomes which contain the letter E.

(c) P(outcome contains the letter E) = $\dfrac{\text{number of favourable outcomes}}{\text{number of possible outcomes}}$

$$= \frac{3}{18} = \frac{1}{6}$$

(d) P(outcome contains the number 6) = $\dfrac{\text{number of favourable outcomes}}{\text{number of possible outcomes}}$

$$= \frac{6}{18} = \frac{1}{3}$$

(e) P(outcome contains a letter E, or 6, or both)

$$= \frac{\text{number of favourable outcomes}}{\text{number of possible outcomes}} = \frac{8}{18} = \frac{4}{9}$$

Q11 (a) U (500)

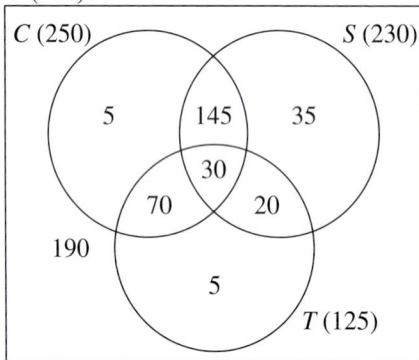

$\#U = 500$, $\#C = 250$, $\#S = 230$ and $\#T = 125$

$\#(C \cap S \cap T) = x = 30$, $\#(C \cap S) = 175$, $\#(S \cap T) = 50$

$\#(C \cap T) = 100$

$\#(C \cap T)/x = 100 - 30 = 70$

$\#(C \cap S)/x = 175 - 30 = 145$

$\#(S \cap T)/x = 50 - 30 = 20$

$\#C$ only $= 250 - 145 - 30 - 70 = 5$

$\#T$ only $= 125 - 70 - 30 - 20 - 125 - 120 = 5$

$\#S$ only $= 230 - 145 - 30 - 20 - 230 - 195 = 35$

$\#(C \cup S \cup T)' = 500 - 5 - 145 - 30 - 70 - 20 - 35 - 5$

$$= 500 - 310 = 190$$

(b) Number of students who did not participate in any of the three sporting activities: $\#(C \cup S \cup T)' = 500 - (5 + 145 + 30 + 70 + 35 + 20 + 5)$

$$= 500 - (310) = 190$$

(c) P(student did not participate in any activity) $= \dfrac{190}{500} = 0{\cdot}38$

(d) P(student participated in at least one activity)

$= 1 - P$(did not particpate in any activity) $= 1 - 0{\cdot}38 = 0{\cdot}62$

(e) P(student participated in at least two activities)

$$= \frac{20 + 30 + 70 + 145}{500}$$

$$= \frac{265}{500} = 0.53$$

Q12 (a) P(arrow hits bullseye) $= 0.4$.

So P(arrow does not hit bullseye)

$= 1 - P$(arrow hits bullseye) $= 1 - 0.4 = 0.6$

So the tree diagram can be drawn to represent this information:

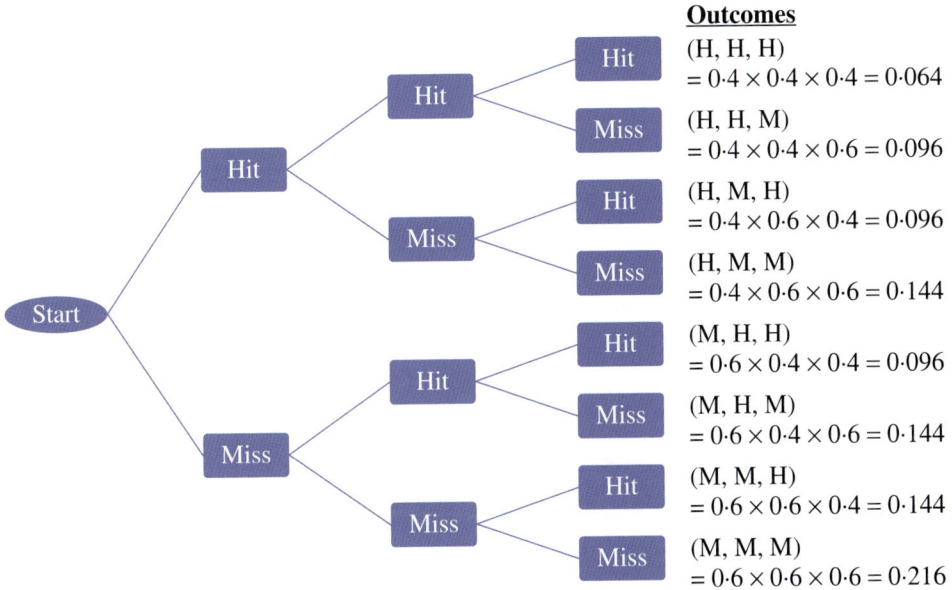

Outcomes

(H, H, H)
$= 0.4 \times 0.4 \times 0.4 = 0.064$

(H, H, M)
$= 0.4 \times 0.4 \times 0.6 = 0.096$

(H, M, H)
$= 0.4 \times 0.6 \times 0.4 = 0.096$

(H, M, M)
$= 0.4 \times 0.6 \times 0.6 = 0.144$

(M, H, H)
$= 0.6 \times 0.4 \times 0.4 = 0.096$

(M, H, M)
$= 0.6 \times 0.4 \times 0.6 = 0.144$

(M, M, H)
$= 0.6 \times 0.6 \times 0.4 = 0.144$

(M, M, M)
$= 0.6 \times 0.6 \times 0.6 = 0.216$

(b) P(all three arrows hit the bullseye) $= 0.4 \times 0.4 \times 0.4 = 0.064$

(c) P(none of the three arrows hit the bullseye) $= 0.6 \times 0.6 \times 0.6 = 0.216$

(d) P(at least one arrow hits the bullseye)
$= 1 - P$(none of the arrows hit the bullseye) $= 1 - 0.216 = 0.784$

Q13 (a)

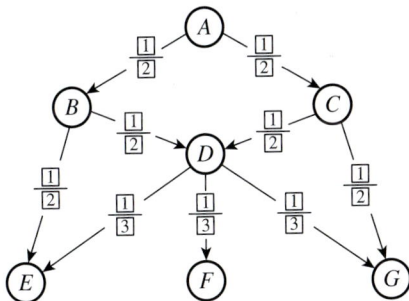

(b) (i) 1. $A \to B \to E$

   2. $A \to B \to D \to E$ } 3 ways

   3. $A \to C \to D \to E$

(ii) 1. $\dfrac{1}{2} \times \dfrac{1}{2} = \dfrac{1}{4}$

   2. $\dfrac{1}{2} \times \dfrac{1}{2} \times \dfrac{1}{3} = \dfrac{1}{12}$ } Probability $= \dfrac{1}{4} + \dfrac{1}{12} + \dfrac{1}{12} = \dfrac{5}{12}$

   3. $\dfrac{1}{2} \times \dfrac{1}{2} \times \dfrac{1}{3} = \dfrac{1}{12}$

Q14 (a) $U\ (54)$

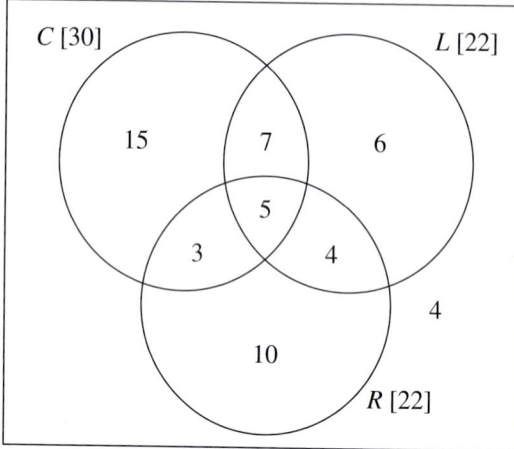

$\#U = 54$, $\#C = 30$, $\#L = 22$ and $\#R = 22$

$\#(C \cap L \cap R) = x = 5$, $\#(C \cap L) = 12$, $\#(L \cap R) = 9$

$\#(C \cap R) = 8$, $\#(C \cap L)/x = 12 - 5 = 7$

$\#(C \cap R)/x = 8 - 5 = 3$

$\#(L \cap R)/x = 9 - 5 = 4$

$\#C$ only $= 30 - 7 - 5 - 3 = 15$

$\#L$ only $= 22 - 7 - 5 - 4 = 22 - 16 = 6$

$\#R$ only $= 22 - 3 - 5 - 4 = 22 - 12 = 10$

$\#(C \cup L \cup R)' = 54 - 15 - 7 - 5 - 3 - 6 - 4 - 10 = 54 - 50 = 4$

(b) Number of people who did not vote in any of the three elections:

$\#(C \cup L \cup R)' = 54 - 15 - 7 - 5 - 3 - 6 - 4 - 10 = 54 - 50 = 4.$

So 4 people did not vote.

P(that a person did not vote) $= \dfrac{4}{54} = \dfrac{2}{27}$

(c) *U* (54)

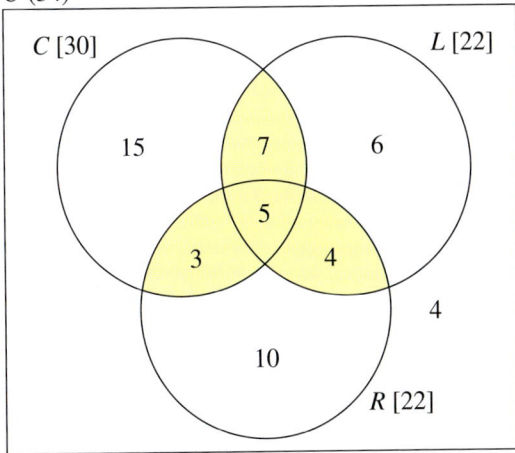

The total number of people who voted for at least two parties was $3 + 5 + 7 + 4 = 19$.

Therefore, the probability a person voted for at least two parties is $\dfrac{19}{54}$.

(d) *U* (54)

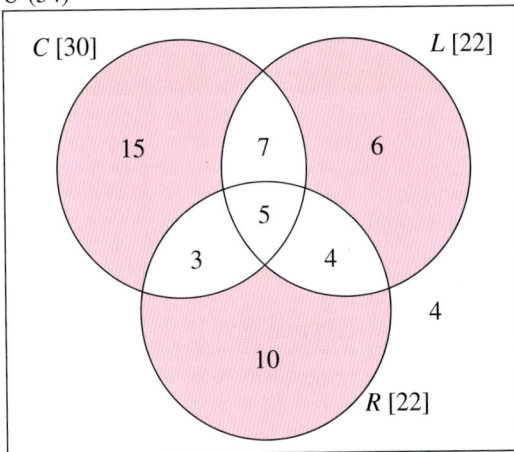

The total number of people who voted for only one party was $15 + 6 + 10 = 31$.

Therefore, the probability a person voted for the same party in all three elections is $\dfrac{31}{54}$.

3 Statistics 1: Statistics Use, Data Types and Sampling

Learning objectives

In this chapter you will learn about:

- Key terminology and information associated with gathering and interpreting statistical data

- The different types of statistical data

- The data handling cycle

- The key information needed when collecting statistical data.

What is statistics?

This revision chapter deals with the key information related to statistics, the methods used to collect data and the different types of data.

Word(s)	Meaning
Statistics	Is about the collection, organisation, presentation and interpretation of data.
Statistician	A person who collects data and turns it into meaningful information, which can be used to plan for the future.
Data	Individual facts, statistics or items of information. Datum is the singular of data. Strictly speaking, books and studies ought to use 'data are' (i.e. plural), but many use 'data is', and this is accepted terminology.
Univariate data	Univariate data looks at one item of data at a time from each topic, for example, height.

Types of data: Categorical and numerical data

Points to note

- When data is collected, it is generally organised as being either **categorical data** or **numerical data**, as shown in the table.

Categorical/Qualitative data	Numerical/Quantitative data
Data that can be described using words only.	Data that can be represented by numbers.
It can be ordered or unordered.	It can be discrete or continuous.

- This data can then be organised further, as shown in the diagram below:

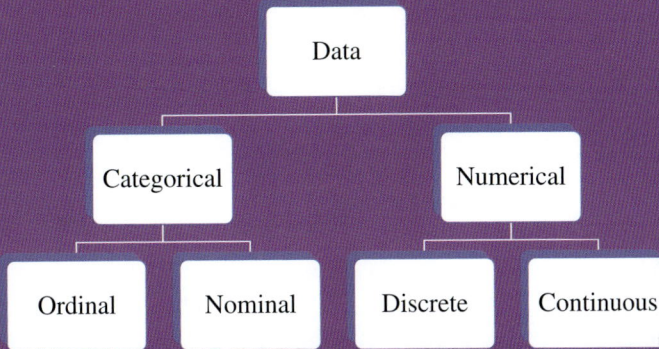

- The meaning and examples of each data type are provided in the table:

Type of Data	Definition	Examples	Suitable graphical representation
Categorical ordinal	Data that: • can be described using words only • can be ordered in some way	• Places in a race: 1st, 2nd, 3rd, etc. • Months of the year • Days of the week • Grades in an exam • Clothes sizes: extra-small, small, medium, large, etc.	• Bar chart • Line plot • Pie chart

Type of Data	Definition	Examples	Suitable graphical representation
Categorical nominal	Data that: • can be described using words only • cannot be ordered in some way	• Favourite colour • Film genre • Animals • Favourite food	• Bar chart • Line plot • Pie chart
Numerical discrete	Data that: • can be represented by numbers • can only have certain values (finite values)	• Family size • Shoe size • Number of pens in your pencil case • Shirt collar size • Number of goals scored	• Bar chart • Pie chart • Line plot • Stem-and-leaf plot
Numerical continuous	Data that: • can be represented by numbers • can involve any real number (infinite values)	• Height • Age • Time • Temperature • Weight • Area • Length	• Histogram

Example

Classify each of the following data as categorical nominal, categorical ordinal, numerical discrete or numerical continuous.

(a) The make of your family car (car manufacturer)

(b) Number of subjects you study in school

(c) Grades achieved in Junior Certificate

(d) Times taken to complete the 200 m men's race in the Olympic Games

Solution

(a) The make of your family car is **categorical nominal**. The answers are not numbers and they cannot be ordered in any particular way.

(b) The number of subjects you study in school is **numerical discrete**. The answers are numbers and they can only have certain values.

(c) Grades achieved in Junior Certificate are **categorical ordinal**. The answers are not numbers and they can be ordered in some way.

(d) Times taken to complete the 200 m men's race in the Olympic Games is **numerical continuous**. The answers are numbers and can have any real value.

Collecting data: Primary and secondary data

Points to note

- Data is collected for:
  - ➲ Market research: To find out what customers like and dislike about certain products available and to plan for future new products that customers might like.
  - ➲ Government research: The Census is carried out every five years to plan for the infrastructure of schools, hospitals, housing, and carry out age-profiling of the population to plan for future pension provision, etc.

- Data that is collected is divided into either **primary data** or **secondary data**, as shown below.

Data type	How it is collected	Advantages	Disadvantages
Primary data is data collected by the person who uses it.	Is collected by means of a survey. The different types of surveys are: 1 Questionnaires 2 Experimental study: • the researcher deliberately influences events and investigates the effects of the intervention	• You collect the data you need • It's accurate • Easy to understand	• Takes time • Need the help of other people • Can be expensive

Data type	How it is collected	Advantages	Disadvantages
	Examples: • Laboratory experiment • Clinical trial **3** Observational study: • the researcher collects information but does not influence events Example: Monitoring behaviour		
Secondary data is data collected by another person	• Books • Magazines • Newspapers • Internet • TV • Central Statistics Office (CSO) • Census at school	• Cheap to collect • Doesn't take a lot of time	• It may not be up to date • May not be accurate • May not provide the information needed • May be biased

Example

For the list of sources shown, identify which are primary and which are secondary data.

Data source	Identify the source as primary (P) or secondary (S) data
TV	
Laboratory experiment	
Magazine	
Books	
Survey	
Questionnaire	
Clinical trial	
Census	

Solution

Data source	Primary (P) or secondary (S) data
TV	S
Laboratory experiment	P
Magazine	S
Books	S
Survey	P
Questionnaire	P
Clinical trial	P
Census	S

The laboratory experiment, survey, questionnaire and clinical trial are the only sources where the researcher collects their own data. These are primary data sources.

The remaining data sources are all secondary data sources, as their data was collected by another person.

The data handling cycle

When carrying out a statistical investigation it is important that the steps carried out can be repeated for every investigation. These steps are known as the **data handling cycle**.

Points to note

The **data handling cycle** follows these steps:

1 Pose a question
2 Collect the data
3 Analyse the data
4 Interpret the results

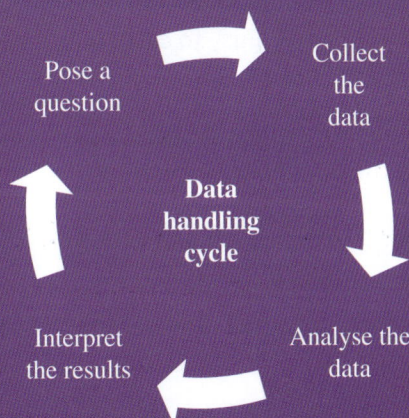

Pose a question → Collect the data

Data handling cycle

Interpret the results ← Analyse the data

Carrying out a survey: Collecting data

A common method of collecting data for a survey is to use a **questionnaire**.

A questionnaire is a set of questions designed to obtain data from individuals.

The four main methods of collecting data, including the advantages and disadvantages of each type, are listed in the table.

Method	Advantages	Disadvantages
Face-to-face interview	People are more likely to answer. More difficult questions can be asked and explained if necessary.	It takes a long time and is not random. The interviewee is more likely to lie. Expensive.
Phone interview	Almost everyone has a phone. Questions can be explained. It's random.	Phone calls can be expensive. It is difficult to get people's phone numbers. Calling people randomly can annoy them.
Postal questionnaire	People might have more time to answer questions at home. Not expensive.	People may not return their questionnaires. Questions cannot be explained. May not be representative of the population.
Online questionnaire	Saves time. Very low cost. Easy to carry out.	Questions cannot be explained. Only people who want to answer will take part.

When designing a questionnaire, use the questions in the table below as a guide to ensure the questionnaire is clear.

Question types	Each question must:	Possible answers
1 Yes/ No answers 2 Tick boxes	1 Be easy to understand 2 Cover every possible answer	1 Must include the most common answer 2 **Should not** be neutral, as people may choose this option to complete a questionnaire quickly

Question types	Each question must:	Possible answers
3 Numbered responses 4 Word responses 5 Questions which require a sentence to be written	3 Be unbiased/ neutral Have a clear meaning 4 Be relevant to the survey 5 Not lead a person to the answer you want	3 Should include an 'other' option when possible 4 May be scaled, so a person can rate their feelings about a question 5 Can be rated, where the person gets to rate/rank the options given

Example

Write down the advantages and disadvantages of carrying out a face-to-face interview.

Solution

Advantages	Disadvantages
The person being interviewed is more likely to answer the questions than if they were asked to post their responses either online or via post.	Interviewing takes a lot of time.
The interviewer can ask more complicated questions.	It may be more expensive than other types of questionnaires.
The interviewer can explain what is meant by a question if needed.	The person being interviewed may not understand the meaning of a question.
An interviewer would be more consistent when recording information.	The person being interviewed is more likely to lie or not answer a question.

Reliability of data

When designing and conducting a survey or questionnaire it is important to ensure that the information collected is not **biased** and is representative of the entire population.

- **More key information related to statistics**

Word(s)	Meaning
Population	The entire group of people, animals or things about which we want information.
Sample	A subset of a population, which we actually collect information from in order to draw conclusions about the whole population.
Census	This is when every member of the population has data collected from them.
Sample survey	A survey based on a sample of people, rather than the entire population.
Bias	A sample is **biased** if individuals or groups from the population are not represented in the sample.
Random sample	Each member of the population has an equal chance of being selected.

- Two of the most important concepts in this list are **bias** and **random sampling**.

Biased samples

A sample is **biased** if individuals or groups from the population are not represented in the sample. For example, if you were carrying out a survey to estimate how many people visit a local tourist attraction, it would be unwise to stand outside the local tourist attraction to get your data. This data would produce a biased sample. To avoid bias, we can use simple random sampling, which is the only type of sampling tested on the JCHL course.

Simple random sampling

To avoid bias, each name in the population should be given a number. A sample of the population can then be selected using the random number generator on a calculator or on a computer. This method is called **simple random sampling**.

- To generate a random number between 1 and 200 on a Casio calculator, use the **RanInt** button on the calculator, and follow the procedure below.

Press (ALPHA) (•) (1) (( ) (2) (0) (0) ( )) (=)

To keep generating a random whole number between 1 and 200 keep pressing (=)

Example

Students in a transition year class wish to carry out a survey of students to find out which mobile phone provider they use. The school has 900 students and they wish to survey 50 students.

(a) What is the population of the school?

(b) What is the sample?

(c) How can they avoid bias?

(d) How should they select the students for the survey?

Solution

(a) The population is the 900 students in the school.

(b) The sample is the 50 students that they wish to survey.

(c) To avoid bias the members of the sample should be selected at random, using simple random sampling.

(d) To select the students for their sample, they should:

- Give each student a number between 1 and 900.

- Select 50 numbers at random using the **RanInt** button on their calculator:

  - Then press ALPHA ● 1) 9 0 0) = repeatedly until they have selected 50 numbers.

- Find the students with the numbers generated and give them the survey.

Exercise

Q1 Explain the meaning of the following words:

(a) Statistics   (b) Data   (c) Univariate data   (d) Population

(e) Sample   (f) Bias   (g) Random sample

Q2 (a) Explain what categorical data and numerical data are.

(b) Provide another name for both categorical data and numerical data.

Q3 Fill in the table giving a minimum of two examples for each data type.

Type of data	Definition	Examples	Suitable graphical representation
Categorical ordinal			
Categorical nominal			
Numerical discrete			
Numerical continuous			

Q4 Complete the table shown for primary and secondary data. List a minimum of one advantage and disadvantage for each.

Data type	How it is collected?	Advantages	Disadvantages
Primary data			
Secondary data			

Q5 What is the difference between an experimental study and an observational study?

Q6 List one advantage and one disadvantage of the following methods of data collection:

(a) Face-to-face interview (b) Telephone interview

(c) Postal questionnaire (d) Online questionnaire

Q7 What are the steps of the data handling cycle?

Q8 How would you get a random sample of 20 people from a population of 100?

Q9 An Gardaí Síochána wants to know how Dublin inner city residents feel about the police service. A questionnaire with several questions about the police is prepared. A sample of 300 mailing addresses in inner city areas is chosen, and a Garda is sent to each address to administer the questionnaire to an adult living there.

Identify the population, variables measured and the sample. In addition, describe the potential bias.

(NCE-MSTL,Q2)

Q10 Eithne is going to survey post-primary Geography teachers in Ireland.

(a) Some of the questions in the survey are shown in the table below. Put a tick (✔) in the correct box to show what type of data each question would give.

Question	Numerical continuous	Numerical discrete	Categorical nominal	Categorical ordinal
How many Geography classes do you teach each week?				
How much do you like teaching Geography? A lot □ A little □ Not at all □				
What subjects (other than Geography) do you teach?				

Eithne is going to send her survey to some of the post-primary schools in Ireland.

(b) Describe how Eithne could select a simple random sample from all the post-primary schools in Ireland.

Eithne is considering sending her survey by email.

(c) State one advantage and one disadvantage of using email to collect data.

(SEC 2015)

Q11 A survey was conducted among third-year students. The answers to each survey question can be classified as one of the data types shown in the table below.

In each row in the table write a short question that you could include in a survey and that will give the type of data stated.

Question	Type of data
(a)	Categorical data where the categories are not ordered
(b)	Ordered categorical data
(c)	Discrete numerical data
(d)	Continuous numerical data

(SEC 2011)

Solutions

Q1 (a) Statistics is about the collection, organisation, presentation and interpretation of data.

(b) Data is individual facts, statistics or items of information.

(c) Univariate data looks at one item of data at a time from each topic, for example, height.

(d) The population is the entire group of people, animal or things about which we want information.

(e) A sample is a subset of a population, which we actually collect information from in order to draw conclusions about the whole population.

(f) A sample is **biased** if individuals or groups from the population are not represented in the sample.

(g) In a random sample each member of the population has an equal chance of being selected.

Q2 (a) Categorical data is data that can be described using words only. It can be ordered or unordered. Numerical data is data that can be represented by numbers. It can be discrete or continuous.

(b) Another name for categorical data is **qualitative**. Another name for numerical data is **quantitative**.

Q3

Type of data	Definition	Examples	Suitable graphical representation
Categorical ordinal	Data that: • can be described using words only • can be ordered in some way	• Places in a race: 1st, 2nd, 3rd, etc. • Months of the year • Days of the week • Grades in an exam • Clothes sizes: extra-small, small, medium, large, etc.	• Bar chart • Line plot • Pie chart

Type of data	Definition	Examples	Suitable graphical representation
Categorical nominal	Data that: • can be described using words only • cannot be ordered in some way	• Favourite colour • Film genre • Animals • Favourite food	• Bar chart • Line plot • Pie chart
Numerical discrete	Data that: • can be represented by numbers • can only have certain values (finite values)	• Family size • Shoe size • Number of pens in your pencil case • Shirt collar size • Number of goals scored	• Bar chart • Pie chart • Line plot • Stem-and-leaf plot
Numerical continuous	Data that: • can be represented by numbers • can involve any real number (infinite values)	• Height • Age • Time • Temperature • Weight • Area • Length	• Histogram

Data type	How it is collected	Advantages	Disadvantages
Primary data is data collected by the person who uses it.	Is collected by means of a survey. The different types of surveys are: **1** Questionnaires **2** Experimental study: • the researcher deliberately influences events and investigates the effects of the intervention Examples: • Laboratory experiment • Clinical trial **3** Observational study: • the researcher collects information but does not influence events Example: • Monitoring behaviour	• You collect the data you need • It's accurate • Easy to understand	• Takes time • Need the help of other people • Can be expensive
Secondary Data is data collected by another person	• Books • Magazines • Newspapers • Internet • TV • Central Statistics Office (CSO) • Census at school	• Cheap to collect • Doesn't take a lot of time	• It may not be up to date • May not be accurate • May not provide the information needed • May be biased

Q5 In an experimental study the researcher deliberately influences events and investigates the effects of the intervention. In an observational study the researcher collects information but does not influence events.

Q6

Method	Advantages	Disadvantages
Face to face	People are more likely to answer. More difficult questions can be asked and explained if needed.	It takes a long time and is not random. The interviewee is more likely to lie. Expensive.
Phone	Almost everyone has a phone. Questions can be explained. It's random.	Phone calls can be expensive. It is difficult to get people's phone numbers. Calling people randomly can annoy them.
Post	People might have more time to answer questions at home. Not expensive.	People may not return their questionnaires. Questions cannot be explained. May not be representative of the population.
Website	Saves time. Very low cost. Easy to carry out.	Questions cannot be explained. Only people who want to answer will take part.

Q7 The data handling cycle follows these steps:

1 Pose a question
2 Collect the data
3 Analyse the data
4 Interpret the results

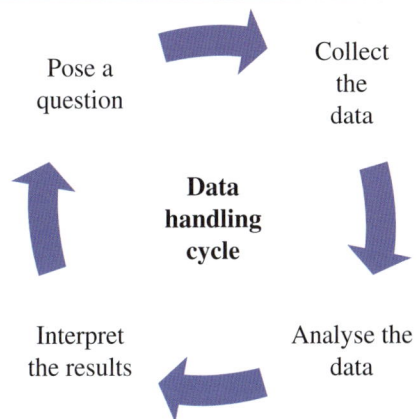

Pose a question
Collect the data

Data handling cycle

Interpret the results
Analyse the data

Q8 We could give each person a number from 1 to 100 and then select 20 numbers using a random method. We could:

- write the 100 numbers on paper, put them in a bag, shake them, and take 20 of them out without looking.
- use the random number generator on your calculator.

Q9 Population: All Dublin inner city residents.

Variable measured: opinion on the police service, for example by a rating scale.

Sample: 300 adults living at the 300 addresses chosen (not given any information on the response rate).

Potential bias: may overestimate positive feedback on police service because a Garda is asking the questions – would be better to have someone neutral or trusted by the community to carry out the survey. Would also need information on the response rate.

Q10 (a)

Question	Numerical continuous	Numerical discrete	Categorical nominal	Categorical ordinal
How many Geography classes do you teach each week?		✓		
How much do you like teaching Geography? A lot A little Not at all ☐ ☐ ☐				✓
What subjects (other than Geography) do you teach?			✓	

(b) Eithne could select a simple random sample from all the post-primary schools in Ireland by:

- Step 1: Getting a list of all of the post-primary schools in Ireland.
- Step 2: Randomly selecting a number of them, e.g. by using a random number generator.

(c) Advantages of using email to collect data include that it is quick, convenient and cheap.

Disadvantages include that not everyone has email, the mail may go to spam, there is a faulty computer or people don't reply.

Q11

Question	Type of data
(a) What subjects do you study at school?	Categorical data where the categories are not ordered
(b) How would you rate your school: Bad/ Good/ Excellent?	Ordered categorical data
(c) What is your shoe size?	Discrete numerical data
(d) What is your height in centimetres?	Continuous numerical data

Statistics 2: Central Tendency and Spread of Data 4

Learning objectives

In this chapter you will learn about:

- The three measures of average/central tendency: Mean, mode and median
- How to calculate the three measures of central tendency from a list of numbers or frequency tables
- The existence of outliers
- The two measures of spread: Range and interquartile range
- How to calculate the measures of spread from a list of numbers or frequency tables.

Measures of central tendency/averages

Points to note

- There are three measures of central tendency/averages on the JCHL course. They are different ways of working out the **average** and these are called the mean, mode and median.

Word(s)	Meaning
Mean	• Is the most commonly used measure of central tendency and is commonly known as the average.
	• Is found by adding (summing) all the values together and dividing by the number of values in the data set.
	$\therefore$ Mean $= \dfrac{\text{sum of the values in the data set}}{\text{number of values in the data set}}$
	• The formula for the mean can be written as:
	$$\mu = \frac{\sum x}{n}$$

Word(s)	Meaning
	○ Σ is pronounced 'sigma' and means 'the sum of'.
	○ Σx means to add up all the data values (x values).
	○ μ is pronounced 'mew' and is the symbol for the mean.
	○ n is the number of values in the data set.
	• From a frequency distribution table, the mean can be calculated using the formula: $$\mu = \frac{\Sigma fx}{\Sigma f}$$
	○ f is the frequency. Frequency is the number of times a value occurs.
	○ x is the data value or mid-interval value in a grouped frequency table.
	• Is used when data is numerical and there are NO extreme values (outliers).
Mode	• The data value that occurs most often in the set of data.
	• It is possible for there to be more than one mode, or there might be no mode at all.
	• It is used when data is categorical.
Ranking	Arranging the values of a set of data in order from the smallest to the largest value.
Median	• The middle data value when all the data has been ranked.
	• Is used when the data is numerical and there are extreme values.
Outlier	• A data value that is much smaller or larger than the other values in the data set.
	• Outliers can skew the mean.

- Note that the mean and the median do not have to be data values of the original data set given. There are advantages and disadvantages when using the mean, mode or median as the central tendency/average.

Central tendency/average	Advantages	Disadvantages
Mean	• Uses all the data • Can be calculated easily • You don't need to order the data	• Includes outlier values • May not exist in the data
Mode	• Easy to find • Is not affected by outliers • The only average used for qualitative/categorical nominal data • The value exists in the data	• Some data sets may not have a mode • More than one mode may exist
Median	• Is not affected by outliers • Easy to find when the data is ordered • Works well with ordinal data	• Data needs to be ranked • Can be hard to calculate • May not exist in the data

Example

Identify **(a)** the mean, **(b)** mode and **(c)** median from the data set:
20, 24, 27, 24, 26, 28, 27, 24, 22.

Solution

(a) The mean is found by adding (sum) all the values together and dividing by the number of values in the data set.

$$\text{Mean} = \frac{\text{sum of all the values}}{\text{number of values}}$$

$$= \frac{20 + 24 + 27 + 24 + 26 + 28 + 27 + 24 + 22}{9}$$

$$= \frac{222}{9} = 24 \cdot \dot{6}$$

So the mean $= 24 \cdot \dot{6}$

(b) The mode is the data value that occurs most often in the set of data.

$$20, \mathbf{24}, 27, \mathbf{24}, 26, 28, 27, \mathbf{24}, 22$$

Since 24 appears the most times, it is the mode.

The mode = 24

(c) The median is the middle number when the data is ranked:

Rank the data: 20, 22, 24, 24, 24, 26, 27, 27, 28

Identify/find the middle number: 20, 22, 24, 24, **24**, 26, 27, 27, 28

The median = 24

Example

A group of 22 students in a Science class recorded the number of whole minutes spent doing experiments during Monday's class. The total amount of time spent was 1230 minutes.

(a) Find the mean number of minutes that each student spent doing experiments on Monday.

(b) Two additional students joined the class and reported that respectively they spent 48 minutes and 50 minutes doing experiments on Monday. Calculate the new mean including these students.

Solution

(a) Mean $= \dfrac{\text{sum of all the values}}{\text{number of values}} = \dfrac{1230}{22} = 55 \cdot 91$ minutes

The mean number of minutes is 55·91 minutes.

(b) Mean $= \dfrac{\text{sum of all the values}}{\text{number of values}} = \dfrac{1230 + 48 + 50}{24} = \dfrac{1328}{24} = 55 \cdot \dot{3}$ minutes.

The new mean is $55 \cdot \dot{3}$ minutes.

Points to note

To find the mean from a frequency/grouped frequency table, follow these steps in the in the order given:

Step 1 Find the mid-interval value of the grouped frequency if needed and label this column x.

Step 2 Multiply the frequencies by the corresponding mid-interval value, fx.

Step 3 Sum the product of the frequencies and the mid-interval values, Σfx.

Step 4 Sum the frequencies, Σf.

Step 5 Divide the sum of the products of the frequencies and the observation/mid-interval values, Σfx, by the sum of the frequencies, Σf.

$$\text{Mean} = \mu = \frac{\Sigma fx}{\Sigma f}$$

Example

The frequency table shows the number of goals scored by a local football team in each game.

Goals scored	Frequency
1	3
2	9
3	4
4	7
5	2

(a) Find the: (i) mean, (ii) mode and (iii) median.

(b) Comment on your results.

Solution

(a) (i) To find the mean, use the formula: mean $= \mu = \dfrac{\Sigma fx}{\Sigma f}$.

Goals scored x	Frequency f	Goals × Frequency fx
1	3	(1)(3) = 3
2	9	(2)(9) = 18
3	4	(3)(4) = 12
4	7	(4)(7) = 28
5	2	(5)(2) = 10
	$\Sigma f = 25$	$\Sigma fx = 71$

Multiply the frequencies by the corresponding number of goals scored, fx

Sum of the product of the frequencies and the corresponding number of goals scored, Σfx

Sum of the frequencies, Σf

$$\text{Mean} = \mu = \frac{\sum fx}{\sum f} = \frac{(1)(3) + (2)(9) + (3)(4) + (4)(7) + (5)(2)}{25} = \frac{71}{25} = 2 \cdot 84$$

Therefore, the mean number of goals scored is 2·84.

(ii) The mode is the data value that occurs most often in the set of data.

The highest frequency is 9, so the mode = 2 goals.

Therefore, the modal number of goals scored is 2.

(iii) The median is the middle number when the data is ranked.

Method 1

Rank the data: 1, 1, 1, 2, 2, 2, 2, 2, 2, 2, 2, 2, 3, 3, 3, 3, 4, 4, 4, 4, 4, 4, 4, 5, 5

Find the middle number: 1, 1, 1, 2, 2, 2, 2, 2, 2, 2, 2, 2, **3**, 3, 3, 3, 4, 4, 4, 4, 4, 4, 4, 5, 5

The median is the 13th data value = 3

Method 2

As the data is already ranked within the frequency table, we must find where the 13th data value lies. It lies in the row highlighted yellow in the table in part **(a)** The median number of goals scored is 3.

(b) The best central tendency/average to use in this case is the median number of goals scored. It shows that in half the matches fewer than 3 goals were sco red and for the other half more than 3 goals were scored.

Example

The frequency table below shows the results from a Maths exam.

Maths percentage	Frequency
0–10	0
10–20	1
20–30	2
30–40	2
40–50	3
50–60	6
60–70	7
70–80	4
80–90	3
90–100	2

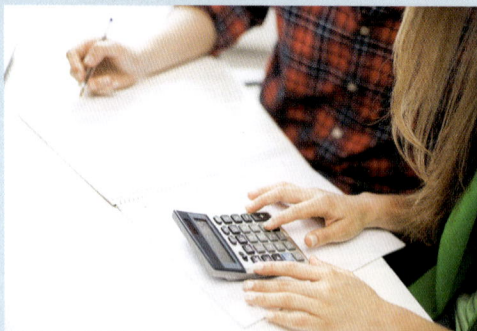

(a) Find the: **(i)** mean, **(ii)** mode and **(iii)** median.

(b) Comment on your results.

Solution

(a) (i) To find the mean use the formula: mean $= \mu = \dfrac{\Sigma fx}{\Sigma f}$

Maths percentage	Frequency f	Mid-interval value x	frequency × mid-interval value	
0–10	0	$\dfrac{0+10}{2} = \dfrac{10}{2} = 5$	$(0)(5) = 0$	Multiply the frequencies by the corresponding mid-interval value, fx
10–20	1	$\dfrac{10+20}{2} = \dfrac{30}{2} = 15$	$(1)(15) = 15$	
20–30	2	$\dfrac{20+30}{2} = \dfrac{50}{2} = 25$	$(2)(25) = 50$	
30–40	2	$\dfrac{30+40}{2} = \dfrac{70}{2} = 35$	$(2)(35) = 70$	
40–50	3	$\dfrac{40+50}{2} = \dfrac{90}{2} = 45$	$(3)(45) = 135$	
50–60	6	55	$(6)(55) = 330$	
60–70	7	65	$(7)(65) = 455$	
70–80	4	75	$(4)(75) = 300$	
80–90	3	85	$(3)(85) = 255$	
90–100	2	95	$(2)(95) = 190$	
	$\Sigma f = 30$		$\Sigma fx = 1800$	

Sum of the frequencies, Σf

Sum of the product of the frequencies and the mid-interval values, Σfx

$$\text{Mean} = \mu = \frac{\Sigma fx}{\Sigma f} = \frac{1800}{30} = 60$$

Therefore, the mean Maths percentage achieved in the class is 60%.

(ii) The mode is the data value that occurs most often in the set of data.

The highest frequency is 7, so the modal percentage score in the Maths test is 65%.

(iii) The median is the middle number when the data is ranked. As the data is already ranked within the frequency table, to find the median value we must find where the 15th data value lies. It lies in the row highlighted yellow in the table in part **(a)(i)**. Therefore, the median Maths percentage is 65%.

(b) The best central tendency/average to use in this case is the median percentage. It does not consider any outlier values (extreme values) and shows that half the class scored less than 65% and over half the class scored more than 65%. This value is also included in the data set. Note that the median and mode are the same value for this data set.

Example

The table below shows the distances travelled by seven paper airplanes after they were thrown.

Airplane	A	B	C	D	E	F	G
Distance (cm)	188	200	250	30	380	330	302

(a) Find the median of the data.

(b) Find the mean of the data.

(c) Airplane D is thrown again and the distance it travels is measured and recorded in place of the original measurement. The median of the data remains unchanged and the mean is now equal to the median. How far did airplane D travel the second time?

(d) What is the minimum distance that airplane D would need to have travelled for the median to have changed?

(SEC 2011)

Solution

(a) The median is the middle number when the data is ranked.

Rank the data and identify the middle number: 30, 188, 200, **250**, 302, 330, 380

The median is the 4th data value = 250.

So, the median distance travelled by the paper airplanes is 250 cm.

(b) Mean = $\dfrac{\text{total distance travelled}}{\text{number of airplanes}} = \dfrac{30 + 188 + 200 + 250 + 302 + 330 + 380}{7}$

$$= \frac{1680}{7}$$

$$= 240 \text{ cm}$$

So, the mean distance travelled by the paper airplanes is 240 cm.

(c) We are told that the new mean equals the median in part **(a)**, so we know that the new mean is 250 cm. We need to use algebra to solve this part of the question.

Let x = distance travelled by airplane D the second time.

$$\text{Mean} = \frac{\text{total distance travelled}}{\text{number of airplanes}} = \frac{x + 188 + 200 + 250 + 302 + 330 + 380}{7} = 250 \text{ cm}$$

$\Rightarrow \dfrac{x + 1650}{7} = 250$ ...multiply by 7

$\Rightarrow x + 1650 = 250(7)$ ...subtract 1650

$\Rightarrow x = 1750 - 1650 \Rightarrow x = 100$

Airplane D travelled 100 cm the second time.

(d) For the median to have changed, Airplane D must travel further than the median Airplane C. Therefore, Airplane D must travel greater then 250 cm, to change the median.

Measures of spread

Points to note

Two measures of spread are covered on the JCHL course: they are the **range** and the **interquartile range**.

Word(s)	Meaning
Range	The difference between the largest and the smallest value. Range = largest value – smallest value
The middle quartile, Q_2	The median.
The lower quartile, Q_1	The median of the numbers to the left of Q_2.
The upper quartile, Q_3	The median of the numbers to the right of Q_2.
Interquartile range	The difference between the upper and lower quartiles. Interquartile range = $Q_3 - Q_1$

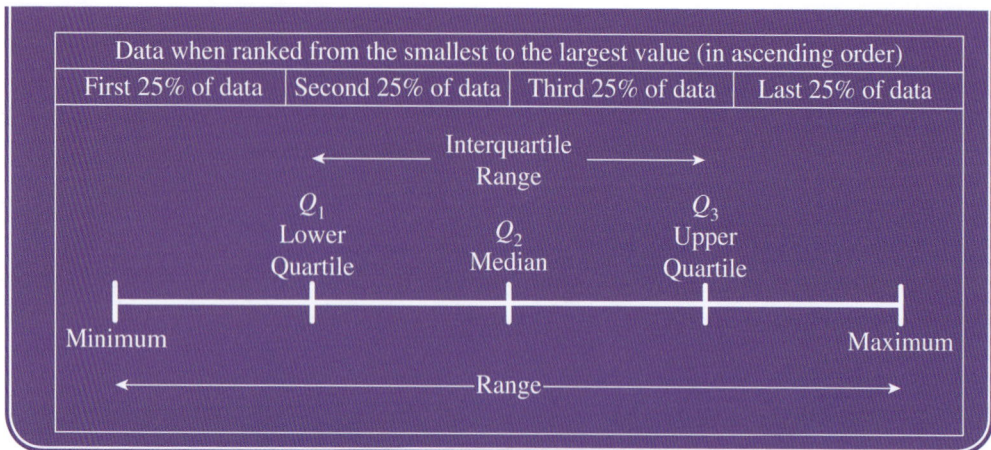

Data when ranked from the smallest to the largest value (in ascending order)			
First 25% of data	Second 25% of data	Third 25% of data	Last 25% of data

Interquartile
Range

Q_1
Lower
Quartile

Q_2
Median

Q_3
Upper
Quartile

Minimum

Maximum

Range

Example

A data set consists of: 12, 14, 16, 18, 20, 22, 24, 26, 28, 30, 52

(a) Find the: **(i)** range, **(ii)** middle quartile, **(iii)** lower quartile, **(iv)** upper quartile, and **(v)** interquartile range.

(b) Comment on the values of the range and the interquartile range.

Solution

(a) **(i)** The **range** is the difference between the largest and the smallest value.

Range = largest value – smallest value = 52 – 12 = 40.

(ii) The **middle quartile** is the median, which is the middle data value when all the data has been ranked. As the data is already ranked, the median is the 6th data value:

12, 14, 16, 18, 20, **22**, 24, 26, 28, 30, 52

The median = 22. Therefore, $Q_2 = 22$.

(iii) The **lower quartile** is the median of the numbers to the left of Q_2. There are five values before the median, so the lower quartile is the 3rd value in the data set: 12, 14, **16**, 18, 20 …

The median = 16. Therefore, $Q_1 = 16$.

(iv) The **upper quartile** is the median of the numbers to the right of Q_2. There are five values after the median, so the upper quartile is the 9th value in the data set: … 24, 26, **28**, 30, 52

The median = 28. Therefore, $Q_3 = 28$.

(v) The **interquartile range** is the difference between the upper and lower quartiles.

Interquartile range = $Q_3 - Q_1 = 28 - 16 = 12$

(b) The range is a larger value than the interquartile range, indicating that the data set has a wide range of values. However, the range includes outliers and so includes the data value 52, which skews the answer. The interquartile range has a smaller value as it ignores outliers/extreme values, so for this case the interquartile range is a better value to use to describe the spread of the data.

Example

A data set consists of: 122, 130, 128, 123, 126, 124, 127, 125, 129

Find the: **(a)** mean, **(b)** mode, **(c)** median, **(d)** range, and **(e)** interquartile range

Solution

(a) Mean = $\dfrac{\text{sum of all the values}}{\text{number of values}}$

$= \dfrac{122 + 130 + 128 + 123 + 126 + 124 + 127 + 125 + 129}{9} = \dfrac{1134}{9} = 126$

(b) The mode is the data value that occurs most often in the set of data.

As there are no repeated values, no mode exists.

(c) The median is the middle data value when all the data has been ranked.

Rank/arrange the numbers in ascending order:

$$122, 123, 124, 125, \mathbf{126}, 127, 128, 129, 130$$

The central number is 126. Therefore, the median = 126.

(d) The range is the difference between the largest and the smallest value.

Range = largest value – smallest value = 130 – 122 = 8

(e) The interquartile range is the difference between the upper and lower quartiles.

First identify Q_1 and Q_3 from the data set.

$$122, 123, 124, 125, \mathbf{126}, 127, 128, 129, 130$$

$Q_1 = 123.5 \qquad Q_2 = 126 \qquad Q_3 = 128.5$

Use either method below to find the interquartile range.

Method 1

- There are four values before the median, so the lower quartile Q_1 is halfway between the 2nd and 3rd value in the data set.

Therefore, $Q_1 = \dfrac{123 + 124}{2} = 123.5 \Rightarrow Q_1 = 123.5$

- There are four values after the median, so the upper quartile Q_3 is halfway between the 7th and 8th value in the data set.

Therefore, $Q_3 = \dfrac{128 + 129}{2} = 128.5 \Rightarrow Q_3 = 128.5$

Method 2

- To find the lower quartile Q_1 multiply the number of data values by $\frac{1}{4}$
  $$\Rightarrow 9\left(\frac{1}{4}\right) = 2{\cdot}25.$$
  As the data value is not a full value, find the data value halfway between the 2nd and 3rd value: $Q_1 = \dfrac{123 + 124}{2} = 123{\cdot}5 \Rightarrow Q_1 = 123{\cdot}5$

- To find the upper quartile Q_3 multiply the number of data values by $\frac{3}{4}$
  $$\Rightarrow 9\left(\frac{3}{4}\right) = 7{\cdot}75$$
  As the data value is not a full value, find the data value halfway between the 7th and 8th value: $Q_3 = \dfrac{128 + 129}{2} = 128{\cdot}5 \Rightarrow Q_3 = 128{\cdot}5$

Now the interquartile range can be calculated.

Interquartile range $= Q_3 - Q_1 = 128{\cdot}5 - 123{\cdot}5 = 5$

Example

A data set consists of: 6, 12, 15, 20, 14, 8, 10, 18, 24, 12

(a) Find the: (i) mean, (ii) mode, (iii) median, (iv) range, and (v) interquartile range.

(b) Comment on the values found for the central tendency and the measures of spread.

Solution

(a) (i) Mean $= \dfrac{\text{sum of all the values}}{\text{number of values}}$

$$= \frac{6 + 12 + 15 + 20 + 14 + 8 + 10 + 18 + 24 + 12}{10} = \frac{139}{10} = 13{\cdot}9$$

Note that the mean value is not a value of the data set.

(ii) The mode is the data value that occurs most often in the set of data.
Mode $= 12$

(iii) The median is the middle data value when all the data has been ranked.

6, 8, 10, 12, 12, 14, 15, 18, 20, 24

Median $= 13$

The median is the middle value: this is halfway between the 5th and 6th value.

The 5th value is 12 and the 6th value is 14.

Hence the median $= \dfrac{12 + 14}{2} = 13.$

(iv) The range is the difference between the largest and the smallest value.

Range = largest value – smallest value = 24 – 6 = 18.

(v) The interquartile range is the difference between the upper and lower quartiles.

First identify Q_1 and Q_3 from the data set.

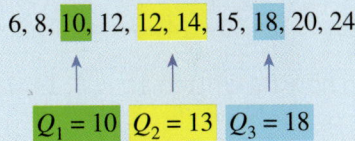

6, 8, 10, 12, 12, 14, 15, 18, 20, 24

$$\uparrow \qquad \uparrow \qquad \uparrow$$

$Q_1 = 10$ $\quad Q_2 = 13$ $\quad Q_3 = 18$

Now the interquartile range can be calculated as = $Q_3 - Q_1$ = 18 – 10 = 8.

(b) All the values for central tendency are between 12 and 13·9. Ignoring outliers, the median is a better value to use to describe the central tendency in this case.

The interquartile range has a smaller value as it ignores outliers/extreme values, so for this case the interquartile range is a better value to use to describe the spread of data.

Example

(a) The following five numbers have a median of 6 and a range of 9. They are given in increasing order: 2, 2, x, 7, y. Find the value of x and the value of y.

(b) The following six numbers have a median of 15, a mean of 18, and a range of 30. They are given in increasing order: a, 8, 14, b, 26, c. Find the value of a, the value of b and the value of c.

(SEC 2016)

Solution

(a) To find the value of x and y, use the information given in the question and solve.

- The median is 6 and is the middle data value when all the data has been ranked.

As the data is already given in increasing order (ranked):   2, 2, **x**, 7, y

Therefore, the median value is $x = 6$.

- The range is 9 and is the difference between the largest and the smallest value.

Range = largest value – smallest value = $y - 2 = 9$

$\therefore y = 9 + 2 = 11$.

(b) To find the values of a, b and c, use the information given in the question and solve.

- The median is 15 and is the middle data value when all the data has been ranked.

As the data is already given in increasing order (ranked): a, 8, **14, b**, 26, c

The median is halfway between 14 and b. Use algebra to find the value of b.

$$\frac{14 + b}{2} = 15 \Rightarrow 14 + b = 2(15) \Rightarrow b = 30 - 14 \Rightarrow b = 16$$

As $b = 16$, the data set can now be written as: a, 8, 14, 16, 26, c

- The mean is 18.

$$\text{Mean} = \frac{\text{sum of all the values}}{\text{number of values}} = 18 \Rightarrow \frac{a + 8 + 14 + 16 + 26 + c}{6} = 18$$

$$\therefore \frac{64 + a + c}{6} = 18 \Rightarrow 64 + a + c = 6(18) \Rightarrow a + c = 108 - 64$$

$\therefore a + c = 44$. Label this as Equation (1).

- The range is 30.

$$\text{Range} = \text{largest value} - \text{smallest value} \Rightarrow c - a = 30$$

$\therefore -a + c = 30$. Label this as Equation (2).

Solve using simultaneous equations. To eliminate a, add Equation (1) and Equation (2).

$$
\begin{array}{ll}
a + c = 44 & (1) \\
\underline{-a + c = 30} & (2) \\
2c = 74 & (3)
\end{array}
$$

Divide Equation (3) by 2 $\Rightarrow c = 37$

Calculate the value of a, by substituting $c = 37$ into Equation (1).

$$a + c = 44 \Rightarrow a + 37 = 44 \Rightarrow a = 44 - 37 \Rightarrow a = 7$$

Therefore $a = 7$, $b = 16$ and $c = 37$.

Exercise

Q1 (a) Which measure of central tendency can have more than one answer?

(b) Which is the most common measure used for central tendency?

(c) Which measures of central tendency do not include outliers?

(d) Which two measures of spread are covered on the JCHL course?

(e) Explain each of the three measures of centre/central tendency on the JCHL course.

(f) Give advantages and disadvantages of the three measures of centre.

(g) Explain each of the two measures of spread covered on the JCHL course.

Q2 A data set consists of: 102, 108, 107, 109, 108, 102, 110, 102

(a) Find the: **(i)** mean, **(ii)** mode, **(iii)** median, **(iv)** range, and **(v)** interquartile range.

(b) Comment on the values found for the central tendency and the measures of spread.

Q3 A data set consists of: 11, 4, 6, 8, 3, 10, 8, 10, 4, 12, 13

(a) Find the: **(i)** mean, **(ii)** mode, **(iii)** median, **(iv)** range, and **(v)** interquartile range.

(b) Comment on the values found for the central tendency and the measures of spread.

Q4 There are ten students in a class. All ten of them sat a test. The table below shows the mean mark, the median mark, and the range of the marks on the test.

	Results of the test	Answers to part (b)
Mean mark	25·1	
Median mark	24	
Range of the marks	14	

The highest mark got by a student on the test was 32.

(a) Use the range to find the lowest mark got by a student on the test.

An external examiner suggested that 2 be added onto each student's mark.

(b) Find what the mean, the median, and the range would be in this case. Fill your answers into the table above.

Bob says: 'Whenever the median of a list of numbers is 24, then at least one of the numbers in the list must be 24.'

(c) Give an example to show that Bob is not correct.

(SEC 2015)

Q5 The size, mean and range of four sets of data, A, B, C and D, are given in the table.

	A	B	C	D
Size (n)	12	50	50	500
Mean (μ)	15	15	55	5
Range	40	50	22	15

Complete the sentences below by inserting the relevant letter in each space.

(a) On average, the data in set _____ are the largest numbers and the data in set _____ are the smallest numbers.

(b) The set that contains more numbers than any other is _____ and the set that contains fewer numbers than any other is _____.

(c) The set with the greatest total is _____.

(d) The data in set _____ have the greatest difference between their highest and lowest values.

Q6 (a) In four games, a soccer player scored 1, x, 4 and 3 goals. The mean number of goals scored by the player per game was 2. Find the number of goals scored in the second game, i.e. the value of x.

(b) Over a period of one month, the owner of a factory recorded the number of days that each of his 50 employees was absent from work. The following table shows the results.

Number of days absent	0	1	2	3	4	5
Number of employees	7	9	11	12	7	4

(i) Find the mean number of days the employees were absent.

(ii) Write down the mode.

(iii) Find the median number of days the employees were absent.

(iv) Calculate the range of days the employees were absent.

(v) Which measure of centre is the most appropriate to use for this data? Explain.

Q7 Katie conducted a survey to determine the ages of the pupils on her school bus. Her results are shown below.

13	14	15	12	14	15
13	14	12	16	15	14
12	12	16	14	16	13
14	15	14	14	13	12
13	12	15	13	12	14

(a) Use this data to complete a frequency table.

(b) Using the frequency table, find:

   (i) the mean age of the pupils on the bus

  (ii) the modal age of the pupils

 (iii) the median age of the pupils.

(c) Calculate the range.

Q8 The salaries, in €, of the different employees working in a call centre are listed below.

22 000	16 500	38 000	26 500	15 000	21 000	15 500	46 000
42 000	9500	32 000	27 000	33 000	36 000	24 000	37 000
65 000	37 000	24 500	23 500	28 000	52 000	33 000	25 000
23 000	16 500	35 000	25 000	33 000	20 000	19 500	16 000

(a) Use this data to complete the grouped frequency table below.

Salary (€1000s)	0–10	10–20	20–30	30–40	40–50	50–60	60–70
Number of employees							

[Note: 10–20 means €10 000 or more but less than €20 000, etc.]

(b) Using mid-interval values, find the mean salary of the employees.

(c) (i) Outline another method which could have been used to calculate the mean salary.

  (ii) Which method is more accurate? Explain your answer.

(SEC 2013)

Q9 (a) 8 is the mean of the five numbers 13, 6, 5, x and 7. Find the value of x.

(b) The weights, in kg, of 125 Junior Certificate students are given in the following frequency table.

Weight in kg	40–45	45–50	50–55	55–60	60–65	65–70	70–75
Number of students	7	9	22	27	24	28	8

[Note: 40–45 means 40 or more but less than 45, etc.]

(i) Calculate the mean weight of the Junior Certificate students.

(ii) Find the modal weight of the students.

(iii) Find the median weight of the students.

(iv) Which measure of centre is the most appropriate to use for this data? Explain.

Solutions

Q1 (a) The measure of centre which can have more than one answer is the mode.

(b) The most common value used for the measure of centre is the mean.

(c) Both the mode and the median do not include outliers/extreme values from the data set.

(d) The two measures of spread covered on the JCHL course are the range and the interquartile range.

(e) The three measures of centre are:

- The mean is the sum of all the data values divided by the number of values in the data set.

- The mode is the data value that occurs most often in the data set. There can be no mode, one mode or more than one modal value.

- The median is the middle number when the data is ranked.

(f)

Central tendency/ average	Advantages	Disadvantages
Mean	• Uses all the data • Can be calculated easily • You don't need to order the data	• Includes outlier values • May not exist in the data
Mode	• Easy to find • Is not affected by outliers • The only average used for qualitative/ categorical nominal data • The value exists in the data	• Some data sets may not have a mode • More than one mode may exist
Median	• Is not affected by outliers • Easy to find when the data is ordered • Works well with ordinal data	• Data needs to be ranked • Can be hard to calculate • May not exist in the data

(g) The two measures of spread are:

• The range is the difference between the largest and the smallest value:

Range = largest value – smallest value

• The interquartile range is the difference between the upper and lower quartiles:

Interquartile range = $Q_3 - Q_1$

Q2 (a) (i) The mean is found by adding (summing) all the values together and dividing by the number of values in the data set.

$$\text{Mean} = \frac{\text{sum of all the values}}{\text{number of values}}$$

$$= \frac{102 + 108 + 107 + 109 + 108 + 102 + 110}{7} = \frac{746}{7} = 106 \cdot 571...$$

The mean is 106·57, accurate to 2 decimal places.

(ii) The mode is the data value that occurs most often in the set of data.

102, 108, 107, 109, 108, 102, 110

In this distribution, 102 and 108 both appear twice, so there are two modes for this set of data.

The modes are 102 and 108.

(iii) The median is the middle number when the data is ranked:

Rank the data: 102, 102, 107, 108, 108, 109, 110

Identify/find the middle number: 102, 102, 107, **108**, 108, 109, 110

The median is the 4th data value. The median is 108.

(iv) The range = largest value − smallest value = 110 − 102 = 8

(v) The interquartile range is the difference between the upper and lower quartiles.

First identify Q_1 and Q_3 from the data set.

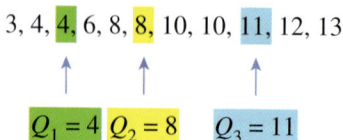

$$102,\ 102,\ 107,\ \mathbf{108},\ 108,\ 109,\ 110$$

$Q_1 = 102 \quad Q_2 = 108 \quad Q_3 = 109$

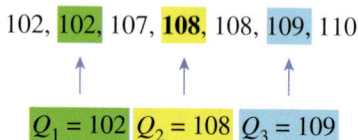

The interquartile range = $Q_3 - Q_1$ = 109 − 102 = 7.

(b) As there are no outliers in this data set, the mean or median values can be used. As there are two values for the mode, these values should not be used.

The interquartile range and range have similar values as there are no outliers/extreme values in the data. So, for this case either value can be used. However, in general the interquartile range is a better value to use to describe the spread of data.

Q3 (a) (i) Mean = $\dfrac{\text{sum of all the values}}{\text{number of values}}$

$$= \frac{11 + 4 + 6 + 8 + 3 + 10 + 8 + 10 + 4 + 12 + 13}{11} = \frac{89}{11} = 8{\cdot}09...$$

(ii) The modes are the data values that occur most often in the set of data. There are three modes for this data set: 4, 8 and 10, which all occur twice.

(iii) The median is the middle value, when the data is ranked. This is the 6th value, which is 8.

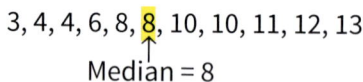

$$3,\ 4,\ 4,\ 6,\ 8,\ \mathbf{8},\ 10,\ 10,\ 11,\ 12,\ 13$$

Median = 8

(iv) The range = largest value − smallest value = 13 − 3 = 10

(v) The interquartile range is the difference between the upper and lower quartiles.

First identify Q_1 and Q_3 from the data set.

$$3,\ 4,\ \mathbf{4},\ 6,\ 8,\ \mathbf{8},\ 10,\ 10,\ \mathbf{11},\ 12,\ 13$$

$Q_1 = 4 \quad Q_2 = 8 \qquad Q_3 = 11$

So the interquartile range = $Q_3 - Q_1$ = 11 − 4 = 7.

(b) Ignoring outliers, the median is a better value to use to describe the central tendency in this case. This value exists in the data set and is close to the mean.

The interquartile range has a smaller value as it ignores outliers/ extreme values, so for this case the interquartile range is a better value to use to describe the spread of data.

Q4 (a) To find the lowest mark scored on the test, use the information provided in the question. The largest mark = 32 and the range of marks = 14.

Range = largest value – smallest value = 32 – lowest mark = 14.

Hence, the lowest mark = 32 – 14 = 18.

(b) If an external examiner requests that 2 is added onto each student's mark then the mean, the median, and the range would change as shown in the table below.

	Results of the test	Answers to part (b)	Explanation
Mean mark	25·1	25·1 + 2 = 27·1	All students get an extra 2 marks
Median mark	24	24 + 2 = 26	All students get an extra 2 marks, so the median increases by 2.
Range of the marks	14	14	The lowest and highest mark both increase by 2, so the range remains the same.

(c) For any data set containing an even number of elements, the median is halfway between two numbers. For example: The set of data: 7, 23, 25, 96 has four elements, so the median is found halfway between the 2nd and 3rd data values. Therefore, the median $= \dfrac{23 + 25}{2} = 24$.

Q5 (a) On average, the data in set $\underline{C}$ are the biggest numbers and the data in set $\underline{D}$ are the smallest numbers. We know this as set C has the biggest mean and set D has the smallest mean, so these numbers contain the biggest and smallest numbers.

(b) The set that contains more numbers than any other is $\underline{D}$ and the set that contains fewer numbers than any other is $\underline{A}$. The size of the data set is given by n.

(c) Total of set A = 12 × 15 = 180   Total of set B = 50 × 15 = 750

Total of set C = 50 × 55 = 2750   Total of set D = 500 × 5 = 2500

So the set with the greatest total is C.

(d) The data in set B have the greatest difference between their highest and lowest values. This is because the range is the biggest value.

Q6 (a) Mean = $\dfrac{\text{sum of all the values}}{\text{number of values}}$

$\therefore$ Mean = $\dfrac{1+x+4+3}{4}=2 \Rightarrow \dfrac{x+8}{4}=2 \Rightarrow x+8=8 \Rightarrow x=0$

The mean number of goals scored was 0 goals.

(b) (i) To find the mean, use the formula: mean = $\mu = \dfrac{\Sigma fx}{\Sigma f}$.

Number of days absent x	Frequency f	Number of days absent × Frequency fx	
0	7	(0)(7) = 0	Multiply the frequencies by the corresponding number of days absent, fx
1	9	(1)(9) = 9	
2	11	(2)(11) = 22	
3	12	(3)(12) = 36	Sum of the product of the frequencies and the corresponding number of days absent, Σfx
4	7	(4)(7) = 28	
5	4	(5)(4) = 20	
	$\Sigma f = 50$	$\Sigma fx = 115$	

Sum of the frequencies, Σf

$\therefore$ Mean = $\mu = \dfrac{\Sigma fx}{\Sigma f} = \dfrac{115}{50} = 2 \cdot 3$.

(ii) The mode is the most common number of days absent. This is 3 days.

(iii) The median number of days that the employees were absent is the middle data value, which is between the 25th and 26th data value. The median number of days absent is 2 days.

(iv) The range = largest value – smallest value = 5 – 0 = 5.

(v) As there are no outliers in this data set, use the mean which is the most common measure of centre. The mean is 2·3 days.

Q7 Katie's results can be colour-coded to help determine frequencies.

13	14	15	12	14	15
13	14	12	16	15	14
12	12	16	14	16	13
14	15	14	14	13	12
13	12	15	13	12	14

(a)

Age of pupil x	Frequency f	Age of pupil on the bus × Frequency fx
12	7	$(12)(7) = 84$
13	6	$(13)(6) = 78$
14	9	$(14)(9) = 126$
15	5	$(15)(5) = 75$
16	3	$(16)(3) = 48$
	$\Sigma f = 30$	$\Sigma fx = 411$

Multiply the frequencies by the corresponding age, fx

Sum of the product of the frequencies and the corresponding age of the pupil, Σfx

(b) Using the frequency table:

   (i) The mean age of the pupils on the bus $\Rightarrow \mu = \dfrac{\Sigma fx}{\Sigma f} = \dfrac{411}{30} = 13\cdot7$

   (ii) The modal age of the pupils is 14.

   (iii) The median age is between the 15th and 16th data value.
   Therefore, the median age is 14.

(c) The range = largest value – smallest value = $16 - 12 = 4$.

Q8 (a)

Salary (€1000s)	0–10	10–20	20–30	30–40	40–50	50–60	60–70
Number of employees	1	6	12	9	2	1	1

(b)

Salary (€1000s)	Number of employees Frequency f	Mid-interval value x	Frequency × mid-interval value fx
0–10	1	5	$(1)(5) = 5$
10–20	6	15	$(6)(15) = 90$
20–30	12	25	$(12)(25) = 300$
30–40	9	35	$(9)(35) = 315$
40–50	2	45	$(2)(45) = 90$
50–60	1	55	$(1)(55) = 55$
60–70	1	65	$(1)(65) = 65$
	$\Sigma f = 32$		$\Sigma fx = 920$

$$\therefore \text{Mean} = \mu = \frac{\Sigma fx}{\Sigma f} = \frac{920}{32} = 28 \cdot 75$$

Therefore, the mean salary earned is €28 750.

(c) (i) Another method which could have been used to calculate the mean salary is to add up all the actual salaries given in the question and divide the answer by 32.

(ii) The second method is more accurate as the mean achieved gives the actual mean for the given salaries. The mid-interval values give a good approximation only.

$$\text{Mean} = \frac{\text{salaries total}}{\text{number of employees}} = \frac{€917\,000}{32} = €28\,656 \cdot 25$$

Q9 (a) Mean $= \dfrac{\text{sum of all the values}}{\text{number of values}}$

$\therefore$ Mean $= \dfrac{13 + 6 + 5 + x + 7}{5} = 8 \Rightarrow \dfrac{x + 31}{5} = 8 \Rightarrow x = 40 - 31 = 9$

(b) **(i)** Create a frequency table to find the mean weight of the Junior Certificate students.

Weight in kg	Number of students Frequency f	Mid-interval value x	Frequency × mid-interval value fx
40–45	7	42·5	(7)(42·5) = 294
45–50	9	47·5	(9)(47·5) = 423
50–55	22	52·5	(22)(52·5) = 1144
55–60	27	57·5	(27)(57·5) = 1539
60–65	24	62·5	(24)(62·5) = 1488
65–70	28	67·5	(28)(67·5) = 1876
70–75	8	72·5	(8)(72·5) = 576
	$\Sigma f = 125$		$\Sigma fx = 7402\cdot5$

$\therefore$ Mean $= \mu = \dfrac{\Sigma fx}{\Sigma f} = \dfrac{7402\cdot5}{125} = 59\cdot22$

(ii) The modal weight of the students is in the range 65–70 kg.

(iii) The median weight of the students is the 63rd data value, which is in the range 55–60 kg.

(iv) The median is the measure of centre which is the most appropriate to use for this data, because extreme outliers exist.

5 Statistics 3: Representation and Interpretation of Statistics

Learning objectives

In this chapter, you will learn about:

- Representing statistical data graphically
- Describing statistical data graphically using measures of centre and spread
- How to create pie charts, bar charts, line plots, histograms with equal intervals, stem-and-leaf plots and back-to-back stem-and-leaf plots
- Using appropriate graphical displays to compare data sets
- Using distributions to compare data.

Representing statistical data graphically

Representing statistical data graphically can be a much more useful way to represent information than a table. For different types of statistical data, we can use different graphical representations.

On the JCHL course, statistical data can be displayed graphically using:

- pie charts
- bar charts
- line plots
- histograms with equal intervals
- stem-and-leaf plots and back-to-back stem-and-leaf plots.

Each graphical display is used for particular types of data as shown in the table below.

Graphical representation	Categorical		Numerical	
	Nominal	Ordinal	Discrete	Continuous
Pie chart	✓	✓	✓	✗
Bar chart	✓	✓	✓	✗
Line/dot plot	✓	✓	✓	✗
Histogram with equal intervals			✓	✓
Stem-and-leaf plot			✓	✓
Back-to-back stem-and-leaf plot			✓	✓

Each graphical representation type is detailed later.

Describing statistical data graphically using measures of centre and spread

A summary of the information learned in Statistics 2 is shown in the table.

Statistics summary		
Statistics terminology	Used for continuous and discrete numerical data	Features and general advice
Measures of centre: • median • mean • mode	Numerical: • The **median** (Q_2) is the middle value from ordered data • The **mean** is the sum of all the data values divided by the number of data values Categorical: • The **mode** is the data value(s) which occurs most frequently	• The median is used for data with outliers • The mean is used for data with a reasonably symmetric distribution* (where there are no outliers) • The mode is used for categorical data
Outliers: affect both the mean and median	An outlier can be identified by eye, as value(s) which are very far away from the main data values	• Take care when deciding whether to ignore outliers, as it will affect the measure of centre chosen

*distributions will be discussed start on the next page

Statistics summary		
Statistics terminology	**Used for continuous and discrete numerical data**	**Features and general advice**

Measures of spread:
 	
• range
 	
• interquartile range
	Numerically:
	
	• Range = maximum value – minimum value
	
	• Interquartile range $(IQR) = Q_3 - Q_1$
	
	  ○ Lower quartile = Q_1
	
	  ○ Upper quartile = Q_3
		• The interquartile range (IQR) is a better indication of spread when data has outliers

In Statistics 2, the measures of centre and spread were found numerically, but graphical displays can also be used to identify these measures, as shown in the table below.

Characteristic	Description	Image
Centre	• Is found at the median of the distribution. • Is found when half the values are on either side.	
Spread	• If the data values cover a wide range, then the spread is large. • If the data values are close together then the spread is smaller.	 1 2 3 4 5 6 7 8 9 More spread 1 2 3 4 5 6 7 8 9 Less spread
Symmetric distribution	• Has an axis of symmetry at the centre of the distribution. • The mean, median and mode all lie on the half way line.	 Normal

Characteristic	Description	Image
Skewed right/ positively skewed distribution	• No axis of symmetry. • The tail is towards the right – as the frequencies are less here. • The mean is drawn towards the tail. • The mode is to the left of the median. • The median is taken as the measure of centre. • Like the shape of the right foot.	
Skewed left/ negatively skewed distribution	• No axis of symmetry. • The tail is towards the left – as the frequencies are less here. • The mean is drawn towards the tail. • The mode is to the right of the median. • The median is taken as the measure of centre. • Like the shape of the left foot.	
Uniform distribution	• Data is uniform across the range of the distribution. • No peaks.	

Representing statistical data using pie charts

Points to note

This table shows the key characteristics/information about pie charts.

Pie chart	Example of chart	Features and advice	Advantages/ disadvantages
Used for: • categorical data • discrete numerical data	Marriage 33% 22% 23% 22% ■ Urban 'Yes' ■ Rural 'Yes' ■ Urban 'No' ■ Rural 'No'	• Include a title • Ensure labels are clear • Add a key if necessary • Add % or number labels • Ensure the total adds up to 100% or the total frequency • Ensure the sectors add to 360°	✓ • Useful to compare categories/ parts as a percentage of the whole ✗ • Hard to draw accurately • Not useful for large number of categories

To draw a pie chart, follow the steps below.

1 Find the total sum of the data frequencies.

2 To calculate the angle for each part of the data, divide the sum of the frequencies by 360°.

3 To find the sector angle, multiply each individual frequency by the value from step 2.

4 Check that the total sum of the angles adds to 360°. If it doesn't, check your calculations.

5 Draw the pie chart, using a compass, protractor and straight edge or ruler. Check that you have included a chart title, noted the frequencies or percentages on each sector, and given a key.

Example

Clara asked all of the students in her school some questions about their eating and exercise. One of Clara's questions was:

How healthy is your diet? Tick one box.

Very healthy	Fairly healthy	Not very healthy	Very unhealthy
☐	☐	☐	☐

She drew a pie chart to show her results. Her results, and the size of each angle in the pie chart, are shown in the table below.

Category	Very healthy	Fairly healthy	Not very healthy	Very unhealthy
Number of students		150	170	
Size of angle (degrees)	96°	90°		

(a) Find the **probability** that a student chosen at random from those surveyed ticked 'Very healthy' **or** 'Fairly healthy'.

(b) Complete the table above. Note: 90° in the pie chart represents 150 students.

(c) Complete the table below to show one question in each case that Clara could ask that would generate each type of data. Each question should be about eating or exercise. One is already filled in.

Type of Data	Question
Numerical continuous	
Numerical discrete	
Categorical ordinal	How healthy is your diet? Tick one box. Very healthy ☐ Fairly healthy ☐ Not very healthy ☐ Very unhealthy ☐
Categorical nominal	

(d) Clara is worried that the students in her school are not a representative sample of all of the students in Ireland. Explain why it is important to have a **representative** sample when doing statistical research.

(SEC 2017)

Solution

(a) The probability that a student chosen at random from those surveyed ticked 'Very healthy' or 'Fairly healthy' can be calculated by adding the size of the angle for both categories and dividing it by 360° (the total number of degrees in a circle).

$$P(\text{a student ticked 'Very healthy' or 'Fairly healthy'}) = \frac{96 + 90}{360} = \frac{186}{360} = \frac{31}{60}$$

(b) To complete the table, it is necessary to calculate the number of students represented by each degree (1°) of the pie chart and the angle which represents 1 student.

Step 1 Calculate the number of students represented by each category of the pie chart.

We know that: 90° = 150 students

$$\therefore 1° = \frac{150}{90} = \frac{5}{3} \text{ students}$$

The total number of students surveyed = $360 \times \frac{5}{3}$ = 600 students

The number of 'Very healthy' students = $96 \times \frac{5}{3}$ = 160 students

The number of 'Very unhealthy' students = 600 − 160 − 150 − 170 = 120 students

Step 2 Calculate the size of the unknown angles in the pie chart.

We know that: 150 students = 90°

$$\therefore 1 \text{ student} = \frac{90°}{150} = 0.6°$$

The size of the angle for 'Not very healthy' students = 170 × 0·6° = 102°

The size of the angle for 'Very unhealthy' students = 120 × 0·6° = 72°

Category	Very healthy	Fairly healthy	Not very healthy	Very unhealthy
Number of students	160	150	170	120
Size of angle (degrees)	96°	90°	102°	72°

Step 3 Finally, check that the total sum of the angles adds to 360° and the total number of students adds to 600.

Number of students = 160 + 150 + 170 + 120 = 600 ✔

Total sum of the angles = 96° + 90° + 102° + 72° = 360° ✔

(c) Note: The sample answers given in the table are not the only ones possible; you can provide any similar question, if it is suitable for the type of data.

Type of Data	Question
Numerical continuous	How much water do you drink each day?
Numerical discrete	How many press-ups can you do in 30 seconds?
Categorical ordinal	How healthy is your diet? Tick one box. Very healthy ☐ Fairly healthy ☐ Not very healthy ☐ Very unhealthy ☐
Categorical nominal	What do you prefer, pizza or salad?

(d) It is important to have a **representative** sample when doing statistical research:

- to ensure that the results are not biased
- so that the results will apply to the whole population, and not just the **sample**
- or any other valid explanation.

Representing statistical data using bar charts

Points to note

- A bar chart is made up of rectangular bars called columns with lengths proportional to the frequencies they represent.
- The bars can be plotted vertically or horizontally. Horizontal bar charts are used when the category names are long.
- A bar chart will have two axes:
  - One axis of the chart shows the specific categories being compared.
  - The other axis represents discrete values that represent the values of the data.

The table below shows key characteristics and information about bar charts.

Bar graphs	Example of chart	Features and advice	Advantages/ disadvantages
Used for: • categorical data • discrete ungrouped numerical data	**Vertical bar chart** Type of transport A = Automobile F = Boat/Ferry W = Walk C = Cycle B = Bus S = Skateboard **Horizontal bar chart** Frequency A = Automobile F = Boat/Ferry W = Walk C = Cycle B = Bus S = Skateboard	• Include a title • Separate columns • Columns must be of equal width separated by equal gaps • Include axes labels • Show units if used • Include key if necessary	✓ • Used for data comparison ✗ • Can be misleading if scale does not begin at 0 • Not useful if there are too many variables

Example

Students in a third-year class were investigating how the number of jelly beans in a box varies for three different brands of jelly beans. Each student counted the number of jelly beans in a box of brand A, B and C. The results are recorded in the tables below.

Brand A

23	25	25	26	26	26	26
27	27	27	27	28	29	29
29	30	30	31	31	31	32
32	32	33	34	35	35	39

Brand B

17	22	22	24	24	25	25
25	25	26	26	26	26	26
26	27	27	27	27	28	29
29	29	29	29	29	30	30

Brand C

25	25	25	26	26	26	26
26	27	27	27	28	28	28
28	28	28	28	28	28	29
29	29	30	30	31	32	32

(a) Display the data in a way that allows you to describe and compare the data for each brand.

(b) If you were to buy a box of jelly beans, which brand would you buy? Give a reason for your answer. In your explanation, you should refer to the mean number of jelly beans per box, and the range or spread of the number of jelly beans per box for each brand.

(SEC 2012/2014)

Solution

(a) Organise the data in a frequency table as shown.

Number of jelly beans	17	22	23	24	25	26	29	30	31	32	33	34	35
Brand A	0	0	1	0	2	2	0	0	0	2	1	1	1
Brand B	1	2	0	2	0	0	5	0	0	0	0	0	0
Brand C	0	0	0	0	3	2	2	2	1	0	0	0	0

Then represent the information on a bar chart as shown below, on three separate bar charts or on a dot plot.

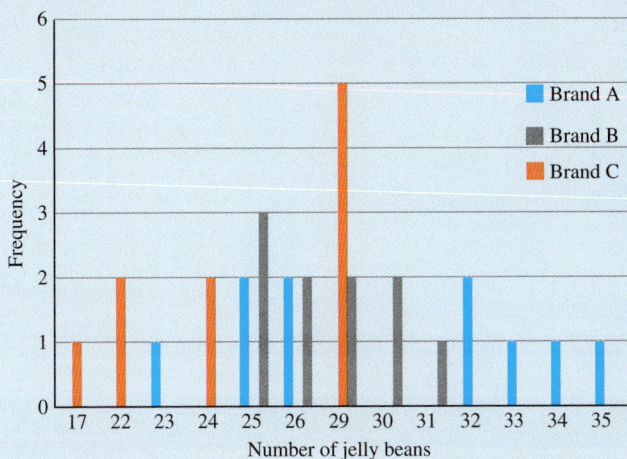

(b) It is best to buy Brand C. For Brand C, the mean number of jelly beans is $\frac{276}{10} = 27 \cdot 6$ jelly beans, compared with a mean of 24·5 jelly beans for Brand B and 29·1 for Brand A. The reason for not picking Brand A, even though it has a greater mean, is because Brand C has a range of 6 (31–25) unlike Brand A (35–23) and Brand B (29–17), which both have a range of 12, double that of Brand C. This means there is a greater difference in the number of jelly beans between the biggest and smallest packages. When buying jelly beans, you would want a consistent number of jelly beans in any brand package; so choose Brand C.

Representing statistical data using line/dot plots

Points to note

- A line or dot plot is made up of dots or x's plotted on a graph.
- Each dot (or x) represents a unit frequency and they are stacked in a column above a category.
- The height of the column represents the frequency of the category.

The table below shows the key characteristics and information about line and dot plots.

Line/dot plots	Example of chart	Features and general advice	Advantages/ disadvantages
Used for: • categorical and discrete numerical data • plotting frequency counts within a small number of categories	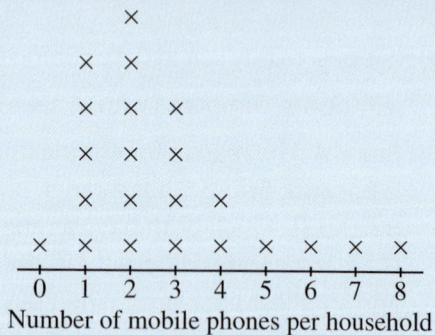 A = Automobile F = Boat/Ferry W = Walk C = Cycle B = Bus S = Skateboard	• Use dots or x's to represent each unit • Include a title and axes labels • Ensure the horizontal scale is accurate	✓ • Quick for small quantities • No need for frequency axis • Ordered so shows shape and spread of distribution ✗ • Need to count for exact total

Example

The dot plot shows the number of mobile phones owned by each family on a street.

(a) How many households on the street are in the sample?

(b) What is the mode of the data?

(c) What is the range?

(d) Describe the distribution. Explain.

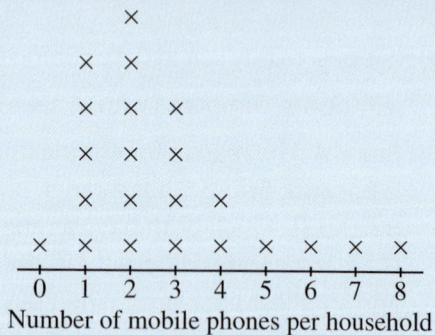

Number of mobile phones per household

Solution

(a) The number of households surveyed in the sample is 22.

(b) The mode of the data is the number of mobile phones that occurs most often, so mode = 2.

(c) The range = maximum value – minimum value = 8 – 0 = 8.

(d) As the categories are quantitative (i.e. numbers), we can describe the skewness of the data in this line/dot plot. Therefore, the distribution is right-skewed with no outliers.

The distribution is right-skewed as the households with the most numbers of mobile phones are on the left-hand side of the distribution. None of the data values are extreme, so there are no outliers.

Representing statistical data using histograms

Points to note

- A histogram is made up of rectangular bars called columns with lengths proportional to the frequencies they represent.

- A histogram will have two axes:

  - One axis of the chart shows the specific numerical data being compared.

  - The other axis represents discrete values (frequency) of the data.

- Visually a histogram differs from a bar chart as its columns touch and there are no gaps.

The table below details the key characteristics and information about histograms.

Histograms	Example of chart	Features and general advice	Advantages/ disadvantages
Used for ungrouped discrete data	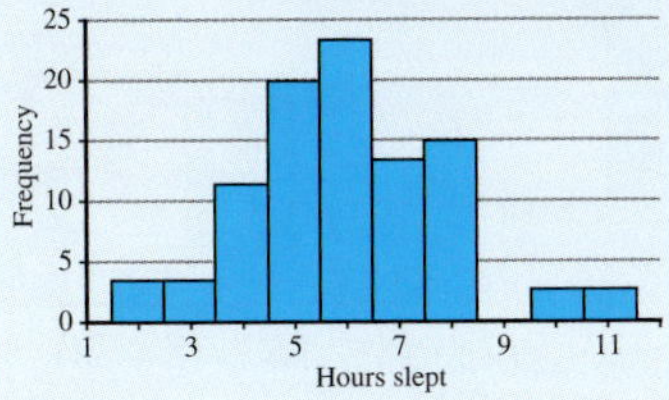	• Columns touch • Category labels are in the middle of each column for discrete ungrouped data	✓ • Shows shape and spread of distribution ✗ • Small data sets only
Used for grouped continuous numerical data	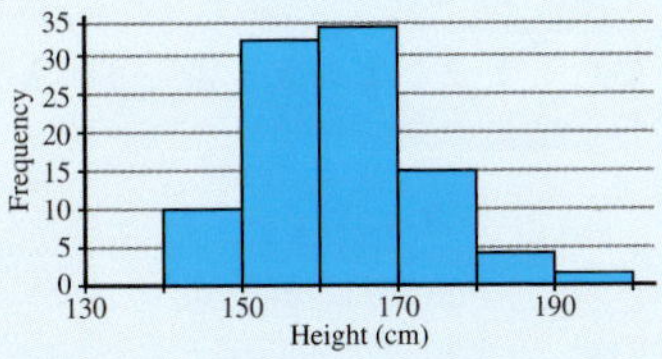	• Category labels are at the beginning of each column for grouped data	✓ • Useful when data has a large range • Shows shape and spread of distribution ✗ • Loss of individual data values

The phase 9 *CensusAtSchool* questionnaire contained the question 'Approximately how long do you spend on social networking sites each week?' The histogram below illustrates the answers given by 100 students, randomly selected from those who completed the survey.

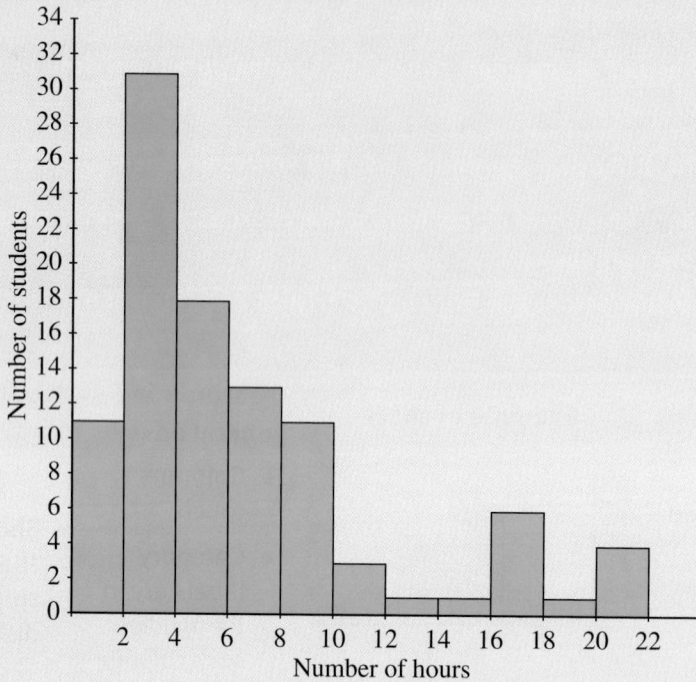

(a) Use the data from the histogram to complete the frequency table below. Note that 2–4, for example, means 2 hours or more but less than 4 hours.

Number of hours	0–2	2–4	4–6	6–8	8–10	10–12	12–14	14–16	16–18	18–20	20–22
Number of students											

(b) What is the modal interval?

(c) Taking mid-interval values, find the mean amount of time spent on social networking sites.

(d) John is conducting a survey on computer usage by students at his school. His questionnaire asks the same question. He plans to carry out his survey by asking the question to twenty first-year boys on the Monday after the mid-term break. Give some reasons why the results from John's question might not be as representative as those in the histogram.

(SEC 2012/2014)

Solution

(a)

Number of hours	0–2	2–4	4–6	6–8	8–10	10–12	12–14	14–16	16–18	18–20	20–22
Number of students	11	31	18	13	11	3	1	1	6	1	4

(b) The modal interval is the interval with the highest frequency. 2–4 has the highest frequency with a value of 31. So the modal number of hours per week that students use social networking sites is more than 2 hours and less than 4 hours.

(c) Taking mid-interval values the frequency table becomes:

Number of hours mid-interval (x)	1	3	5	7	9	11	13	15	17	19	21	Total
Number of Students (f)	11	31	18	13	11	3	1	1	6	1	4	$\sum f = 100$
$f(x)$	11	93	90	91	99	33	13	15	102	19	84	$\sum f(x) = 650$

$$\text{Mean} = \frac{\text{sum of all the values}}{\text{number of values}} = \frac{\sum f(x)}{\sum f} = \frac{650}{100} = 6{\cdot}5$$

(d) The results from John's question might not be as representative as those in the histogram because John is asking first years, who are less likely to be using social networking sites. Also, John surveyed only boys, and thus his survey will be further biased. He is also asking right after the mid-term break, when social networking site usage is generally higher.

Example

From the histograms shown, decide if these statements are true. Explain your answer.

1 Both data sets are symmetric.　　　**2** Labels on the x-axis are quantitative.

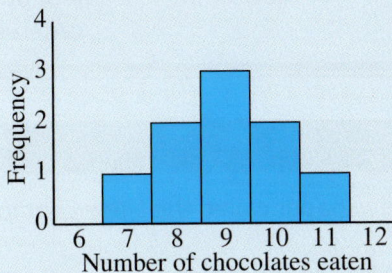

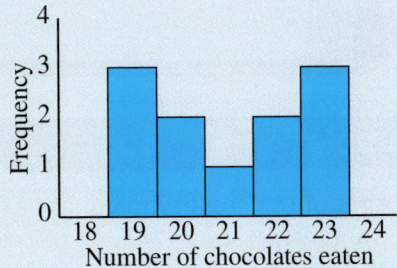

Solution

Both statements are true, as both histograms:

- are mirror images of each other through the centre, so both are symmetric.
- both the x-axis labels start 'Number of...' and so both are quantitative.

Representing statistical data using stem-and-leaf plots

The table below gives the key characteristics and information about stem-and-leaf plots.

Stem-and-leaf plots	Example of chart	Features and advice	Advantages/ disadvantages
Used for discrete and continuous numerical data.	The age of a sample of 20 people 1 | 6 7 9 2 | 0 1 3 4 6 8 9 3 | 3 4 4 5 8 4 | 2 6 5 | 0 7 6 | 3 Key: 1|6 = 16 years	• Ordered data • Include a title • Include a key • **All** stems in the range must be included even if there is no leaf	✓ • Quick to draw • Shows shape and spread • Useful display to identify median (and quartiles) ✗ • Data must first be ordered

Example

The ages of 18 people who bought a local newspaper called the *Liffey Champion* are recorded below:

71	34	15	35	46	63	23	57	26
24	47	58	50	19	42	38	62	83

(a) Represent the data on a stem-and-leaf plot.

(b) How many people under the age of 30 bought the *Liffey Champion*?

(c) Find the median age of the 18 people.

(d) The next person who buys the *Liffey Champion* is 58 years of age. Put a tick (✓) in the box that describes how this will affect the range. Give a reason for your answer.

Range will decrease	Range will increase	Range will stay the same
☐	☐	☐

Solution

(a) The data given is represented on the stem-and-leaf plot.

```
1 | 5  9
2 | 3  4  6
3 | 4  5  8
4 | 2  6  7
5 | 0  7  8
6 | 2  3
7 | 1
8 | 3
```

Key: 1|5 = 15 years

(b) The highlighted cells show the number of people under 30 who bought the newspaper.

```
1 | 5  9
2 | 3  4  6
3 | 4  5  8
4 | 2  6  7
5 | 0  7  8
6 | 2  3
7 | 1
8 | 3
```

Key: 1|5 = 15 years

Therefore, the number of people < 30 years = 5.

(c) To find the median age, rank/order the ages and find the middle number(s). As the data contains an even number of people, take the average (mean) of the two middle numbers.

Ages (ordered): 15, 19, 23, 24, 26, 34, 35, 38, 42, 46, 47, 50, 57, 58, 62, 63, 71, 83

$$\Rightarrow \text{Median} = \frac{42 + 46}{2} = \frac{88}{2} = 44 \text{ years.}$$

(d) If the next person who buys the *Liffey Champion* is 58 years of age, then the range will remain the same as 58 lies within the existing range of the data.

Range will decrease	Range will increase	Range will stay the same
☐	☐	☑

- Range (original) = maximum – minimum = 83 – 15 = 68 years.

- Range (revised) = 83 – 15 = 68 years.

  The range remains the same.

Representing statistical data using back-to-back stem-and-leaf plots

Points to note

- Back-to-back stem-and-leaf plots are used to compare two sets of data graphically.

- The centre of a back-to-back stem-and-leaf plot contains the stem.

- The leaves representing one data set extend to the right, and leaves representing the other data set extend to the left.

The table below provides key characteristics about back-to-back stem-and-leaf plots.

Back-to-back stem-and-leaf plots	Example of chart	Features and advice	Advantages/ disadvantages
Used for discrete and continuous numerical data.	Money carried by students Boys · Girls 7 | 0 | 1 | 1 | 1 146 | 2 | 268 458 | 3 | 3446689 122289 | 4 | 436 3479 | 5 | 4 258 | 6 | 13 | 7 |	• As for stem-and-leaf plots • Need to always read leaves from the stem out	✔ • Ordered so shows shape and spread of distribution • Useful for comparison ✘ • Data must first be ordered

Example

The ages of the Academy Award winners for best male actor and best female actor (at the time they won the award) from 1992 to 2011 are as follows:

Male actor	54 52 37 38 32 45 60 46 40 36 47 29 43 37 38 45 50 48 60 50
Female actor	42 29 33 36 45 49 39 26 25 33 35 35 28 30 29 61 32 33 45 29

(a) Represent the data on a back-to-back stem-and-leaf plot.

(b) State one similarity and one difference that can be observed between the ages of the male and female winners.

(c) Mary says, 'The female winners were younger than the male winners.'
Investigate this statement in relation to:

    (i) the mean age of the male winners and mean age of the female winners;

    (ii) the median age of the male winners and the median age of the female winners.

(d) Find the interquartile ranges of the ages of the male winners and of the female winners.

(SEC 2012)

Solution

(a)

Male actors		Female actors
9	2	5 6 8 9 9 9
8 8 7 7 6 2	3	0 2 3 3 3 5 5 6 9
8 7 6 5 5 3	4	2 5 5 9
4 2 0 0	5	
0 0	6	1

Key: 2|5 is 25 years old

(b)

Similarities between the ages of the male and the female actors	Differences between the ages of the male and the female actors
They have the same shape (are right-skewed)	Outlier in female winners
No one over 61	No female in her 50s
No one won under the age of 25	The female winners are younger
Their ranges are similar	

(c) **(i)** To check Mary's statement, find the mean age of both the male and female winners.

Male mean age

$$= \frac{29+32+36+37+37+38+38+40+43+45+45+46+47+48+50+50+52+54+60+60}{20}$$

$$= \frac{887}{20} = 44 \cdot 35.$$

The mean male age is 44·35 years old.

Female mean age

$$= \frac{42+29+33+36+45+49+39+26+25+33+35+35+28+30+29+61+32+33+45+29}{20}$$

$$= \frac{714}{20} = 35 \cdot 7.$$

The mean female age is 35·7 years old.

The mean age of female winners is lower, so the statement is true for mean age.

(ii) To check if Mary's statement is true in relation to the median, find the median age of both the male and female winners.

Rank/order the ages and find the middle number.

Male	29 32 36 37 37 38 38 40 43 **45 45** 46 47 48 50 50 52 54 60 60

Female	25 26 28 29 29 29 30 32 33 **33 33** 35 35 36 39 42 45 45 49 61

- Male median age $= \dfrac{(45 + 45)}{2} = 45$ • Female median age $= \dfrac{(33 + 33)}{2} = 33$

The median age of female winners is lower, so the statement is true for median age.

(d) Find the interquartile ranges of the ages of both the male and female winners.

Rank/order the ages and find the lower and upper quartiles.

Male	29 32 36 37 **37 38** 38 40 43 45 45 46 47 48 **50 50** 52 54 60 60

Female	25 26 28 29 **29 29** 30 32 33 33 33 35 35 36 **39 42** 45 45 49 61

Male • Q_1 age $= \dfrac{(37 + 38)}{2} = 37{\cdot}5$ • Q_3 age $= \dfrac{(50 + 50)}{2} = 50$ • $Q_3 - Q_1 = 50 - 37{\cdot}5 = 12{\cdot}5$

Female • Q_1 age $= \dfrac{(29 + 29)}{2} = 29$ • Q_3 age $= \dfrac{(39 + 42)}{2} = 40{\cdot}5$ • $Q_3 - Q_1 = 40{\cdot}5 - 29 = 11{\cdot}5$

Exercise

Q1 60 students were asked how they travelled to school. The following table is a summary of the results.

Type of transport	Public transport	Car	Bicycle	Walk
Number of people	22	14	13	11

(a) Display the data on a pie chart, showing clearly how the size of each angle is calculated.

(b) Why is this an appropriate method to display this data?

(c) What percentage of students travel to school by public transport? Give your answer correct to the nearest whole number.

Q2 The pie chart shows how Mary spends her time over a typical 24-hour period.

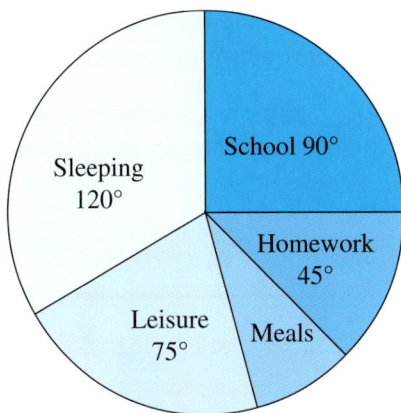

Copy and complete the following table in your answer book.

Activity	Sleeping	School	Homework	Meals	Leisure
Number of hours					

(SEC 2012)

Q3 In total 7150 second level school students from 216 schools completed the 2011/2012 phase 11 *CensusAtSchool* questionnaire. The questionnaire contained a question relating to where students keep their mobile phones while sleeping.

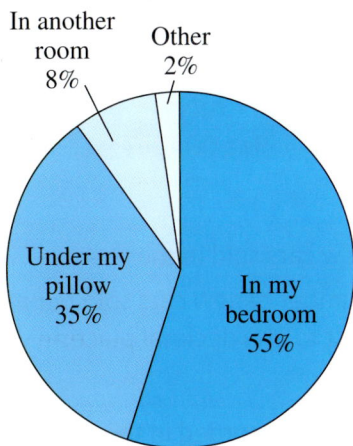

Phone location while sleeping – Female

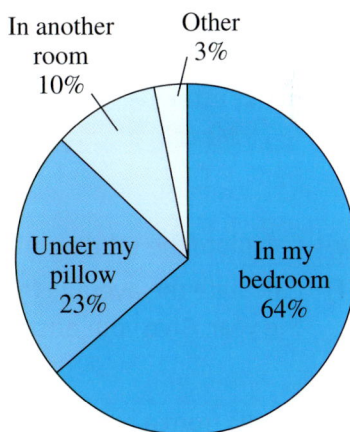

Phone location while sleeping – Male

(a) Given that this question was answered by 4171 girls and 2979 boys, calculate how many female students kept their mobile phones under their pillows.

(b) Calculate the overall percentage of students who kept their mobile phones under their pillows.

(c) A new pie chart is to be drawn showing the mobile phone location for all students. Calculate the measure of the angle that would represent the students who kept their mobile phones under their pillows.

(SEC 2013)

Q4 The diagram shows the number of new cars sold in a garage in one year.

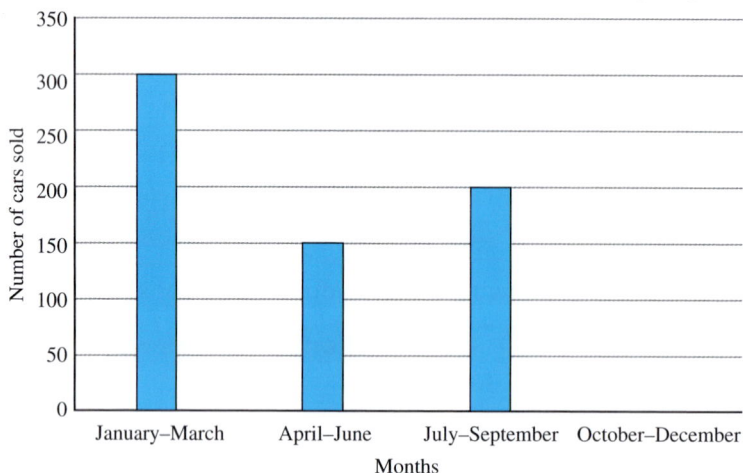

(a) How many new cars were sold in the months April–June?

In the months October–December, there were exactly half as many new cars sold as in April–June.

(b) How many new cars were sold in October–December?

(c) Draw the bar for October–December on the diagram.

(d) In which quarter were most new cars sold? Put a tick (✓) in the correct box.

January–March	April–June	July–September	October–December
☐	☐	☐	☐

(e) Calculate the total number of new cars sold in the year.

(f) Calculate the average (mean) number of new cars sold per month in the year. Give your answer correct to one decimal place.

(SEC 2015)

Q5 The results from a recent Science test are recorded in the table below:

Grade	A	B	C	D	E	F
Number of students	4	9	12	3	1	1

(a) How many students sat the class test?

(b) Represent the information graphically in a bar chart.

(c) What was the modal grade?

(d) What percentage of students got a grade C or above?

Q6 At a Garda checkpoint, the speed of 100 vehicles passing was recorded. The following were the results. Note that 20–40, for example, means 20 or more but less than 40.

Speed in km/hr	0–20	20–40	40–60	60–80	80–100
Number of cars	8	24	40	18	10

(a) Using mid-interval values, calculate the mean speed of the 100 vehicles.

(b) Display the above data on a histogram.

(c) Describe the shape of the distribution of the histogram.

Q7 The weights, in kg, of 125 Junior Certificate students are given in the following frequency table. Note that 40–50, for example, means 40 or more but less than 50.

Weight in kg	40–45	45–50	50–55	55–60	60–65	65–70	70–75
Number of students	3	13	22	27	30	22	8

(a) Using mid-interval values, calculate the mean weight of the Junior Certificate students.

(b) Display the above data on a histogram.

(c) Describe the shape of the distribution of the histogram.

Q8 A professional golfer plays 50 rounds of golf over a season. The following were the number of shots taken in each round:

69	66	70	70	71	70	68	71	76	72
69	74	75	73	77	70	73	74	66	74
69	74	74	70	75	73	69	76	80	72
73	69	79	72	69	74	79	73	77	72
69	67	70	69	68	70	70	71	68	66

(a) Complete the following frequency table. Note that 66–69, for example, means 66 or more but less than 69.

Number of shots per round	66–69	69–72	72–75	75–81
Number of rounds				

(b) Using mid-interval values, calculate the mean number of shots per round, giving your answer correct to the nearest whole number.

(c) Draw a histogram to represent this information.

(d) Describe the shape of the distribution of the histogram.

(SEC 2008)

Q9 A class of 30 students were asked to write down their favourite colour. The results are shown in the table.

Colour	Red	Orange	Yellow	Green	Blue	Pink	Black
Number of students	4	2	3	5	7	6	3

(a) Draw a dot plot to represent this information.

(b) What is the modal colour?

(c) Is it appropriate to talk about the shape of this distribution? Explain.

Q10 In a survey a number of people were asked the question: 'How many phone calls do you make on average each day?' The results are shown in the following dot plot.

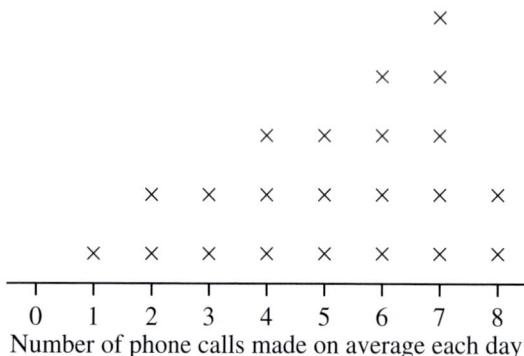

Number of phone calls made on average each day

(a) How many people were surveyed?

(b) What is the mean number of calls made per day?

(c) What is the median number of calls made per day?

(d) Is it appropriate to talk about the shape of this distribution? Explain.

Q11 Data showing the ages of all people who attended a local council meeting is shown in the stem-and-leaf plot.

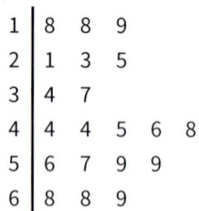

```
1 | 8  8  9
2 | 1  3  5
3 | 4  7
4 | 4  4  5  6  8
5 | 6  7  9  9
6 | 8  8  9
```
Key: 1|8 = 18 years

(a) How many people attended the meeting?

(b) What is the range of ages of the people who attended the meeting?

(c) What is the median age of the people who attended the meeting?

(d) Find the interquartile range of the data.

Q12 A group of students was asked how many text messages each had sent the previous day. The results were:

14	32	6	17	19	15	3	35	42	25
9	28	34	18	40	11	16	28	31	7

(a) How many students were in the group?

(b) Represent the data on a stem-and-leaf plot.

(c) Find the mode of the data.

(d) Find the mean of the data.

(e) What percentage of students sent more than 30 texts?

(SEC 2013)

Q13 The ages of the 30 people who took part in an aerobics class are as follows:

18	24	32	37	9	13	22	41	51	49
15	42	37	58	48	53	27	54	42	24
33	48	56	17	61	37	63	45	20	39

The ages of the 30 people who took part in a swimming class are as follows:

16	22	29	7	36	45	12	38	52	13
33	41	24	35	51	8	47	22	14	24
42	62	15	24	23	31	53	36	48	18

(a) Represent this data on a back-to-back stem-and-leaf plot.

Aerobics class		Swimming class
	0	
	1	
	2	
	3	
	4	
	5	
	6	
	Key :	

(b) Use your diagram to identify the median in each case.

(c) What other measure of central tendency could have been used when examining this data?

(d) Based on the data make one observation about the ages of the two groups.

(SEC 2013)

Solutions

Q1 (a)

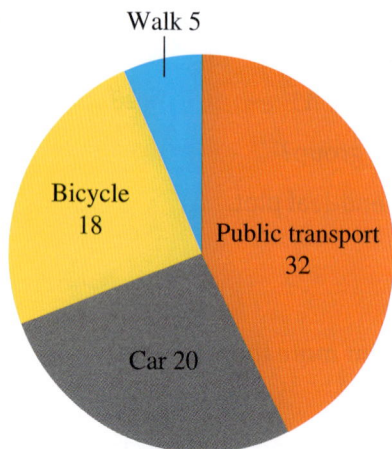

Walk 5
Bicycle 18
Public transport 32
Car 20

We know that 60 students = 360° $\Rightarrow$ 1 student = $\dfrac{360°}{60}$ = 6°

The 'public transport' angle = 32 × 6° = 192°

The 'car' angle = 20 × 6° = 120°

The 'bicycle' angle = 3 × 6° = 18°

The 'walk' angle = 5 × 6° = 30°

(b) This is an appropriate method to display the data as the angles are not close in size and there are not too many categories.

(c) The percentage of students who travel to school by public transport

$= \dfrac{32}{60}$ × 100 = 53·$\dot{3}$ = 53% to the nearest whole number.

Q2 Use the pie chart to calculate the number of hours spent on different activities in 24 hours.

The number of hours spent sleeping = $\dfrac{120}{360}$ × 24 = 8 hours

The number of hours spent at school = $\dfrac{90}{360}$ × 24 = 6 hours

The number of hours spent doing homework = $\dfrac{45}{360}$ × 24 = 3 hours

The number of hours spent eating meals = $\dfrac{360 - 120 - 90 - 45 - 75}{360}$ × 24

$= \dfrac{30}{360}$ × 24 = 2 hours

The number of hours spent enjoying leisure activities = $\dfrac{75}{360}$ × 24 = 5 hours

Activity	Sleeping	School	Homework	Meals	Leisure
Number of hours	8	6	3	2	5

Q3 (a) The number of female students who keep their mobile phones under their pillows

= 35% of 4171

= 4171 × 35% = 4171 × 0·35 = 1459·85 = 1460 female students.

(b) To calculate the overall percentage of students who keep their mobile phones under their pillows, follow the steps below.

1 Find the total number of students = 7150

2 Find the number of male students who keep their mobile phones under their pillows = 23% of 2979 = 2979 × 23% = 685·17 ≈ 686 male students

3 Find the total number of students who keep their mobile phones under their pillows = 1460 + 686 = 2146

4 Calculate the overall percentage of students who kept their mobile phones under their pillows = $\frac{2146}{7150}$ × 100 = 30·01 = 30%

(c) The measure of the angle that would represent the students who keep their mobile phones under their pillows = 30% of 360° = 0·3 × 360 = 108°

Q4 (a) The number of new cars that were sold in the months April–June was 150.

(b) The number of new cars sold in October to December is exactly half that from April to June. Therefore, the number of cars sold from October to December is 150 ÷ 2 = 75.

(c) The bar for October to December is shown on the bar chart.

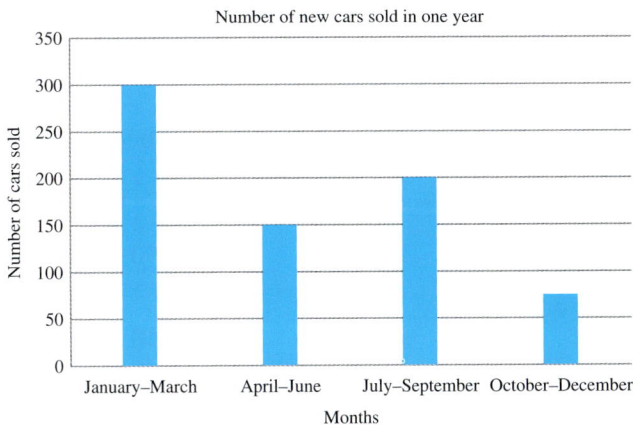

Number of new cars sold in one year

(d) Most new cars were sold from January to March.

January–March	April–June	July–September	October–December
☑	☐	☐	☐

(e) The total number of new cars sold in the year = 300 + 150 + 200 + 75 = 725.

(f) The average (mean) number of new cars sold per month in the year, correct to one decimal place is: $\frac{725}{12}$ = 60·41$\dot{6}$ = 60·4 cars to 1 d.p.

Q5 (a) 30 students did the class test.

(b)

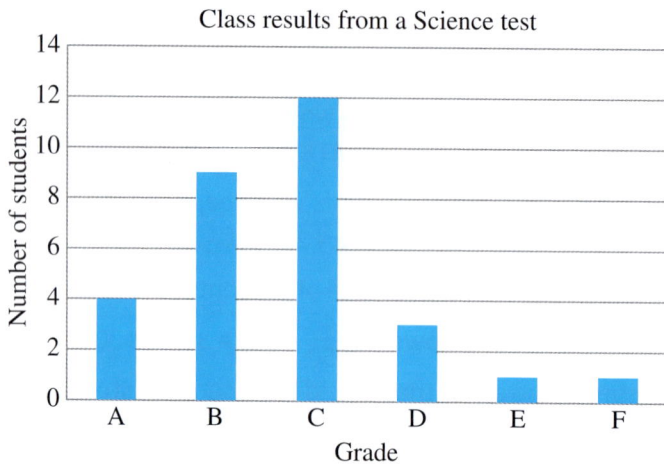

Class results from a Science test

(c) The modal grade is C, as it is the grade that most students achieved in the test.

(d) The percentage of students who got a grade C or above

$$= \frac{\text{number of students who got a grade C or above}}{\text{number of students who sat the test}} \times 100 = \frac{25}{30} \times 100$$

$$= 83 \cdot \dot{3} \%$$

Q6 (a) Taking mid-interval values of the frequency table becomes:

Speed in km/hr	0–20	20–40	40–60	60–80	80–100	Total
Mid-interval speed (x)	10	30	50	70	90	
Number of cars (f)	8	24	40	18	10	$\Sigma f = 100$
$f(x)$	80	720	2000	1260	900	$\Sigma f(x) = 4960$

$$\text{Mean} = \frac{\text{sum of all the values}}{\text{number of values}} = \frac{\Sigma f(x)}{\Sigma f} = \frac{4960}{100} = 49 \cdot 6$$

Hence, the mean speed of the cars passing the checkpoint is 49·6 km/hr

(b) The speed of 100 vehicles passing a Garda checkpoint

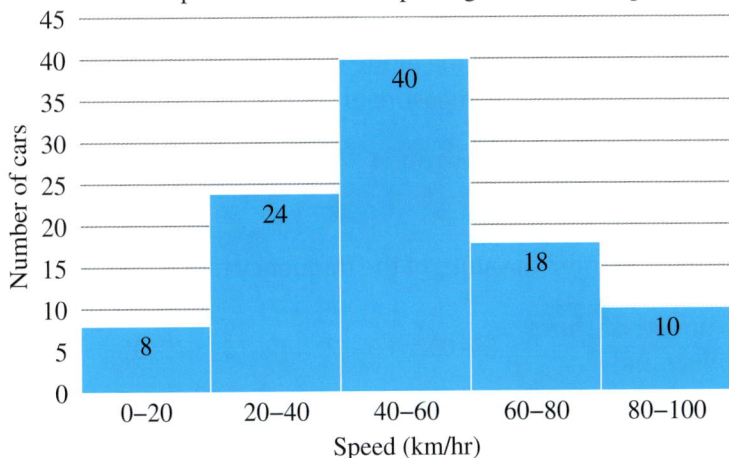

Number of cars (y-axis): 0, 5, 10, 15, 20, 25, 30, 35, 40, 45

Bars: 0–20: 8; 20–40: 24; 40–60: 40; 60–80: 18; 80–100: 10

Speed (km/hr)

(c) The distribution can be described as nearly symmetric. As such, the values of the mean, median and mode are very close together.

Q7 (a) Taking mid-interval values of the frequency table becomes:

Weight in kg	40–45	45–50	50–55	55–60	60–65	65–70	70–75	Total
Mid-interval weight (x)	42·5	47·5	52·5	57·5	62·5	67·5	72·5	
Number of students (f)	3	13	22	27	30	22	8	$\Sigma f = 125$
$f(x)$	127·5	617·5	1155	1552·5	1875	1485	580	$\Sigma f(x) =$ 7392·5

$$\text{Mean} = \frac{\text{sum of all the values}}{\text{number of values}} = \frac{\Sigma f(x)}{\Sigma f} = \frac{7392·5}{125} = 59·14 \text{ kg}$$

(b) The weights, in kilograms, of 125 Junior Certificate students

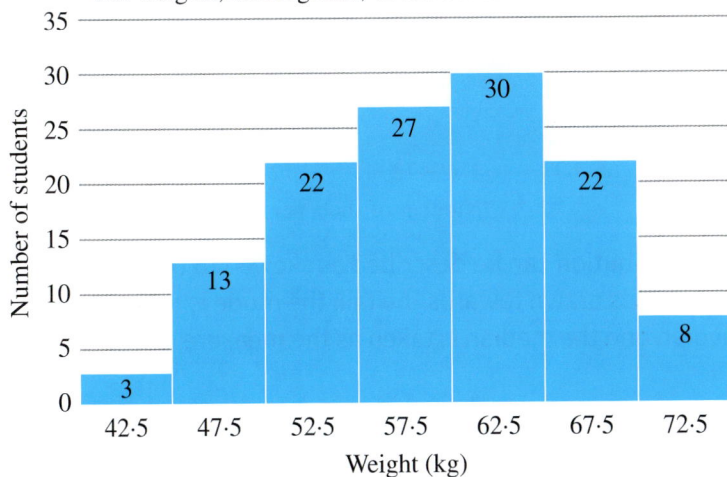

Number of students (y-axis): 0, 5, 10, 15, 20, 25, 30, 35

Bars: 42·5: 3; 47·5: 13; 52·5: 22; 57·5: 27; 62·5: 30; 67·5: 22; 72·5: 8

Weight (kg)

(c) The distribution could be described as skewed to the left as most of the weights are on the right side of the chart. In such cases the mean is drawn towards the tail, the mode is to the right of the median and the median is taken as the measure of centre.

Q8 (a)

Number of shots per round	66–69	69–72	72–75	75–81
Number of rounds	7	19	15	9

(b) Taking mid-interval values of the frequency table becomes:

Number of shots per round	66–69	69–72	72–75	75–81	Total
Mid-interval value (x)	67·5	70·5	73·5	78	
Number of rounds (f)	7	19	15	9	$\Sigma f = 50$
$f(x)$	472·5	1339·5	1102·5	702	$\Sigma f(x) = 3616·5$

$$\text{Mean} = \frac{\text{sum of all the values}}{\text{number of values}} = \frac{\Sigma f(x)}{\Sigma f} = \frac{3616·5}{50} = 72·33 \approx 72 \text{ to the}$$

nearest whole number

(c)

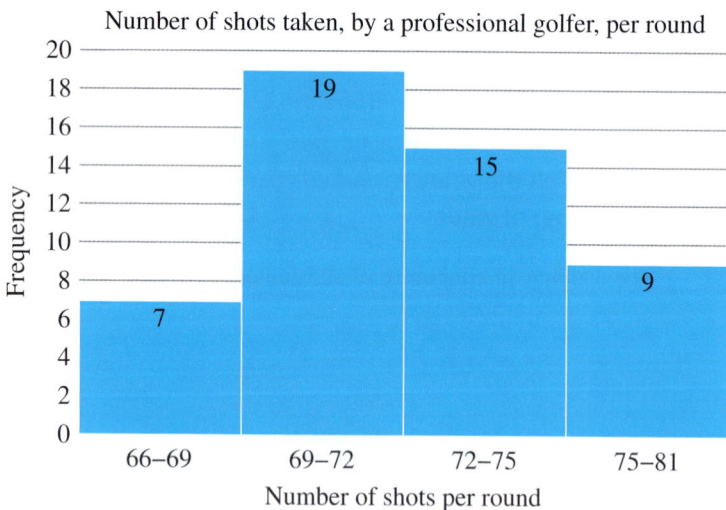

Number of shots taken, by a professional golfer, per round

(d) The distribution can be described as skewed to the left. In such cases the mean is drawn towards the tail, the mode is to the left of the median and the median is taken as the measure of centre.

Q9 (a)

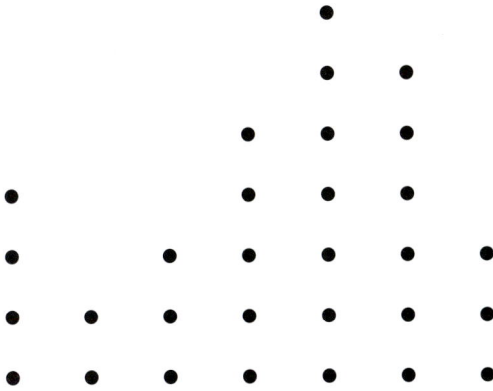

Red　Orange　Yellow　Green　Blue　Pink　Black

(b) The modal colour is blue, as it was chosen most often by the students.

(c) No, it is not appropriate to talk about the shape of this distribution, as the category is a qualitative variable. The shape of a distribution can only be discussed in relation to quantitative variable.

Q10 (a) 22 people were surveyed.

(b) The mean number of calls

$$= \frac{\Sigma f(x)}{\Sigma f} = \frac{1 + 2(2) + 2(3) + 3(4) + 3(5) + 4(6) + 5(7) + 2(8)}{22} = \frac{113}{22} = 5 \cdot 13\overset{..}{6}3$$

(c) The median number of calls made per day $= \frac{5 + 6}{2} = 5 \cdot 5$ calls.

(d) It is appropriate to talk about the shape of this distribution, as the category is a quantitative variable. When the mean is to the left of the median the data is said to be skewed to the left or negatively skewed. The mode affects the height of the curve.

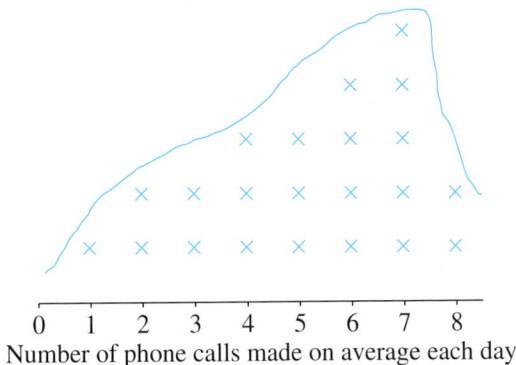

0　1　2　3　4　5　6　7　8
Number of phone calls made on average each day

Q11 (a) 20 people attended the meeting.

(b) The range = maximum age – minimum age = 69 – 18 = 51 years.

18 18 19 21 **23 25** 34 37 44 **44 45** 46 48 56 **57 59** 59 68 68 69

(c) The median age is half way between 44 and 45. Therefore the median is 44·5 years old.

18 18 19 21 23 25 34 37 44 **44 45** 46 48 56 57 59 59 68 68 69

(d) The interquartile range of the data = $Q_3 - Q_1$

Lower quartile, $Q_1 = \dfrac{23 + 25}{2} = 24$

Upper quartile, $Q_3 = \dfrac{57 + 59}{2} = 58$

Interquartile range = $Q_3 - Q_1 = 58 - 24 = 34$ years old.

Q12 (a) There were 20 students in the group.

(b)

0	3	6	7	9			
1	1	4	5	6	7	8	9
2	5	8	8				
3	1	2	4	5			
4	0	2					

Key : 1|8 = 18 years

(c) The mode of the data is the value which occurs the most. Therefore, the mode is 28. The modal number of texts sent is 28.

(d) The mean of the data is the sum of all the data values divided by the number of students.

Mean $= \dfrac{14 + 32 + 6 + 17 + 19 + 15 + 3 + 35 + 42 + 25 + 9 + 2 + 34 + 18 + 40 + 11 + 16 + 28 + 31 + 7}{20} = \dfrac{430}{20}$

$= 21\cdot5$

The mean number of texts sent is 21·5 texts.

(e) The percentage of students who sent more than 30 texts

$= \dfrac{\text{number of students who sent more than 30 texts}}{\text{number of students}} \times 100 = \dfrac{6}{20} \times 100 = 30\%$

Q13 (a)

Aerobics class		Swimming class
9	0	7 8
8 7 5 3	1	2 3 4 5 6 8
7 4 4 2 0	2	2 2 3 4 4 4 9
9 7 7 7 3 2	3	1 3 5 6 6 8
9 8 8 5 2 2 1	4	1 2 5 7 8
8 6 4 3 1	5	1 2 3
	6	2

Key: 1|5 means 15

(b) Aerobics median: $\dfrac{37 + 39}{2} = 38$ years old.

Swimming median: $\dfrac{29 + 31}{2} = 30$ years old.

(c) Another measure of central tendency which could have been used when examining this data is either the mean or the mode.

(d) One observation that can be made from the data is that an older age group take the aerobics class (or a younger age group take the swimming class).

6 Geometry 1: Theorems, Axioms and Corollaries

Learning objectives

In this chapter you will learn:

- Key terminology
- All axioms, theorems and corollaries on the Junior Certificate course.

Key terminology associated with geometry

Key Terminology

Words	Meaning
Axiom	An axiom is a statement accepted without proof.
Theorem	A theorem is a statement which can be proved from the axioms by logical argument.
Converse	The converse of a statement is the reverse order of the given statement. For example: **Statement:** If a shape has three straight sides, then the shape is a triangle. **Converse statement:** If a shape is a triangle, then it is a shape with three straight sides.
Corollary	A corollary is a statement which can be made following a given theorem.
Proof	A proof involves writing well-structured, logical steps that use axioms and previously proved theorems to arrive at a conclusion about a statement.

Collinear	If three or more points lie on the same line, they are collinear.
Congruent ≡	Two triangles are congruent if all the sides and angles of one triangle are equal to the corresponding sides and angles of the other triangle.
Implies ⇒	Implies means that there is a logical link from one statement to the next statement.

Axioms

Axioms	Statement	Diagram
Axiom 1	**Two points axiom**	

There is exactly one line through any two given points on a plane.

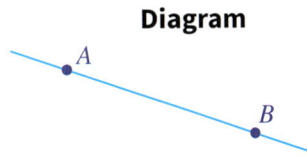

Axiom 2 **Ruler axiom**

The distance between any two given points has the following properties:

1 The distance $|AB|$ is never negative.

2 $|AB| = |BA|$.

3 If C lies on AB, between A and B, then $|AB| = |AC| + |CB|$.

4 Given any ray from A, and given any real number $k \geq 0$, there is a unique point B on the ray whose distance from A is k.

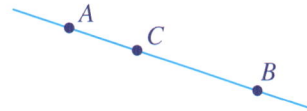

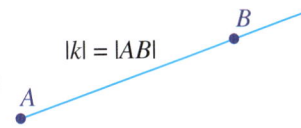

$|k| = |AB|$

Axiom 3 **Protractor axiom**

The number of degrees in any given angle has these properties:

1 A straight angle has 180°.

2 Given a ray $[AB$, and a number d between 0 and 180, there is exactly one ray from A on each side of the line AB that makes an (ordinary) angle having d degrees with the ray $[AB$.

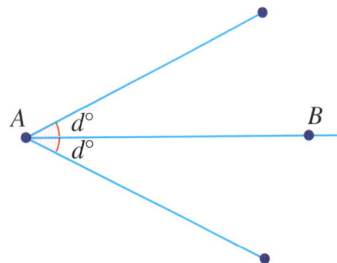

3 If D is a point inside an angle $\angle BAC$, then:

$$|\angle BAC| = |\angle BAD| + |\angle DAC|$$

From the diagram we can state

$$|\angle BAD| = x°$$

$$|\angle DAC| = y°$$

$$\therefore \; |\angle BAC| = x° + y°$$

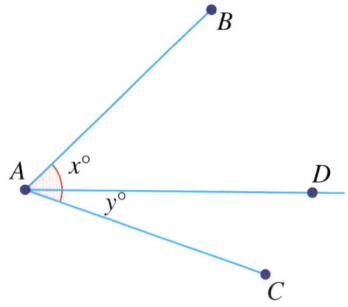

Axiom 4   Congruent triangles

Two triangles are congruent if they satisfy any one of the following statements:

- SSS (Side, Side, Side) – all three sides in both triangles are equal.

1 (SSS)

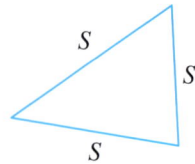

- ASA (Angle, Side, Angle) – two angles and one side in both triangles are equal.

2 (ASA)

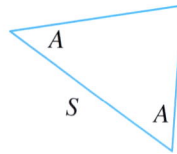

- SAS (Side, Angle, Side) – two sides and one angle in both triangles are equal.

3 (SAS)

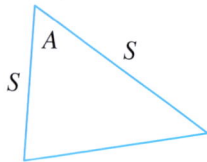

- RHS (Right angle, Hypotenuse, other Side) – right angle, hypotenuse and any other side in both triangles are equal.

4 (RHS)

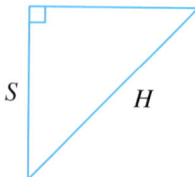

Axiom 5   Axiom of parallels

Given any line l and a point P, there is exactly one line through P that is parallel to l.

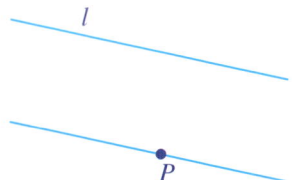

Theorems

Theorem 1   Vertically opposite angles

Vertically opposite angles are equal in measure.

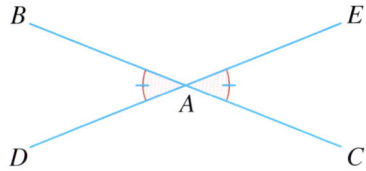

$\angle BAD = \angle EAC$

Theorem 2   Isosceles triangles

1 In an isosceles triangle the angles opposite the equal sides are equal.

2 Conversely, if two angles are equal, then the triangle is isosceles.

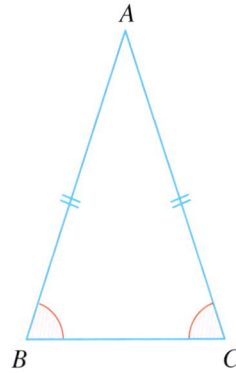

$\angle ABC = \angle ACB$

$|BA| = |AC|$

Theorem 3   Alternate angles

Suppose that A and D are on opposite sides of the line BC.

1 If $|\angle ABC| = |\angle BCD|$, then $AB||CD$. In other words, if a transversal makes equal alternate angles on two lines, then the lines are parallel.

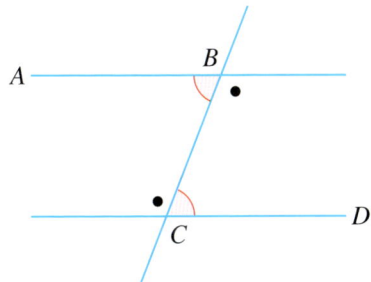

2 Conversely, if $AB \| CD$, then $|\angle ABC| = |\angle BCD|$. In other words, if two lines are parallel, then any transversal will make equal alternate angles with them.

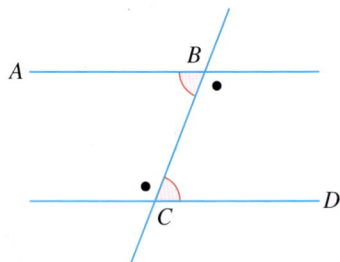

Theorem 4   **Angles in a triangle**

The angles in any triangle add to 180°.

This can be expressed as:

$A° + B° + C° = 180°$

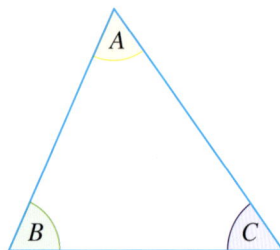

Theorem 5   **Corresponding angles**

Two lines are parallel if and only if for any transversal, corresponding angles are equal.

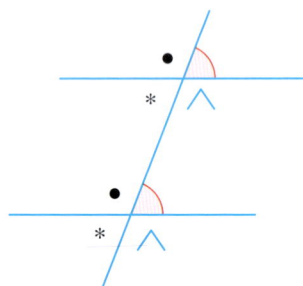

Theorem 6   **Exterior angle**

Each exterior angle of a triangle is equal to the sum of the interior opposite angles.

This can be expressed as:

$A° + B° = D°$

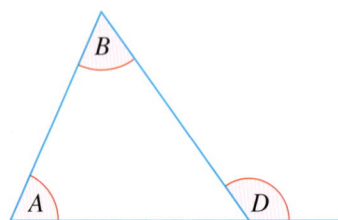

Theorem 7 and Theorem 8   Not covered on the Junior Certificate course

Theorem 9   **Parallelograms**

In a parallelogram, opposite sides are equal, and opposite angles are equal.

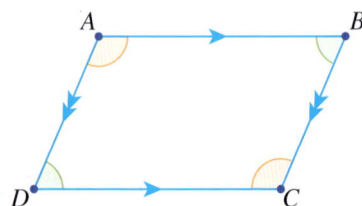

Theorem 10	**Diagonals of a parallelogram**

The diagonals of a parallelogram bisect one another.

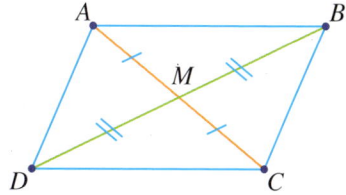

Theorem 11	**Transversals**

If three parallel lines cut off equal segments on some transversal line, then they will cut off equal segments on any other transversal.

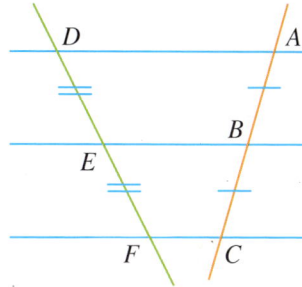

Theorem 12	**Proportional sides**

Let $\triangle ABC$ be a triangle. If a line l is parallel to BC and cuts $[AB]$ in the ratio $s{:}t$, then it also cuts $[AC]$ in the same ratio.

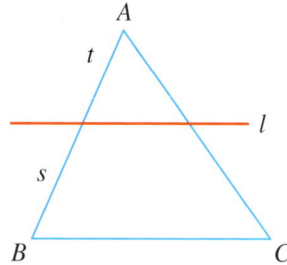

Theorem 13	**Similar triangles**

If two triangles $\triangle ABC$ and $\triangle A'B'C'$ are similar, then their sides are proportional, in order: $\dfrac{|AB|}{|A'B'|} = \dfrac{|BC|}{|B'C'|} = \dfrac{|CA|}{|C'A'|}$

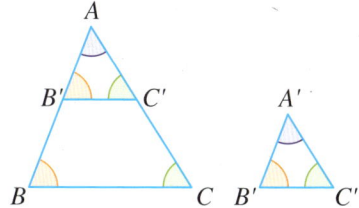

OR

$$\dfrac{|A'B'|}{|AB|} = \dfrac{|B'C'|}{|BC|} = \dfrac{|C'A'|}{|CA|}$$

Theorem 14	**Pythagoras' Theorem**

In a right-angled triangle the square of the hypotenuse is equal to the sum of the squares of the other two sides.

Theorem 15	**Converse to Pythagoras**

If the square of one side of a triangle is equal to the sum of the squares of the other two sides, then the angle opposite the first side is a right angle.

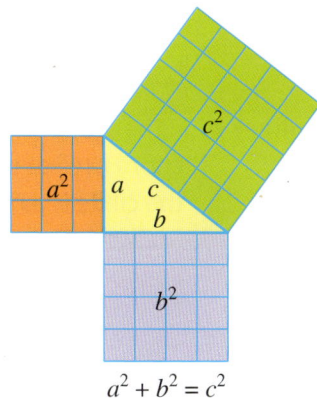

$$a^2 + b^2 = c^2$$

Theorem 16   Circle theorem

The angle at the centre of a circle standing on a given arc is twice the angle at any point of the circle standing on the same arc.

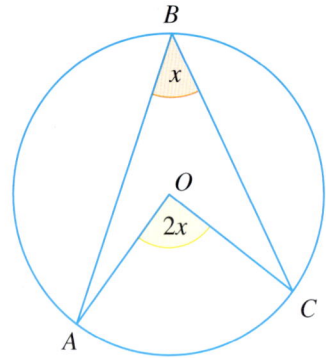

Corollaries

Corollary 1   A diagonal divides a parallelogram into two congruent triangles.

$\triangle ABD \equiv \triangle CDB$

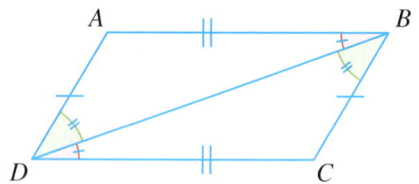

Remember

Note: ≡ means congruent.

Corollary 2   All angles at points of a circle, standing on the same arc, are equal, (and conversely).

$|\angle CAD| = |\angle CBD|$

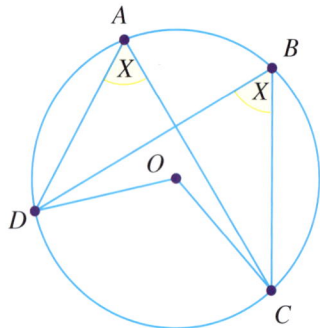

Corollary 3   Each angle in a semi-circle is a right angle.

$|\angle ABC| = 90°$

Corollary 4   If the angle standing on a chord [AC] at some point of the circle is a right-angle, then [AC] is a diameter.

$|\angle ABC| = 90°$

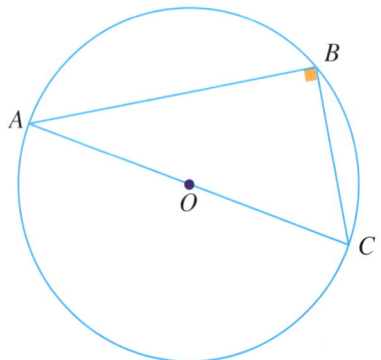

Corollary 5   If *ABCD* is a cyclic quadrilateral, then opposite angles sum to 180°, (and conversely).

$$|\angle 1| + |\angle 3| = 180°$$

$$|\angle 2| + |\angle 4| = 180°$$

Note: A cyclic quadrilateral is any quadrilateral inside a circle which has all vertices touching the circle.

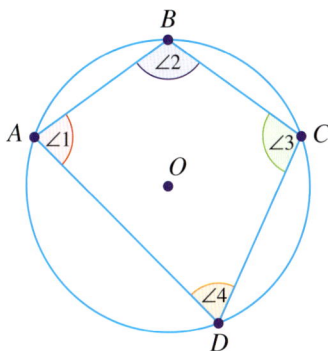

Formal proof of theorems

Formal proof of Theorem 4

Theorem: The angles in any triangle add to 180°.

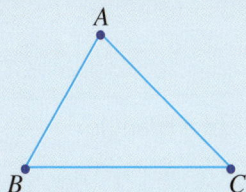

Given: △*ABC*

To prove: $|\angle ABC| + |\angle BAC| + |\angle ACB| = 180°$

Constructions: Draw line *DE* through *A* which is parallel to *BC*.
Label angles 1, 2, 3, 4 and 5.

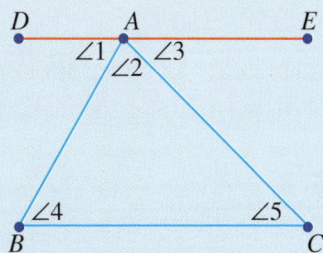

Proof

Statement

$|\angle 1| + |\angle 2| + |\angle 3| = 180°$ ... (Straight line)

$|\angle 1| = |\angle 4|$ ... (Alternate angles)

$|\angle 3| = |\angle 5|$ ... (Alternate angles)

$\Rightarrow |\angle 1| + |\angle 2| + |\angle 3| = 180°$

$\Rightarrow |\angle 4| + |\angle 2| + |\angle 5| = 180°$

Q.E.D.

Formal proof of Theorem 6

Theorem: Each exterior angle of a triangle is equal to the sum of the interior opposite angles.

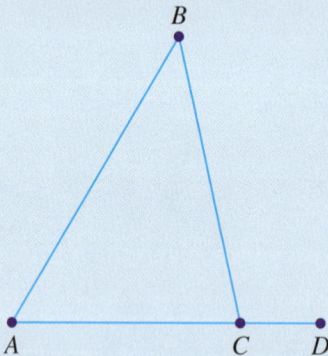

Given: $\triangle ABC$ with line segment $[AC]$ extended to D.

To prove: $|\angle BAC| + |\angle ABC| = |\angle BCD|$

Constructions: Label angles 1, 2, 3 and 4.

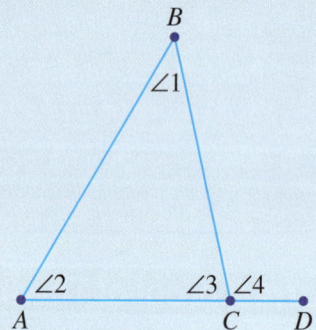

Proof

Statement

$|\angle 1| + |\angle 2| + |\angle 3| = 180°$ ... (Interior angles of a triangle)

$|\angle 3| + |\angle 4| = 180°$ ... (Straight line)

$\therefore |\angle 1| + |\angle 2| + |\angle 3| = |\angle 3| + |\angle 4|$ ... (Both sides of the equation equal 180°)

$\therefore |\angle 1| + |\angle 2| = |\angle 4|$ ... (Subtract $|\angle 3|$ from both sides)

Q.E.D.

Theorem: In a parallelogram, opposite sides are equal, and opposite angles are equal.

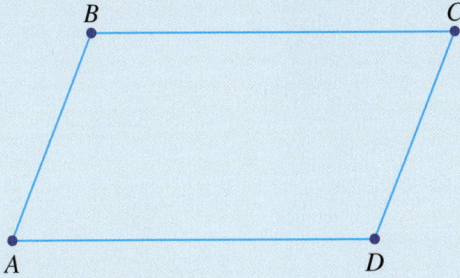

Given: Parallelogram $ABCD$

To prove: $|AB| = |CD|, |BC| = |AD|, |\angle ABC| = |\angle ADC|$ and $|\angle BAD| = |\angle BCD|$

Constructions: A line segment $[AC]$, a diagonal of the parallelogram. Label angles 1, 2, 3 and 4.

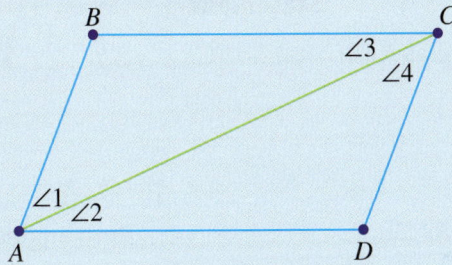

Proof

Statement

$|\angle 1| = |\angle 4|$ ... (Alternate angles)

$|\angle 2| = |\angle 3|$ ... (Alternate angles)

$|AC| = |AC|$ ... (Common side)

$\therefore \triangle ABC$ is congruent to $\triangle ACD$ ... (ASA)

$\Rightarrow |AB| = |CD|$ and $|BC| = |AD|$ ... (Corresponding sides in congruent triangles)

and $|\angle ADC| = |\angle ABC|$ ... (Corresponding angles in congruent triangles)

$\Rightarrow |\angle 1| + |\angle 2| = |\angle 3| + |\angle 4|$ ... (Because $|\angle 1| = |\angle 4|$ and $|\angle 2| = |\angle 3|$)

$\therefore |\angle BAD| = |\angle BCD|$

Q.E.D.

Theorem: In a right-angled triangle, the square of the hypotenuse is equal to the sum of the squares of the other two sides.

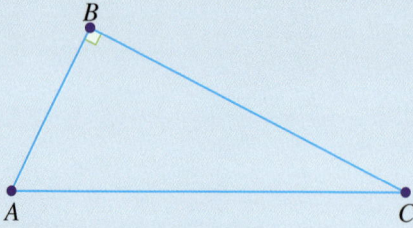

Given: $\triangle ABC$, with $|\angle ABC| = 90°$

To prove: $|AC|^2 = |AB|^2 + |BC|^2$

Constructions: Segment $[BD]$, which is perpendicular to AC.

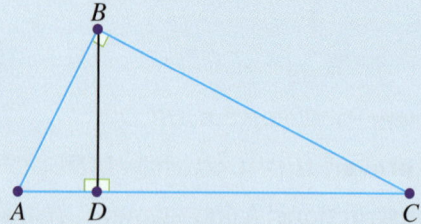

Proof

Statement

Step 1 – Study the triangles $\triangle ABD$ and $\triangle ABC$

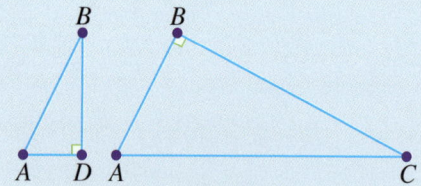

$|\angle ADB| = |\angle ABC|$ ... (Both angles are 90°)

$|\angle BAD| = |\angle BAC|$ ... (Common angle)

$\therefore \triangle ABD$ is similar to $\triangle ABC$

$\therefore \dfrac{|AB|}{|AC|} = \dfrac{|AD|}{|AB|}$ ... (From Theorem 13)

$\Rightarrow |AB|^2 = |AC| \times |AD|$

Step 2 – Study the triangles $\triangle ABC$ and $\triangle BCD$

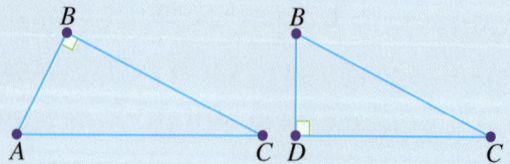

$|\angle ABC| = |\angle BDC|$ ... (Both angles are 90°)

$|\angle BAD| = |\angle BAC|$ ... (Common angle)

$\therefore \triangle ABC$ is similar to $\triangle BCD$

$\therefore \dfrac{|BC|}{|DC|} = \dfrac{|AC|}{|BC|}$ ... (From Theorem 13)

$\Rightarrow |BC|^2 = |DC| \times |AC|$

Step 3 – combine Step 1 and Step 2:

$$|AB|^2 = |AC| \times |AD| \qquad \text{... (Step 1)}$$

$$|BC|^2 = |DC| \times |AC| \qquad \text{... (Step 1)}$$

Adding these equations:

$$|AB|^2 + |BC|^2 = (|AC| \times |AD|) + (|DC| \times |AC|)$$

$$|AB|^2 + |BC|^2 = |AC|(|AD| + |DC|) \qquad \text{... (Factoring out } |AC| \text{ as common)}$$

$$|AB|^2 + |BC|^2 = |AC|(|AC|) \qquad \text{... (Because } |AD| + |DC| = |AC|)$$

$$\therefore |AB|^2 + |BC|^2 = |AC|^2$$

Q.E.D.

Formal proof of Theorem 19

Theorem: The angle at the centre of a circle standing on a given arc is twice the angle at any point on the circle standing on the same arc.

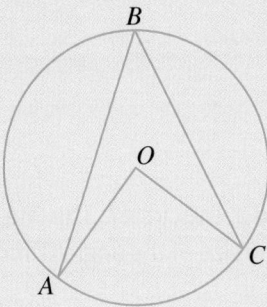

Given: Circle with centre O and points A, B and C on the circumference of the circle.

To prove: $|\angle AOC| = 2|\angle ABC|$

Constructions: A line segment $[BD]$ which passes through O and label angles 1, 2, 3, 4, 5 and 6.

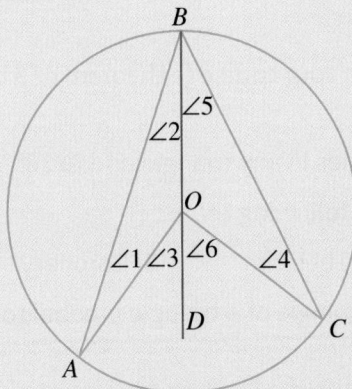

Proof

Statement

$|OA| = |OB|$ ... (Common radii)

$|\angle 1| = |\angle 2|$ ... (Base angles in an isosceles triangle)

$|\angle 1| + |\angle 2| = |\angle 3|$ ... (Exterior angle of $\triangle ABO$)

$\therefore\ 2|\angle 2| = |\angle 3|$ ... (Because $|\angle 1| = |\angle 2|$)

Similarly,

$2|\angle 5| = |\angle 6|$

Adding these two equations:

$2|\angle 2| + 2|\angle 5| = |\angle 3| + |\angle 6|$

$2(|\angle 2| + |\angle 5|) = |\angle 3| + |\angle 6|$ ... (Factoring out 2 as common)

As $|\angle 2| + |\angle 5| = |\angle ABC|$ and $|\angle 3| + |\angle 6| = |\angle AOC|$

$2|\angle ABC| = |\angle AOC|$

Q.E.D.

Exercise

Q1 The diagram shows the triangle RST inscribed in the circle k. The line segment $[RS]$ is a diameter of the circle. Gavin says: 'The size of the angle W must be 90°.'

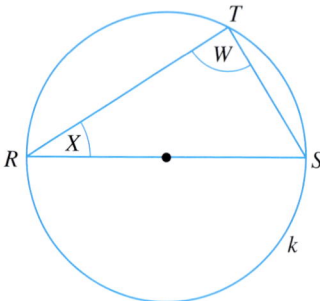

State one result on your course (a theorem or a corollary) that shows that Gavin is correct.

Q2 Prove that the angles in any triangle add to 180°.

Q3 Define each of the following terms:

     1 Axiom   **2** Theorem   **3** Corollary

Q4 Prove that exterior angle of a triangle is equal to the sum of the interior opposite angles.

Q5 Define each of the following terms:

    1 Proof   **2** Collinear   **3** Congruent

Q6 Prove that in a parallelogram, opposite sides are equal, and opposite angles are equal.

Q7 Prove that in a right-angled triangle, the square of the hypotenuse is the sum of the squares of the other two sides.

Q8 Prove that the angle at the centre of a circle standing on a given arc is twice the angle at any point of the circle standing on the same arc.

Solutions

Q1 Corollary 3: Each angle in a semi-circle is a right-angle; or Corollary 4: If the angle standing on a chord [BC] at some point of the circle is a right-angle, then [BC] is a diameter.

Q2 See formal proof of **Theorem 4:** The angles in any triangle add to 180°.

Q3

1 Axiom	An axiom is a statement accepted without proof.
2 Theorem	A theorem is a statement which can be proved from the axioms by logical argument.
3 Corollary	A corollary is a statement which can be made following a given theorem.

Q4 See formal proof of **Theorem 6:** Each exterior angle of a triangle is equal to the sum of the interior opposite angles.

Q5

1 Proof	A proof involves writing well-structured, logical steps that use axioms and previously proved theorems to arrive at a conclusion about a statement.
2 Collinear	If three or more points lie on the same line, they are collinear.
3 Congruent	Two triangles are congruent if all the sides and angles of one triangle are equal to the corresponding sides and angles of the other triangle.

Q6 See formal proof of **Theorem 9:** In a parallelogram, opposite sides are equal, and opposite angles are equal.

Q7 See formal proof of **Theorem 14:** In a right-angled triangle, the square of the hypotenuse is equal to the sum of the squares of the other two sides.

Q8 See formal proof of **Theorem 19:** The angle at the centre of a circle standing on a given arc is twice the angle at any point on the circle standing on the same arc.

7 Geometry 2: Applications of Theorems, Axioms and Corollaries

Learning objectives

In this chapter you will study:

How to apply theorems, axioms and corollaries to:

- Solve for missing angles
- Solve for missing sides
- Prove given statements.

Key notes

- It is essential to be extremely familiar with all theorems, axioms and corollaries covered in Chapter 6 to be able to answer application-based problems.

- It is important to note that there can be more than one method of solving geometric-based problems.

Using theorems, axioms and corollaries to solve for missing angles

Example

Find the measure of the angles 1, 2, 3, 4, 5 and 6 and give reasons for your answers.

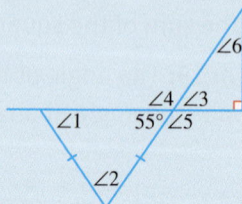

Solution

$|\angle 1| = 55°$ ... (Base angles of an isosceles triangle)

$\Rightarrow |\angle 2| = 180° - (55° + 55°) = 70°$

$|\angle 3| = 55°$ ... (Vertically opposite angles)

$|\angle 4| = 180° - 55° = 125°$ ... (Straight line)

$|\angle 5| = |\angle 4| = 125°$ ... (Vertically opposite angles)

$|\angle 6| + |\angle 3| + 90° = 180°$

$|\angle 6| = 180° - (55° + 90°) = 35°$

Example

In the parallelogram $ABCD$, $|\angle ABC| = 114°$ and $|\angle CAD| = 47°$.
Find $|\angle CAB|$.

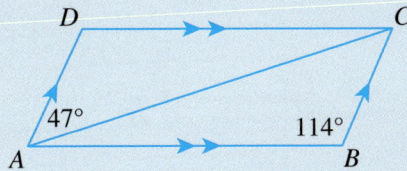

(SEC 2004)

Solution

$|\angle ABC| = |\angle ADC| = 114°$ ... (Opposite angles in a parallelogram)

$|\angle DAB| + |\angle DCB| = 360° - 2(114°) = 132°$

But $|\angle DAB| = |\angle DCB|$ ... (Opposite angles in a parallelogram)

$\therefore |\angle DAB| = \dfrac{132}{2} = 66°$

$|\angle CAB| = |\angle DAB| - |\angle DAC|$

$\therefore |\angle CAB| = 66° - 47° = 19°$

Example

$[AB]$ is a diameter of the circle, C is the centre
of the circle and $|AD| = |BD|$.
Find $|\angle CAD|$.

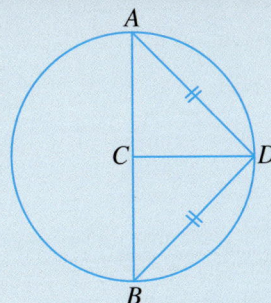

Solution

From the diagram:

$\lvert\angle ADB\rvert = 90°$	... (Angle in a semi-circle)
$\lvert\angle BAD\rvert = \lvert\angle ABD\rvert$	... (Because $\triangle ABD$ is an isosceles triangle)
$\lvert\angle BAD\rvert + \lvert\angle ABD\rvert = 90°$	... (Angles in a triangle add up to 180°)
$\lvert\angle BAD\rvert = \lvert\angle CAD\rvert$	
$\Rightarrow \lvert\angle CAD\rvert = 45°$	

Example

In the given diagram $m \parallel p$. Find $\lvert\angle BAC\rvert$ and $\lvert\angle AED\rvert$.

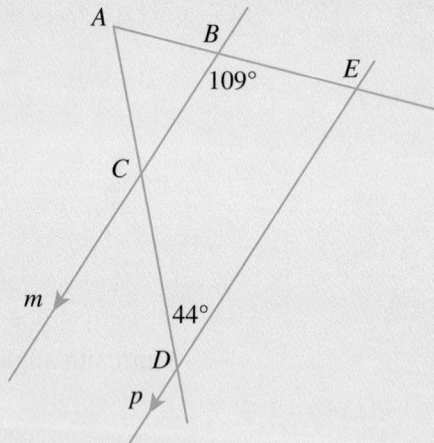

Solution

From the diagram:

$\lvert\angle ABC\rvert = 180° - 109° = 71°$	... (Straight line)
$\lvert\angle CDE\rvert = \lvert\angle ACB\rvert = 44°$	... (Corresponding angles)
$\lvert\angle BAC\rvert = 180° - (71° + 44°) = 65°$	... (Sum of the angles in a triangle)
$\lvert\angle AED\rvert = \lvert\angle ABC\rvert = 71°$	... (Corresponding angles)

[AB] is a diameter of the circle of centre O. C and D are points on the circle. [AB] and [CD] intersect at K and $|\angle CDB| = 38°$.

Find $|\angle ABC|$.

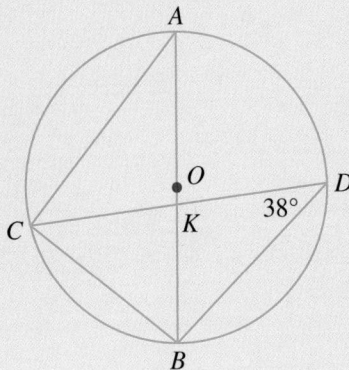

Solution

From the diagram:

$|\angle CDB| = |\angle CAB| = 38°$	... (Angles standing on the same arc)
$|\angle ACB| = 90°$	... (Angle in a semi-circle)
$|\angle ABC| + |\angle CAB| + |\angle ACB| = 180°$	... (Sum of the angles in a triangle)

$|\angle ABC| + 38° + 90° = 180°$

$|\angle ABC| = 180° - (38° + 90°)$

$\therefore |\angle ABC| = 52°$

Using theorems, axioms and corollaries to solve for missing sides

Example

Given that transversals RT and PQ cut three parallel lines which are the same distance apart from one another, find the value of x such that $|RT| + |PQ| = 30$.

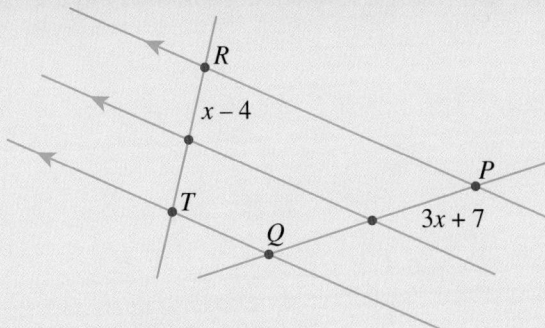

Solution

Given that transversals RT and PQ cut three parallel lines which are the same distance apart, we can fill in the missing segments.

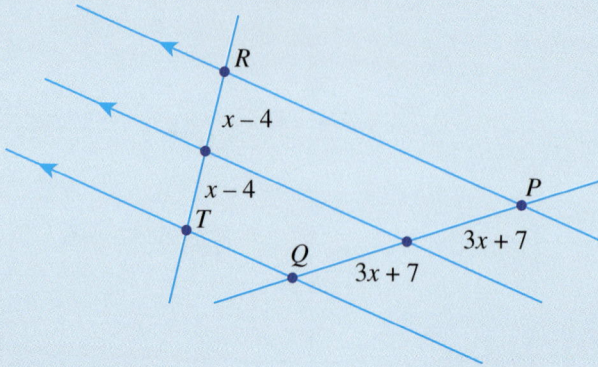

From the diagram:

$|RT| = x - 4 + x - 4$

$|RT| = 2x - 8$

$|PQ| = 3x + 7 + 3x + 7$

$|PQ| = 6x + 14$

Given that $|RT| + |PQ| = 30$, we can rewrite this equation and solve for x:

$2x - 8 + 6x + 14 = 30$

$8x + 6 = 30$

$8x = 30 - 6$

$8x = 24$

$\dfrac{8x}{8} = \dfrac{24}{8}$

$\therefore x = 3$

Example

The two triangles shown are similar. Find the value of x.

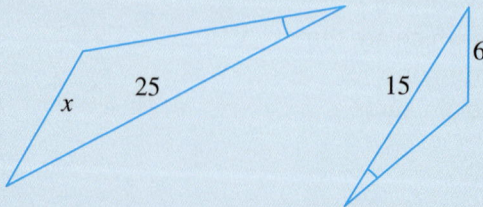

(SEC 2013)

Solution

Identifying corresponding sides to solve for the unknown side:

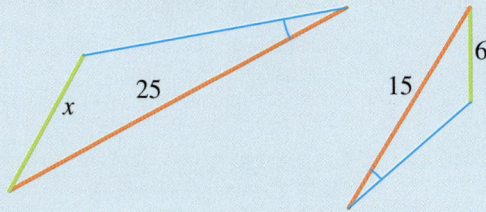

$$\frac{x}{6} = \frac{25}{15}$$

Multiply both sides by 6 to solve for x.

$$6\left(\frac{x}{6}\right) = 6\left(\frac{25}{15}\right)$$

$$\Rightarrow x = \frac{150}{15} = 10$$

Example

In the triangle PQR, $[XY]$ is parallel to $[QR]$. $|PQ| = 14$ cm, $|QR| = 21$ cm and $|PX| = 10$ cm.
Find $|XY|$.

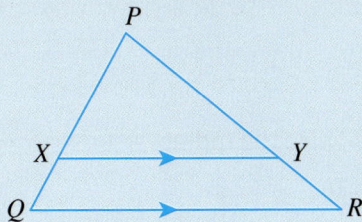

Solution

Since $[XY]$ is parallel to $[QR]$:

$$\frac{|XY|}{|QR|} = \frac{|PX|}{|PQ|}$$ ... (Corresponding sides in similar triangles)

Fill in known values and solve for the required side:

$$\frac{|XY|}{21} = \frac{10}{14}$$

$$|XY| = 21 \times \frac{10}{14}$$

$$\therefore |XY| = 15 \text{ cm}$$

Example

A circle, centre C, has a chord $[AB]$ of length 8. D is a point on $[AB]$ and $[CD]$ is perpendicular to $[AB]$ and $|CD| = 3$. Find the length of a diameter of the circle.

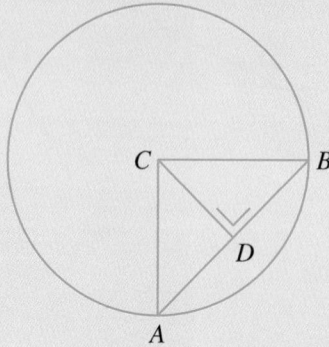

(SEC 2004)

Solution

$\triangle ABC$ is an isosceles triangle as $|AC| = |CB|$ because they are both radii of the circle. $[CD]$ bisects $[AB]$ which means $|AD| = |DB| = 4$.

Using Pythagoras' Theorem:

$|AC|^2 = |AD|^2 + |CD|^2$

$|AC|^2 = (4)^2 + (3)^2$

$|AC|^2 = 16 + 9 = 25$

$|AC| = \sqrt{25} = 5$

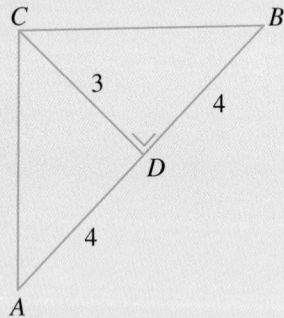

The diameter of the circle is twice the radius.

$\therefore$ Diameter $= 2|AC| = 2(5) = 10$

Example

A surveyor wants to calculate the distance across a lake. The lake is surrounded by woods. Three paths have been constructed to provide access to the lake from a road AC as shown in the diagram. The lengths of the paths from the road to the lake are as follows.

$|AE| = 120$ m.

$|BE| = 80$ m.

$|CD| = 200$ m.

(a) Explain how these measurements can be used to find $|ED|$.

(b) Calculate $|ED|$, the distance across the lake.

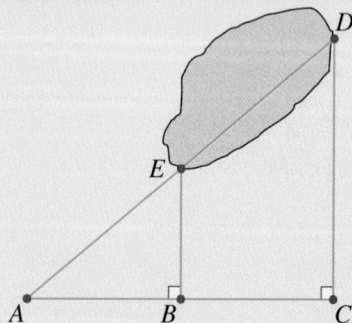

(SEC 2014)

Solution

(a) The two triangles $\triangle AEB$ and $\triangle ADC$ are similar since they have the same three angles (they are 'equiangular'). This means that the corresponding sides are proportional to one another. Therefore:

$$\frac{|AD|}{|AE|} = \frac{|CD|}{|BE|},$$

which can be solved for $|AD|$.

Then, from the diagram: $|ED| = |AD| - |AE|$.

(b) From part **(a)**, we can insert the given information into the equation and solve for the missing side.

$$\frac{|AD|}{120} = \frac{200}{80}$$

Multiply both sides by 120 and solve for $|AD|$.

$$120\left(\frac{|AD|}{120}\right) = 120\left(\frac{200}{80}\right)$$

$$|AD| = 120\left(\frac{200}{80}\right)$$

$$\therefore |AD| = 300$$

$$|ED| = |AD| - |AE|$$

$$\therefore |ED| = 300 - 120 = 180 \text{ m}$$

Using theorems, axioms and corollaries to prove a given statement

Example

$ABCD$ is a parallelogram. AE and CF are perpendicular to BD as shown.

Prove the triangles ABE and CDF are congruent.

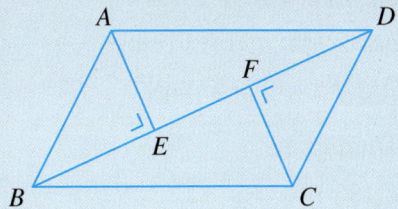

Solution

In triangles ABE and CDF:

$|\angle BEA| = |\angle DFC| = 90°$	... (Given in the question)
$|\angle ABE| = |\angle CDF|$	... (Alternate angles)
$|AB| = |DC|$	... (Opposite sides of a parallelogram)

$\therefore$ The triangles ABE and DCF are congruent as ASA holds true.

Q.E.D.

Prove that $x + y + z = 360°$.

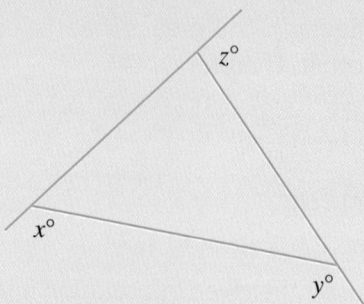

(SEC 2012)

Solution

Label the angles inside the triangle.

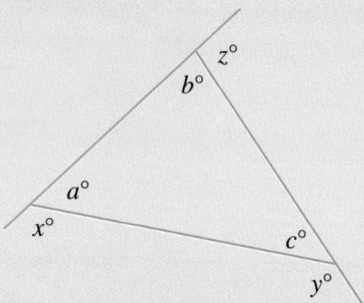

We can state that:

$b° + c° = x°$	… (Exterior angle of a triangle)
$a° + b° = y°$	… (Exterior angle of a triangle)
$a° + c° = z°$	… (Exterior angle of a triangle)

Adding the three equations gives:

$2a° + 2b° + 2c° = x° + y° + z°$

$2(a° + b° + c°) = x° + y° + z°$

But $a° + b° + c° = 180°$ … (Sum of the angles of a triangle)

Therefore:

$2(180°) = x° + y° + z°$

$360° = x° + y° + z°$

Q.E.D.

A, B, C and D are four points on a circle as shown. $[AD]$ bisects $\angle BAC$. P is the point of intersection of AD and BC.

(a) Show that $\triangle ADB$ and $\triangle APC$ are similar.

(b) Show that $|AC| \cdot |BD| = |AD| \cdot |PC|$.

Solution

(a) To show that $\triangle ADB$ and $\triangle APC$ are similar, we can show that the two triangles have the same angles (equiangular).

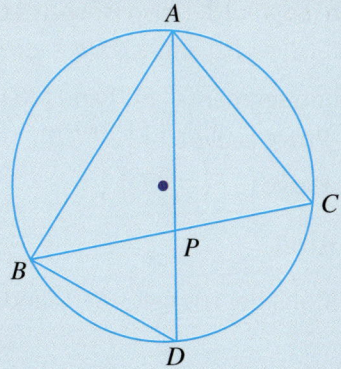

Label the angles in $\triangle ADB$ and $\triangle APC$.

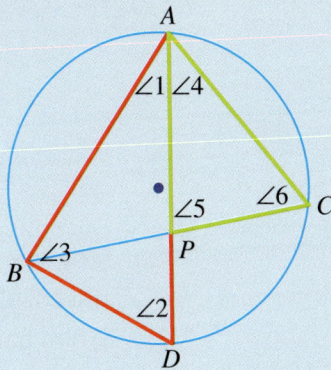

(SEC 2014)

From the labelled diagram:

$|\angle 1| = |\angle 4|$ ... (Given that $[AD]$ bisects $\angle BAC$)

$|\angle 2| = |\angle 6|$ ... (Both angles standing on the same arc AB)

But $|\angle 1| + |\angle 2| + |\angle 3| = 180° = |\angle 4| + |\angle 5| + |\angle 6|$

$\Rightarrow |\angle 3| = |\angle 5|$

Therefore $\triangle ADB$ and $\triangle APC$ are similar triangles or equiangular triangles.

(b) Since the two triangles are similar, corresponding sides must be in proportion to one another. Therefore:

$$\frac{|AC|}{|AD|} = \frac{|PC|}{|BD|}$$

Multiplying both sides by $|AD| \cdot |BD|$ and simplifying:

$$\left(|AD| \cdot |BD| \right) \frac{|AC|}{|AD|} = \frac{|PC|}{|BD|} \left(|AD| \cdot |BD| \right)$$

$$\therefore |BD| \cdot |AC| = |AD| \cdot |PC|$$

Q.E.D.

Example

The triangle ABC is an isosceles triangle, with $|AB| = |AC|$ and $\angle CDB = \angle BEC = 90°$.

The line segments $[EC]$ and $[BD]$ intersect at F.

(a) Prove $|\angle DBC| = |\angle ECB|$.

(b) Prove $|EF| = |FD|$.

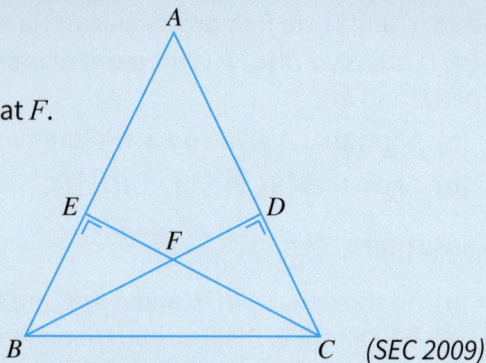

(SEC 2009)

Solution

(a) Consider triangles BCD and CBE.

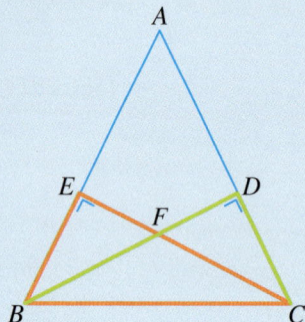

$|\angle BCD| = |\angle CBE|$ ... (Triangle ABC is isosceles)

$|\angle CDB| = |\angle BEC|$ ... (Given information)

$\therefore |\angle DBC| = |\angle ECB|$ ... (Third pair of angles must be equal)

(b) Consider triangles BEF and CDF.

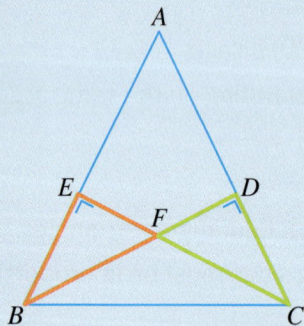

$|\angle EFB| = |\angle DFC|$ ... (Vertically opposite angles)

$|\angle BEF| = |\angle CDF| = 90°$ ... (Given information)

$\therefore |\angle EBF| = |\angle DCF|$ ... (Third pair of angles must be equal)

From part (a):

In $\triangle BCF, |\angle FBC| = |\angle FCB|$

$\therefore |BF| = |CF|$

Hence $\triangle BEF$ is congruent to $\triangle CDF$ ... (ASA)

$\therefore |EF| = |FD|$ ... (Corresponding sides)

Q.E.D.

Exercise

Q1 The diagram below shows a parallelogram and one exterior angle. Find the value of a and the value of b.

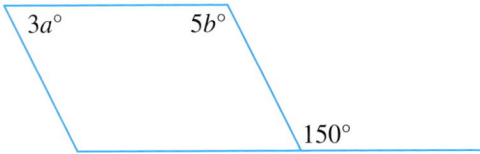

$3a°$ $5b°$

$150°$

(SEC 2012)

Q2 If l_1, l_2 and l_3 are parallel lines, find the measure of the angles α, β and γ.

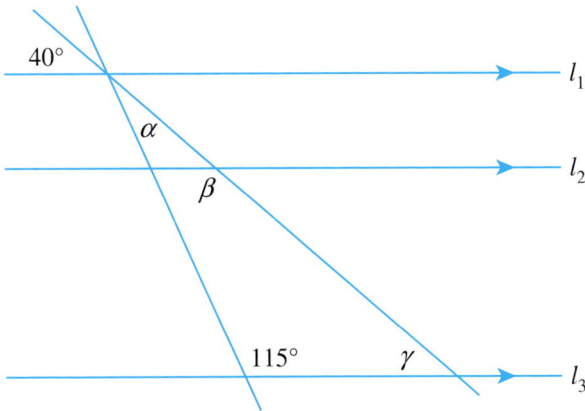

$40°$

α

β

l_1

l_2

$115°$ γ

l_3

(SEC 2013)

Q3 P, Q, R and S are points on a circle with centre O. $\angle PRS = 32°$, as shown.

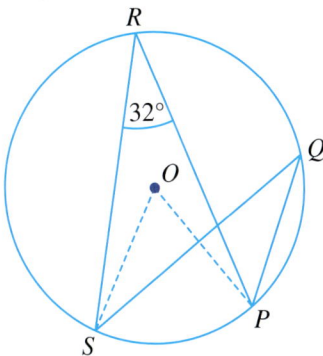

R

$32°$

O

Q

P

S

(a) Find $|\angle SOP|$.

(b) Find $|\angle SQP|$.

(SEC 2014)

Q4 In the triangle ABC, $[DE]$ is parallel to $[CB]$, $|AD| = 4$ cm, $|AC| = 14$ cm and $|AE| = 5$ cm. Find $|EB|$.

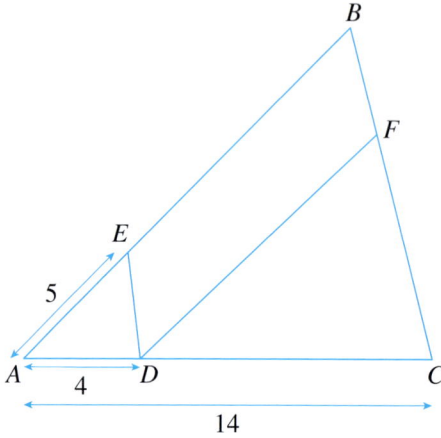

(SEC 2010)

Q5 A, B, C and D are points on a circle, as shown below. $[AC]$ and $[BD]$ are diameters of the circle. Prove that $ABCD$ is a rectangle.

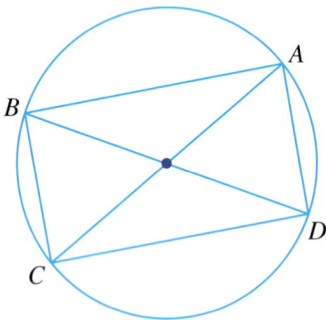

(SEC 2014)

Q6 If $l_1 \parallel l_2$, find the sizes of the angles α, β and γ in the following diagram.

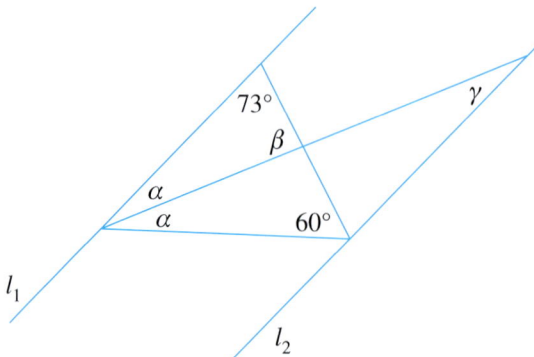

(SEC 2013)

Q7 The points A, B, C and D are shown on the diagram.
They are all on the circle k.
$|AB| = |AD|$ and $|BC| = |DC|$, as shown.
The sizes of some of the angles are marked.

(a) Calculate the value of x.

(b) Calculate the value of y. Show all of your working.

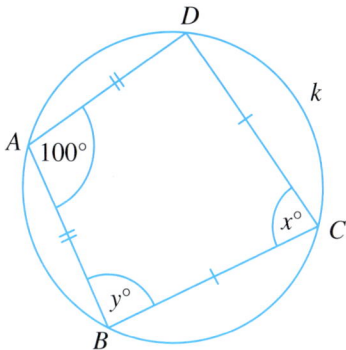

(SEC 2016)

Q8 AB is parallel to CD. BC and AD intersect at the point E.

(a) Prove that the triangles ABE and CDE are equiangular.

(b) Given that $|AB| = 12$ cm, $|BE| = 8$ cm and $|CD| = 7$ cm, find $|EC|$ correct to one decimal place.

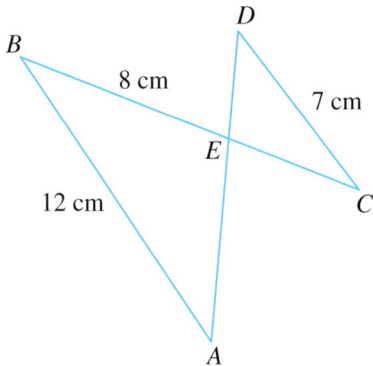

(SEC 2011)

Solutions

Q1 Labelling the unknown angles:

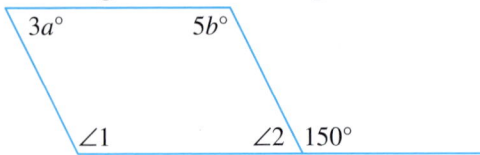

$|\angle 1| = 150°$ ... (Corresponding angles as opposite sides of a parallelogram are parallel)

$5b° = 150°$ ... (Opposite angles of a parallelogram are equal)

$\Rightarrow b° = \dfrac{150°}{5} = 30°$

$|\angle 2| + 150° = 180°$ ... (Straight line)

$|\angle 2| = 180° - 150° = 30°$

$3a° = 30°$ ... (Opposite angles of a parallelogram are equal)

$\Rightarrow a° = \dfrac{30°}{3} = 10°$

Q2

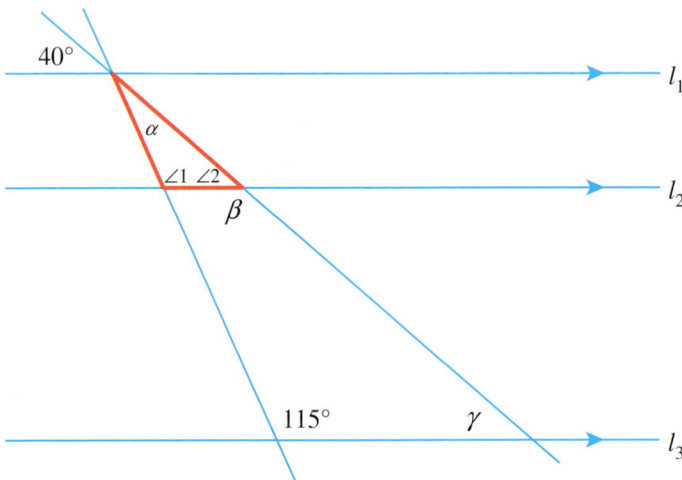

Considering the triangle highlighted:

$\alpha + |\angle 1| + |\angle 2| = 180°$

$|\angle 1| = 115°$ ... (Corresponding angles)

$|\angle 2| = 40°$ ... (Corresponding angles)

$\alpha + 115° + 40° = 180°$

$\therefore \alpha = 180° - (115° + 40°)$

$\therefore \alpha = 180° - 155° = 25°$

$\beta = 180° - 40° = 140°$ ... (Straight line)

$\gamma = 40°$ ... (Corresponding angles with $|\angle 2| = 40°$)

Q3 (a) Given that the angle at the centre of a circle standing on a given arc is twice the angle at any point of the circle standing on the same arc:

$$|\angle SOP| = 2 \times 32° = 64°$$

(b) $|\angle SRP| = |\angle SOP| = 32°$ … (Angles standing on the same arc)

Q4 Since $[DE]$ is parallel to $[CB]$:

$$\frac{|AB|}{|AE|} = \frac{|AC|}{|AD|}$$

Filling in the given information:

$$\frac{|AB|}{5} = \frac{14}{4}$$

$$5\left(\frac{|AB|}{5}\right) = 5\left(\frac{14}{4}\right)$$

$$|AB| = 5\left(\frac{14}{4}\right) = \frac{70}{4}$$

$$\therefore |AB| = 17{\cdot}5$$

From the diagram, $|EB| = |AB| - |AE|$.

$$|EB| = 17{\cdot}5 - 5 = 12{\cdot}5$$

Q5 Consider triangle ABC

$\angle ABC = 90°$ … (Angle in a semi-circle)

Consider triangle BCD

$|\angle BCD| = 90°$ … (Angle in a semi-circle)

Consider triangle ACD

$|\angle ADC| = 90°$ … (Angle in a semi-circle)

Consider triangle ABD

$|\angle BAD| = 90°$ … (Angle in a semi-circle)

$\therefore ABCD$ is a rectangle.

Q.E.D.

Q6

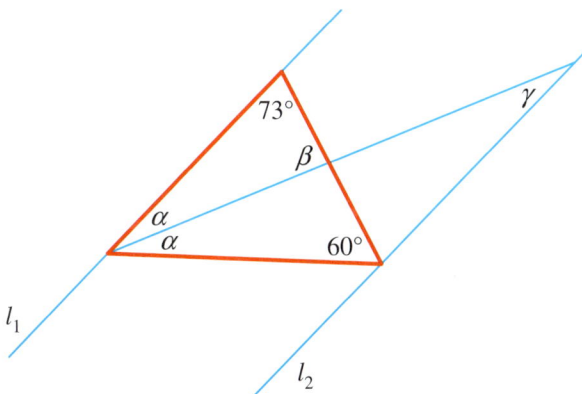

Considering the triangle highlighted we can state that:

$73° + 60° + 2\alpha = 180°$ ... (Sum of the angles of a triangle)

$133° + 2\alpha = 180°$

$2\alpha = 180° - 133°$

$2\alpha = 47°$

$\alpha = \dfrac{47°}{2} = 23.5°$

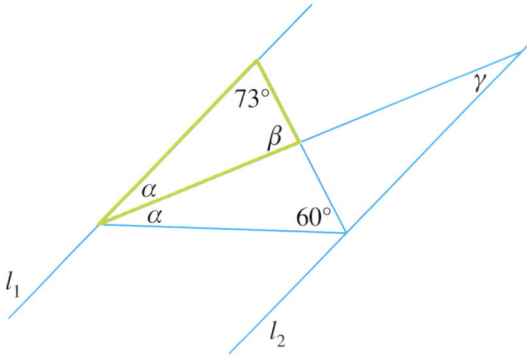

Considering the triangle highlighted:

$73° + \alpha + \beta = 180°$ ... (Sum of the angles of a triangle)

$73° + 23·5° + \beta = 180°$

$96·5° + \beta = 180°$

$\beta = 180° - 96·5°$

$\beta = 83·5°$

Given that $l_1 \parallel l_2$:

$\alpha = \gamma$

$\Rightarrow \gamma = 23·5°$ (Alternate angles)

Q7 (a) $x = 180° - 100° = 80°$ ... (Opposite angles in a cyclic quadrilateral add to 180°)

(b) Constructing the diagonal AC gives triangle ABC.

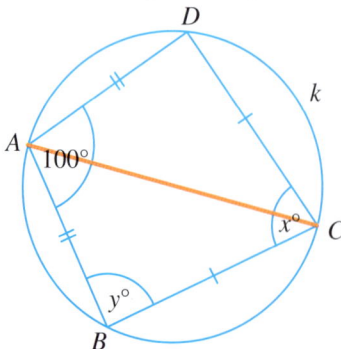

$$y + \frac{100°}{2} + \frac{80°}{2} = 180° \qquad \text{... (The sum of the angles in a triangle)}$$

$y + 50° + 40° = 180°$

$y + 90° = 180°$

$\Rightarrow y = 90°$

Q8 (a) Given that AB is parallel to CD:

$|\angle AEB| = |\angle CED|$ ... (Vertically opposite angles)

$|\angle ABE| = |\angle DCE|$ ... (Alternate angles)

$|\angle BAE| = |\angle CDE|$ ... (Alternate angles)

Therefore, the triangles ABE and CDE are equiangular.

(b) Since the triangles ABE and CDE are similar we can state that:

$$\frac{|EC|}{|BE|} = \frac{|CD|}{|AB|}$$

Filling in the given information and solving for $|EC|$:

$$\frac{|EC|}{8} = \frac{7}{12}$$

$$|EC| = 8\left(\frac{7}{12}\right)$$

$$|EC| = 4 \cdot 666... \simeq 4 \cdot 7 \text{ cm to 1 d.p.}$$

8 Geometry 3: Constructions

Learning objectives

In this chapter, you will study each of the following constructions:

1. Bisector of a given angle, using only a compass and straight edge
2. Perpendicular bisector of a segment, using only a compass and straight edge
3. Line perpendicular to a given line *l*, passing through a given point not on *l*
4. Line perpendicular to a given line *l*, passing through a given point on *l*
5. Line parallel to a given line, through a given point
6. Division of a line segment into three equal segments, without measuring it
7. Division of a line segment into any number of equal segments, without measuring it
8. Line segment of a given length on a given ray
9. Angle of a given number of degrees with a given ray as one arm
10. Triangle, given lengths of three sides
11. Triangle, given a side, angle and side (SAS) data
12. Triangle, given an angle, a side and an angle (ASA) data
13. Right-angled triangle, given the length of the hypotenuse and one other side
14. Right-angled triangle, given one side and one of the acute angles
15. Rectangle, given side lengths

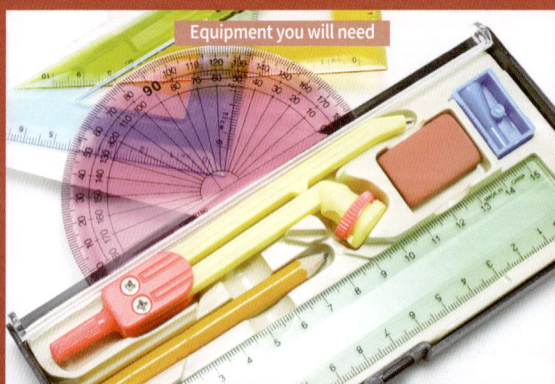

Equipment you will need

Constructions

Construction 1

Bisector of a given angle, using only a compass and straight edge

Example

Construct the bisector of the angle at the vertex labelled B, using only a compass and straight edge.

Solution

Step 1 Position your compass at B and draw an arc which crosses $[AB]$ and $[BC]$.

Step 2 Position your compass at each of the points of intersection and draw two arcs (same distance set for both arcs) that intersect.

Step 3 Draw a line from B through the point of intersection. This is the bisector of the given angle.

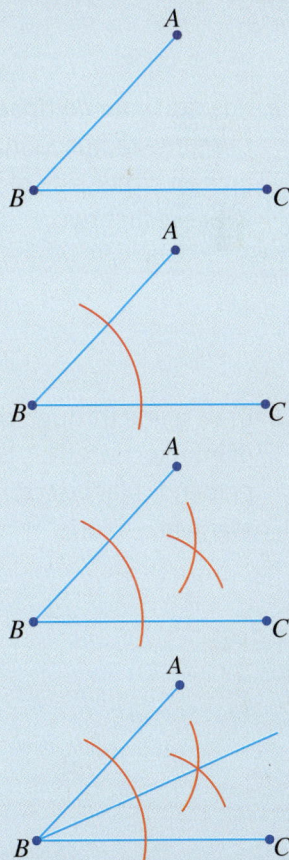

Construction 2

Perpendicular bisector of a segment, using only a compass and straight edge

Example

Construct the perpendicular bisector of the given line segment [PQ], using only a compass and straight edge.

$P \bullet \!\!\!-\!\!\!-\!\!\!-\!\!\!-\!\!\!-\!\!\!-\!\!\!-\!\!\!- \bullet Q$

Solution

Step 1 Position your compass at P, set the radius to be more than half of the distance between P and Q, and draw two arcs, one either side of the given line segment.

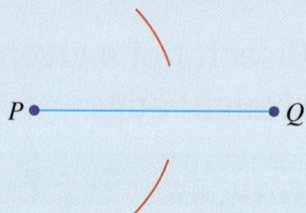

$P \bullet \!\!\!-\!\!\!-\!\!\!-\!\!\!-\!\!\!-\!\!\!-\!\!\!-\!\!\!- \bullet Q$

Step 2 Position your compass at Q, and using the same radius as in Step 1, draw two more arcs on either side of [PQ], which intersect with the first two.

$P \bullet \!\!\!-\!\!\!-\!\!\!-\!\!\!-\!\!\!-\!\!\!-\!\!\!-\!\!\!- \bullet Q$

Step 3 Draw a line through the two points of intersection. This line is the perpendicular bisector of the given line segment.

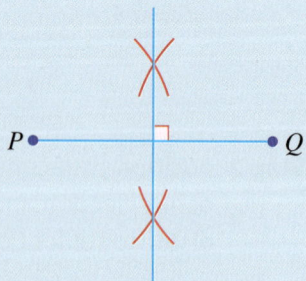

$P \bullet \!\!\!-\!\!\!-\!\!\!-\!\!\!-\!\!\!-\!\!\!-\!\!\!-\!\!\!- \bullet Q$

Construction 3

Line perpendicular to a given line, passing through a given point not on the line

Example

Construct a line perpendicular to the given line AB, passing through the given point C that is not on the line.

Solution

Step 1 Position your compass at C, draw an arc of a circle that intersects the given line segment $[AB]$ at two points. Label the points D and E.

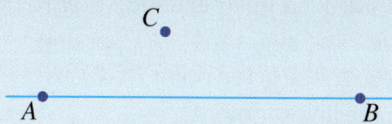

Step 2 Position your compass at D and draw an arc below the line which is over half the distance to E.

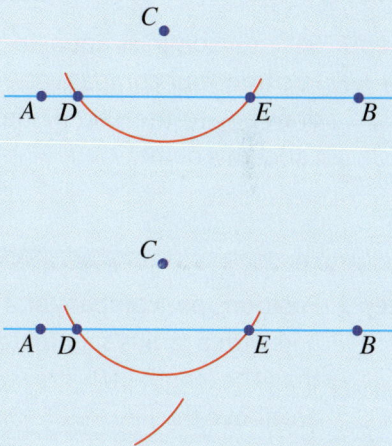

Step 3 Position your compass at E, with the same radius as in Step 2, and draw an arc to intersect the arc just drawn. Label the intersection point P.

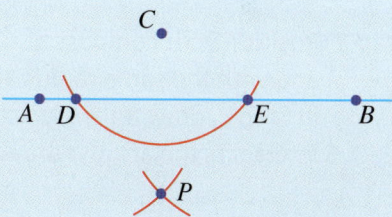

Step 4 Draw a line through P and C. This line is perpendicular to the given line AB.

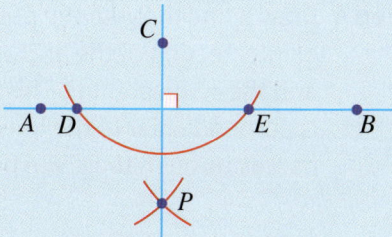

Construction 4

Line perpendicular to a given line, passing through a given point on the given line

Example

Construct a line perpendicular to the given line segment [AB], passing through the given point P which is on the line segment.

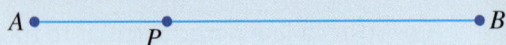

Solution

Step 1 Set your compass equal to |AP|. Position your compass at P and draw an arc intersecting the line. Label this point C.

Step 2 Position your compass at A and with a radius set greater than the length |AP|, draw an arc above the line.

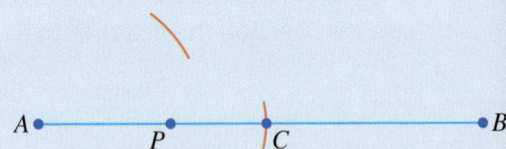

Step 3 Position your compass at C and with the same radius as in Step 2, draw an arc which intersects the arc just drawn.

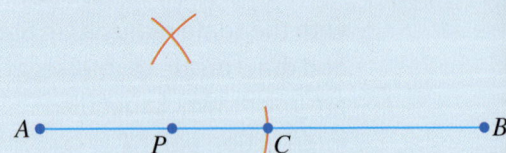

Step 4 Draw a line through the point of intersection of the arcs and the given point P. This line is perpendicular to the line and passes through the given point P.

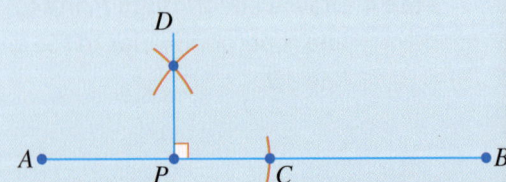

Construction 5

Line parallel to a given line, through a given point

Example

Construct a line parallel to the given line AB, through the given point R.

Solution

Step 1 Mark off any two points on the line AB. Label them C and D.

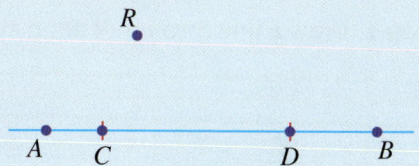

Step 2 Position your compass at R with radius length $|CD|$, draw an arc above the given line AB.

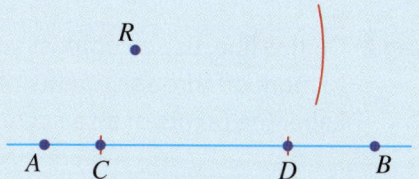

Step 3 Position your compass at D with radius length $|RC|$, and draw an arc to intersect the first arc.

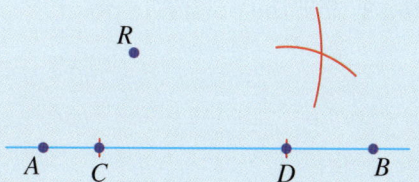

Step 4 Draw a line through R and the point of intersection of the two arcs. This line is parallel to the given line AB.

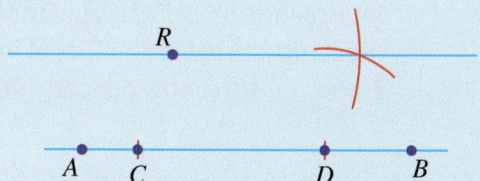

Construction 6

Division of a line segment into three equal segments, without measuring it

Divide the given line segment [AB] into
three equal segments, without measuring it.

A •————————————————• B

Solution

Step 1 Draw a line through A at an acute angle to [AB].

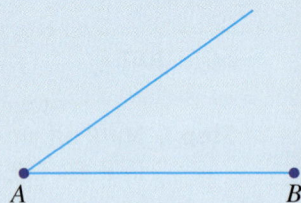

Step 2 On this line, use a compass with a set radius
to mark off three segments of equal length.
Label the points of intersection C, D and E.

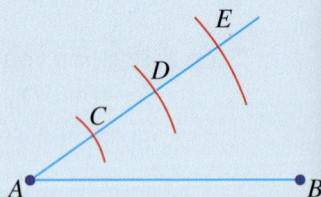

Step 3 Join the point E to point B.

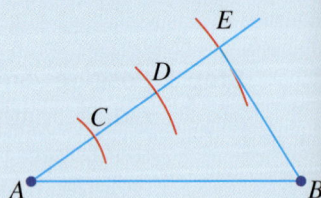

Step 4 Draw two more lines from the points of
intersection on [AE] parallel to [EB] to
meet [AB]. Label this points of intersection
F and G. [AB] is now divided into three equal parts.

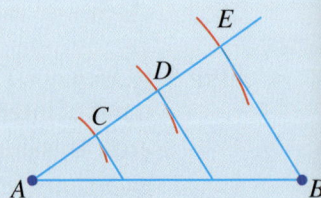

Construction 7

Division of a line segment into any number of equal segments, without measuring it

Divide the given line segment [AB] into five equal segments, without measuring it.

Solution

Step 1 Draw a line through A at an acute angle to [AB].

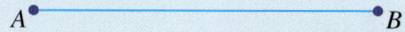

Step 2 On this line, use a compass with a set radius to mark off five segments of equal length. Label the points of intersection C, D, E, F and G.

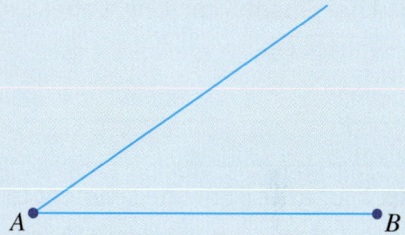

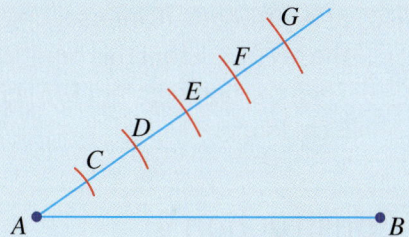

Step 3 Join the point G to point B.

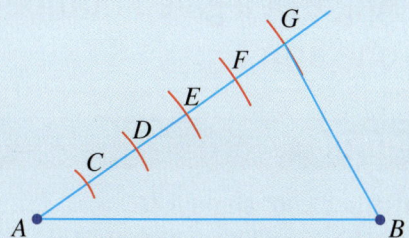

Step 4 Draw four more lines from the points of intersection on [AG] parallel to [GB] to meet [AB]. Label these points of intersection H, I, J and K. [AB] is now divided into five equal parts.

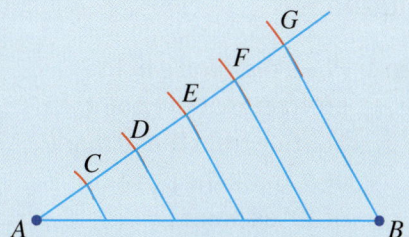

Construction 8

Line segment of a given length on a given ray

Example

Construct a line segment of length 5 cm on the given ray [AB.

$$A \bullet \underline{\hspace{6cm}} \bullet B$$

Solution

Step 1 Using a ruler, draw a line segment 5 cm long. Label it [CD].

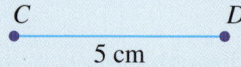

$$C \bullet \underline{\hspace{3cm}} \bullet D$$
5 cm

$$A \bullet \underline{\hspace{6cm}} \bullet B$$

Step 2 Use the 5 cm line segment to set your compass to a radius of 5 cm. Place your compass at A, draw an arc intersecting the ray [AB. Label this point E. Then the line segment [AE] is 5 cm long.

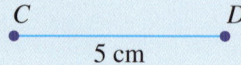

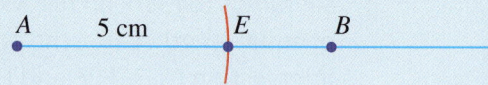

$$C \bullet \underline{\hspace{3cm}} \bullet D$$
5 cm

$$A \bullet \underline{\hspace{2cm}} E \quad \bullet B$$
5 cm

Construction 9

Angle of a given number of degrees with a given ray as one arm

Example

Construct a 40° angle BAC using the given line segment [AB].

$$A \bullet \underline{\hspace{7cm}} \bullet B$$

Solution

Step 1 Place the centre of the protractor at the point A. Starting from the 0° mark at B, mark the position of 40° as point C.

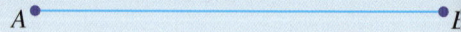

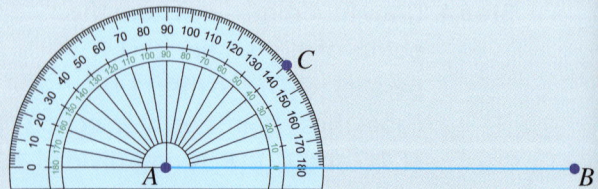

Step 2 Draw a ray from point A through point C. This forms an angle of 40°.

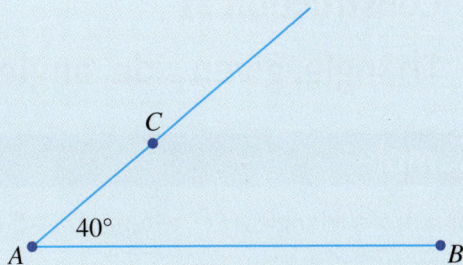

C

40°

A B

Construction 10

Triangle, given lengths of three sides

Example

Construct a triangle with sides 7 cm, 9 cm and 4 cm.

Solution

Step 1 Using the longest side as the base, draw a straight line 9 cm long. Label one end A and the other B.

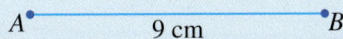

A 9 cm B

Step 2 Set the compass to a radius of 7 cm. Place the compass point at the point A and draw an arc above the line segment.

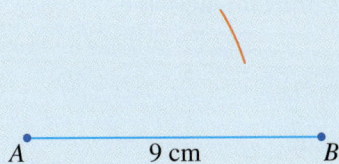

A 9 cm B

Step 3 Set the compass to a radius of 4 cm. Place the compass point at the point B and draw an arc above the line segment which intersects with the first arc drawn.

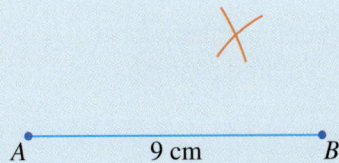

A 9 cm B

Step 4 Draw straight lines from A and B to the point of intersection. This is the required triangle.

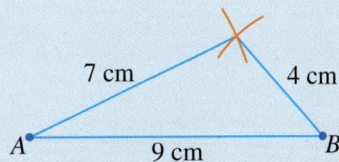

7 cm   4 cm

A 9 cm B

Construction 11

Triangle, given side, angle, side (SAS)

Example

Construct a triangle ABC, where $|AB| = 9$ cm, $|AC| = 7$ cm and $|\angle BAC| = 40°$.

Solution

Step 1 Using the longest side as the base, draw a line 9 cm long and label one end A and the other end B.

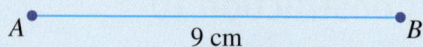

Step 2 Use a protractor to draw an angle of 40° at point A.

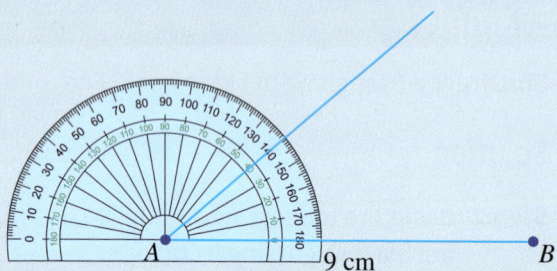

Step 3 Mark off a length of 7 cm on this line and label it C.

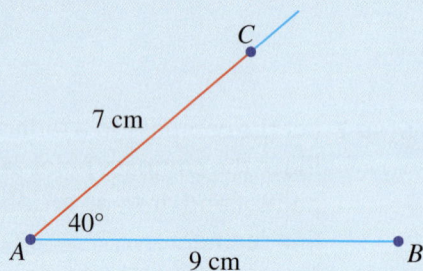

Step 4 Join end points to form the required triangle.

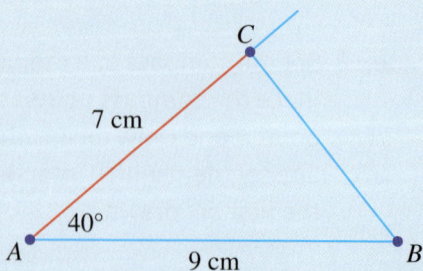

Construction 12

Triangle, given angle, side, angle (ASA)

Example

Construct a triangle ABC, where $|AB| = 8$ cm, $|\angle ABC| = 30°$ and $|\angle BAC| = 100°$.

Solution

Step 1 Draw a line 8 cm long and label one end A and the other end B.

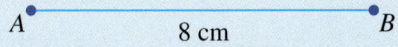

A ———— 8 cm ———— B

Step 2 Use a protractor to draw the angle 30° at point B and draw the angle 100° at point A.

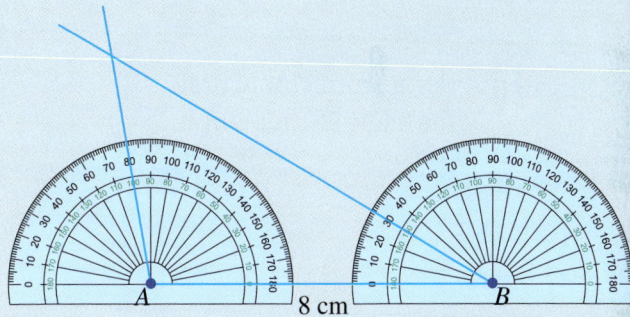

Step 3 Label the point of intersection of these two arms C. The triangle ABC is the required triangle.

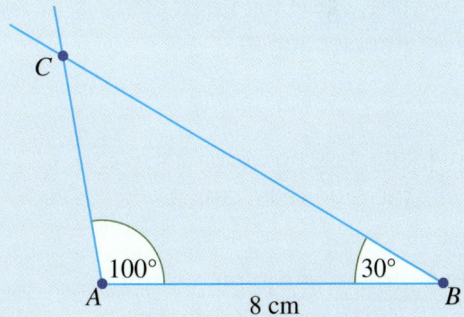

Construction 13

Right-angled triangle, given the length of the hypotenuse and one other side

Example

Construct a triangle ABC, where $|\angle CAB| = 90°$, $|AC| = 4$ cm and $|BC| = 7$ cm.

Solution

Step 1 Using the shortest side as the base, draw a line 4 cm long. Label one end A and the other end C.

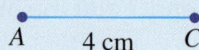

Step 2 Use a protractor to draw the angle 90° at point A.

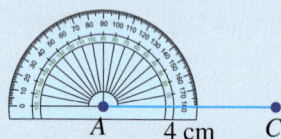

Step 3 Position your compass at C and with a distance of 7 cm set, draw an arc cutting the vertical line. Label the point of intersection B.

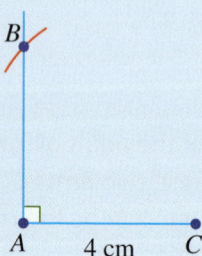

Step 4 Draw a line joining C to B. The triangle ABC is the required triangle.

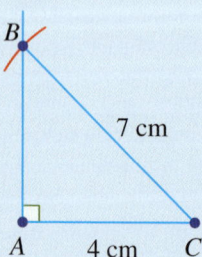

Construction 14

Right-angled triangle, given one side and one of the acute angles

Example

Construct a triangle ABC, where $|\angle ABC| = 30°$, $|\angle BAC| = 90°$ and $|AB| = 8$ cm.

Solution

Step 1 Draw a line 8 cm long and label one end A and the other end B.

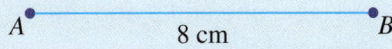

Step 2 Use a protractor to draw a 90° angle at point A. Then use the protractor to draw a 30° angle at point B.

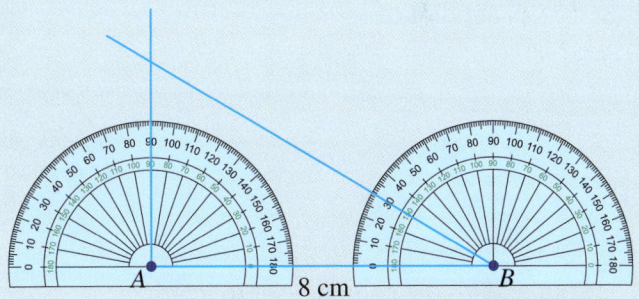

Step 3 Label the point of intersection of these two arms C. The triangle ABC is the required triangle.

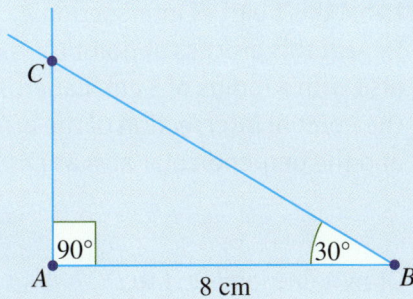

Construction 15

Rectangle, given side lengths

Example

Construct the rectangle $ABCD$ given that $|AB| = 5$ cm and $|BC| = 7$ cm.

Solution

Step 1 Using the longest side as the base, draw a line 7 cm long and label one end B and the other end C.

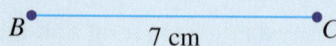

Step 2 Use a protractor to draw a 90° angle at point B and at point C.

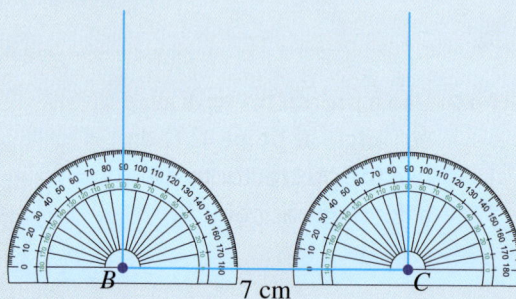

Step 3 With the compass set to a radius of 5 cm, draw an arc from point B which cuts the perpendicular arm. Label this point of intersection A. Repeat this process at point C, also with a radius of 5 cm. Label the point of intersection of the arc and the perpendicular arm as D.

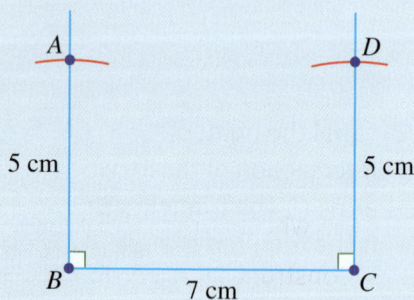

Step 4 Draw a line joining A to D. This completes the required rectangle $ABCD$.

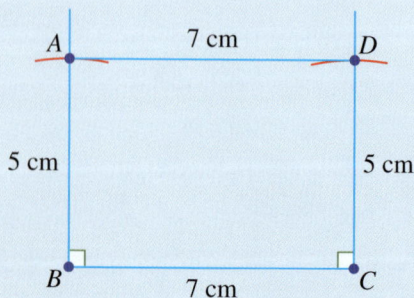

Exercise

Q1 (a) Construct a line segment [AB] where |AB| = 6 cm and place a point C anywhere on this line segment.

(b) Construct a line perpendicular to the line segment [AB], passing through the point C on [AB].

Q2 (a) Construct a line segment [XY] where |XY| = 10 cm.

(b) Construct the perpendicular bisector of the line [XY], using only a compass and straight edge.

Q3 (a) Construct a line segment [ST] where |ST| = 12 cm.

(b) Divide the line segment [ST] into five equal segments, without measuring it.

Q4 Construct the rectangle CDEF given that |CD| = 4 cm and |DE| = 6 cm.

Q5 (a) Construct a line segment [PQ] where |PQ| = 8 cm and place a point R anywhere above the line segment.

(b) Construct a line parallel to the line segment, through the point R.

Q6 (a) Construct a line segment [AB] where |AB| = 7 cm.

(b) Construct a 60° angle on the line segment [AB].

(c) Construct the bisector of the 60° angle, using only a compass and straight edge.

Q7 (a) Construct a triangle of sides 6 cm, 7 cm and 10 cm.

(b) Construct a triangle ABC where |AB| = 10 cm, |AC| = 5 cm and | ∠BAC| = 50°.

(c) Construct a triangle PQR where |PQ| = 8 cm, | ∠RPQ| = 40° and | ∠PQR| = 80°.

Q8 (a) Construct a line segment [AB] where |AB| = 8 cm and place a point P anywhere above the line segment.

(b) Construct a line perpendicular to the given line segment [AB], passing through the point P.

Q9 Construct a triangle ABC where |∠ABC | = 90°, | ∠BAC| = 55° and |AB| = 7 cm.

Q10 (a) Construct a line segment [ST] where |ST| = 12 cm.

(b) Divide the given line segment into three equal segments, without measuring it.

Q11 Construct a triangle PQR, where | ∠QPR| = 90°, |PQ| = 4 cm and |QR| = 7 cm.

Q12 (a) Construct a ray [AB.

(b) Construct a line segment of length 3 cm on the ray [AB.

Solutions

Q1 (a)

A•————C•————6 cm————•B

(b)

A•————C•——|——•D————•B

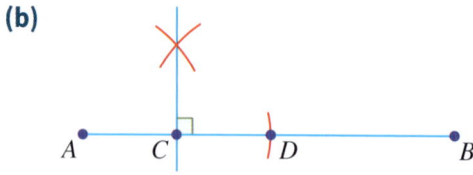

See Construction 4 for step-by-step instructions on how to construct this diagram.

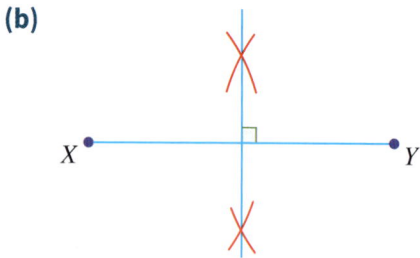

Q2 (a)

X•————10 cm————•Y

(b)

X•————|————•Y

See Construction 2 for step-by-step instructions on how to construct this diagram.

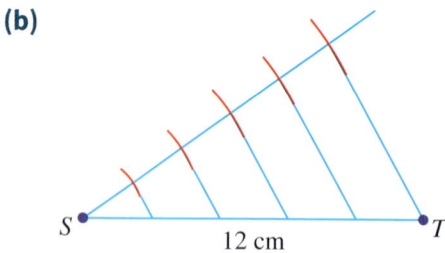

Q3 (a)

S•————12 cm————•T

(b)

S•————12 cm————•T

See Construction 7 for step-by-step instructions on how to construct this diagram.

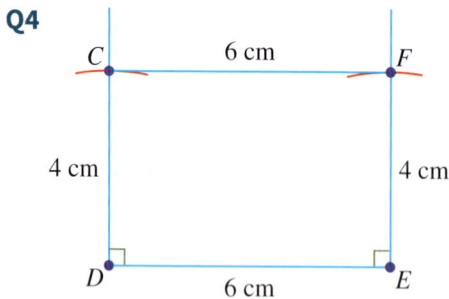

Q4

C•————6 cm————•F
4 cm   4 cm
D•————6 cm————•E

See Construction 15 for step-by-step instructions on how to construct this diagram.

Q5 (a)

(b)

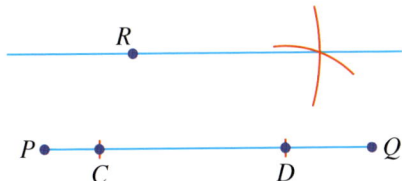

See Construction 5 for step-by-step instructions on how to construct this diagram.

Q6 (a)

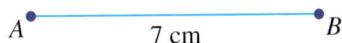

(b)

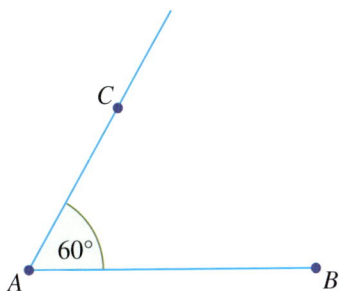

See Construction 9 for step-by-step instructions on how to construct this diagram.

(c)

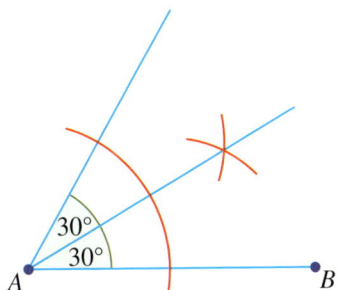

See Construction 1 for step-by-step instructions on how to construct this diagram.

Q7 (a)

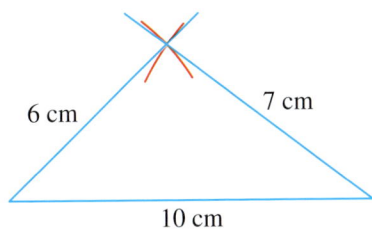

See Construction 10 for step-by-step instructions on how to construct this diagram.

(b)

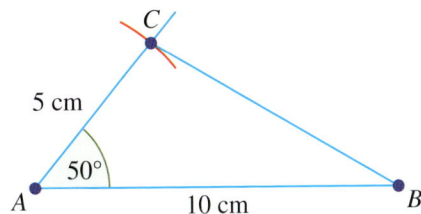

See Construction 11 for step-by-step instructions on how to construct this diagram.

(c)

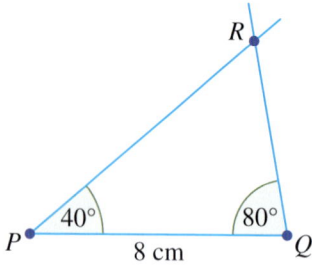

See Construction 12 for step-by-step instructions on how to construct this diagram.

Q8 (a)

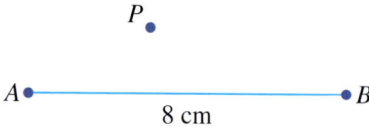

(b)

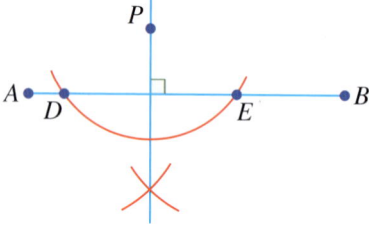

See Construction 3 for step-by-step instructions on how to construct this diagram.

Q9

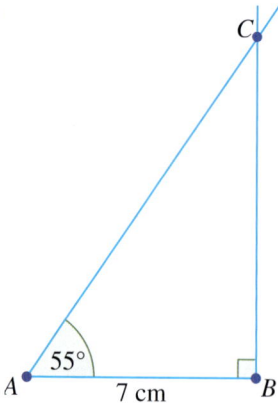

See Construction 14 for step-by-step instructions on how to construct this diagram.

Q10 (a) $S \bullet\!\!-\!\!-\!\!-\!\!-\!\!-\!\!-\!\!-\!\!-\!\!-\!\!\bullet T$

12 cm

(b)

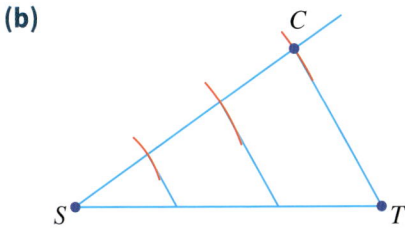

See Construction 6 for step-by-step instructions on how to construct this diagram.

Q11

7 cm

4 cm

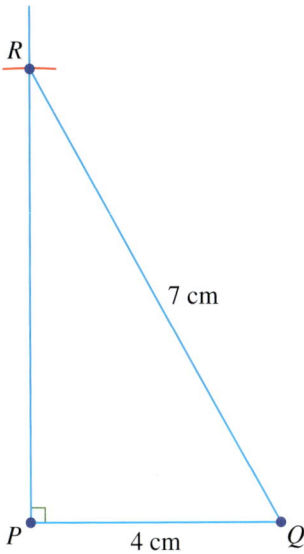

See Construction 13 for step-by-step instructions on how to construct this diagram.

Q12 (a) $A \bullet\!\!-\!\!-\!\!-\!\!-\!\!-\!\!-\!\!-\!\!-\!\!\bullet B$

(b) $C \bullet\!\!-\!\!-\!\!-\!\!-\!\!-\!\!-\!\!\bullet D$

3 cm

A 3 cm E B

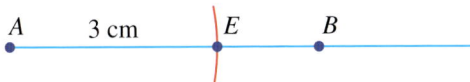

See Construction 8 for step-by-step instructions on how to construct this diagram.

9 Coordinate Geometry of the Line

Learning objectives

In this chapter you will learn about:

- The coordinate plane
- The distance between two points
- The midpoint between two points
- The slope of a line
- The equation of a line
- Parallel and perpendicular lines.

The coordinate plane

The coordinate plane is a two-dimensional surface which has two axes, the horizontal axis called the x-axis and the vertical axis called the y-axis. In this chapter we use the coordinate plane to plot points in the form (x, y) and show how the coordinates can be used to draw lines.

The coordinate plane can be divided into four quadrants, as shown in the figure.

Note that the quadrants are labelled in an anticlockwise direction.

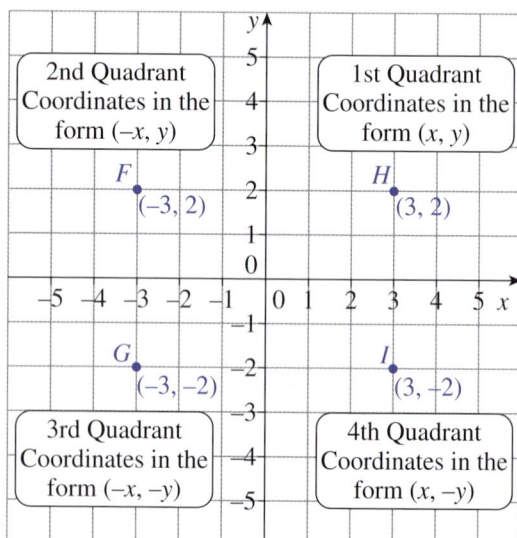

2nd Quadrant
Coordinates in the form $(-x, y)$

1st Quadrant
Coordinates in the form (x, y)

F $(-3, 2)$

H $(3, 2)$

G $(-3, -2)$

I $(3, -2)$

3rd Quadrant
Coordinates in the form $(-x, -y)$

4th Quadrant
Coordinates in the form $(x, -y)$

Distance between two given points

The distance between two points can also be referred to as the length of a given line segment. The formula is derived by forming a right-angled triangle and applying Pythagoras' Theorem.

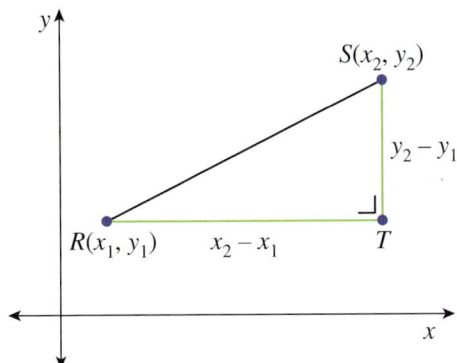

Let:

$|RT| = x_2 - x_1$

$|ST| = y_2 - y_1$

Now Pythagoras' Theorem can be applied to find $|RS|$.

$|RS|^2 = |RT|^2 + |ST|^2$

Hence, by taking the square root of both sides of the equation:

$|RS| = \sqrt{(x_2 - x_1)^2 + (y_2 - y_1)^2}$

> ## Point to note
>
> The length of the line segment $|AB|$ given $A(x_1, y_1)$ and $B(x_2, y_2)$
> can be found using the formula $|AB| = \sqrt{(x_2 - x_1)^2 + (y_2 - y_1)^2}$.
> *In the *Formulae and Tables* booklet.
>
>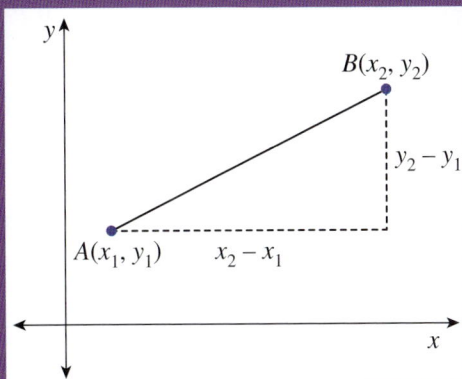

Example

Given the points $A(4, -4)$ and $B(-1, 8)$, find $|AB|$.

Solution

Label one of the points (x_1, y_1) and the other point (x_2, y_2).

$$(x_1, \ y_1) \qquad (x_2, y_2)$$
$$\Updownarrow \ \Updownarrow \qquad\qquad \Updownarrow \ \Updownarrow$$
$$(4, -4) \qquad (-1, 8)$$

Substitute this information into the distance formula and simplify.

$$|AB| = \sqrt{(x_2 - x_1)^2 + (y_2 - y_1)^2}$$
$$= \sqrt{(-1 - 4)^2 + (8 - (-4))^2}$$
$$= \sqrt{(-5)^2 + (12)^2}$$
$$= \sqrt{25 + 144} = \sqrt{169} = 13$$

Hence $|AB| = 13$.

The midpoint between two given points

The midpoint between two points can also be referred to as the midpoint of a line segment. It is the halfway point between the given points.

Point to note

The midpoint P of the line segment $|AB|$, given the points $R(x_1, y_1)$ and $S(x_2, y_2)$, can be found using the formula $P = \left(\dfrac{x_1 + x_2}{2}, \dfrac{y_1 + y_2}{2} \right)$.

*In the *Formulae and Tables* booklet.

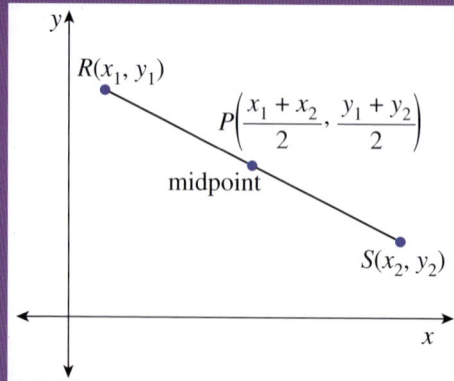

Find the midpoint between $S(7, -2)$ and $T(-11, 8)$.

Solution

Label one of the points (x_1, y_1) and the other point (x_2, y_2).

$$(x_1, y_1) \qquad (x_2, y_2)$$
$$\Updownarrow \Updownarrow \qquad \Updownarrow \Updownarrow$$
$$(7, -2) \qquad (-11, 8)$$

Substitute this information into the midpoint formula and simplify.

$$\text{Midpoint} = \left(\frac{x_1 + x_2}{2}, \frac{y_1 + y_2}{2} \right)$$
$$= \left(\frac{7 + (-11)}{2}, \frac{(-2) + 8}{2} \right)$$
$$= \left(\frac{-4}{2}, \frac{6}{2} \right)$$
$$= (-2, 3)$$

The slope of a line

The slope of a line represents the steepness of the line. Another way of thinking about the slope is that it represents the rate of change of one variable with respect to another variable. A line may be:

- positive sloping;
- horizontal or vertical;
- negative sloping.

Positive sloping

When the value of x increases and the value of y increases, the graph slants upward. (Positive slope.)

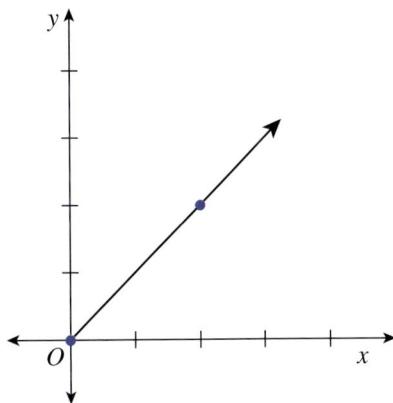

Horizontal

When the value of x increases and the value of y remains constant, the graph will be a horizontal line. (The slope equals zero.)

Vertical

When the value of y increases and the value of x remains constant, the graph will be a vertical line. (The slope is undefined.)

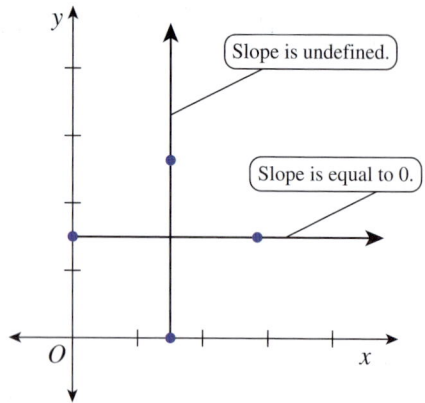

Slope is undefined.

Slope is equal to 0.

> ### Remember
> A vertical line has undefined slope because all points on the line have the same x-coordinates. Due to this fact, when we calculate the slope using the formula $m = \dfrac{y_2 - y_1}{x_2 - x_1}$ it will always produce a denominator of 0, which makes the slope undefined.

Negative sloping

When the value of x increases and the value of y decreases, the graph slants downward. (Negative slope.)

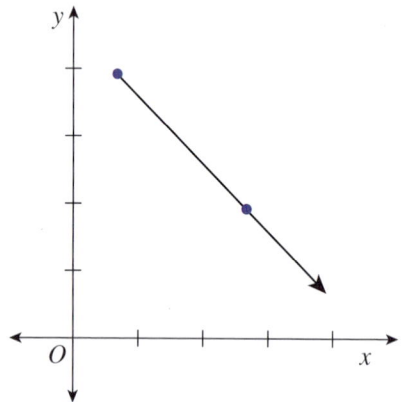

Calculating the value of the slope

> ### Points to note
> - The slope is denoted by m, which is calculated by $m = \dfrac{\text{rise}}{\text{run}}$, where 'rise' means the increase in 'height' or the increase in y, and 'run' means the increase in 'length' or the increase in x.
>
> - The slope, m, of the line which passes through the points $A(x_1, y_1)$ and $B(x_2, y_2)$ is given by the formula $m = \dfrac{y_2 - y_1}{x_2 - x_1}$.
>
>   *In the *Formulae and Tables* booklet.

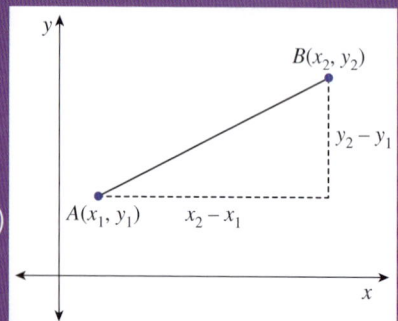

Find the slope of the line PQ given $P(-6, 3)$ and $Q(4, 7)$.

Solution

Label one of the points (x_1, y_1) and the other point (x_2, y_2).

$$\begin{array}{cc} (x_1, y_1) & (x_2, y_2) \\ \Updownarrow \ \Updownarrow & \Updownarrow \ \Updownarrow \\ (-6, 3) & (4, 7) \end{array}$$

Substitute this information into the slope formula and simplify.

$$m = \frac{y_2 - y_1}{x_2 - x_1}$$

$$= \frac{7 - 3}{4 - (-6)}$$

$$= \frac{4}{10} = \frac{2}{5}$$

The equation of a line

The equation of a line is an algebraic equation that describes a given line. There are three forms of equation which can be used to describe a line:

- $y = mx + c$
- $y - y_1 = m(x - x_1)$
- $ax + by + c = 0$

The equation of a line in the form $y = mx + c$

In this equation:

- m represents the slope of the line,

- c represents the y-intercept (i.e. where the line crosses the y-axis), and

- x and y are the coordinates of any point on the line.

  This formula is given in the *Formulae and Tables* booklet.

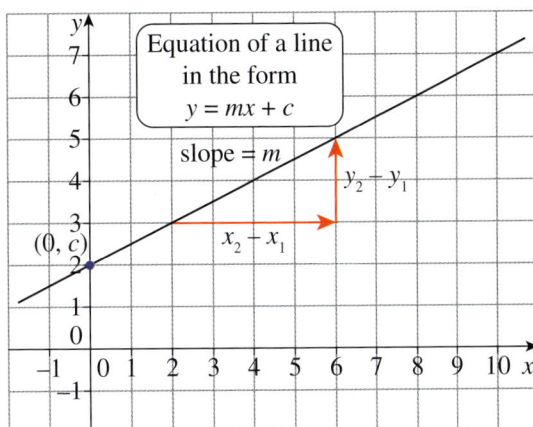

Equation of a line in the form $y = mx + c$

slope $= m$

$(0, c)$

$y_2 - y_1$

$x_2 - x_1$

Example

Given the graph of the line AB, find the equation of the line AB.

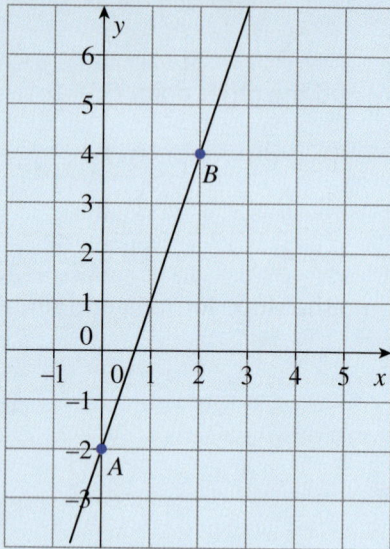

Solution

From the graph, A is at $(0, -2)$ and B is at $(2, 4)$.

Set (x_1, y_1) and (x_2, y_2) as follows:

(x_1, y_1) $\quad$ (x_2, y_2)

$\updownarrow \updownarrow$ $\qquad$ $\updownarrow \updownarrow$

$(0, -2)$ $\quad$ $(2, 4)$

First find the slope, m.

$$m = \frac{y_2 - y_1}{x_2 - x_1}$$

$$= \frac{4 - (-2)}{2 - 0}$$

$$= \frac{6}{2}$$

$$= 3$$

From the given diagram, the y-intercept is point A, $(0, -2)$.

Now substitute the slope and the y-intercept point into the formula $y = mx + c$.

$$y = mx + c$$

$$= 3x + (-2)$$

$$\Rightarrow y = 3x - 2$$

Example

The coordinate diagram represents the lines l_1, l_2, l_3 and l_4. The table to the right contains the equation of each line. Match each of the lines to its correct equation.

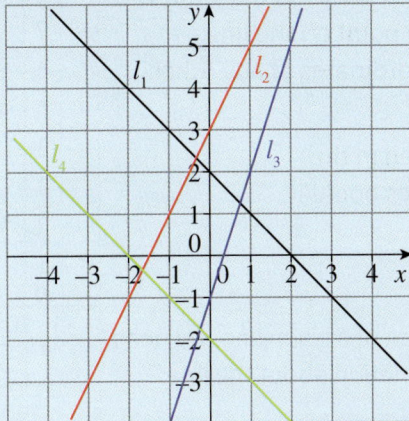

Equation
$y = 2x + 3$
$y = -x - 2$
$y = -x + 2$
$y = 3x - 1$

Solution

From the graph, relevant 'run' and 'rise' figures can be measured and the y-intercepts noted. Then in each case the values for m and c can be substituted into the equation $y = mx + c$ to obtain the equation of the line.

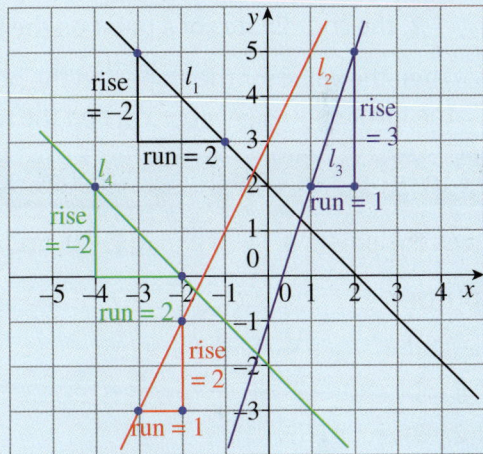

The line l_1:

Slope $m = \dfrac{\text{rise}}{\text{run}} = \dfrac{-2}{2} = -1$

y-intercept $= (0, 2)$

Substituting into the equation of a line in the form $y = mx + c$

$\Rightarrow l_1: y = -x + 2$

The line l_2:

Slope $m = \dfrac{\text{rise}}{\text{run}} = \dfrac{2}{1} = 2$

y-intercept $= (0, 3)$

Substituting into the equation of a line in the form $y = mx + c$

$\Rightarrow l_2: y = 2x + 3$

The line l_3:

Slope $m = \dfrac{\text{rise}}{\text{run}} = \dfrac{3}{1} = 3$

y-intercept $= (0, -1)$

Substituting into the equation of a line in the form $y = mx + c$

$\Rightarrow l_3: y = 3x - 1$

The line l_4:

Slope $m = \dfrac{\text{rise}}{\text{run}} = \dfrac{-2}{2} = -1$

y-intercept $= (0, -2)$

Substituting into the equation of a line in the form $y = mx + c$

$\Rightarrow l_4: y = -x - 2$

The equation of a line in the form $y - y_1 = m(x - x_1)$

In this equation, m represents the slope of the line, (x_1, y_1) is a point on the line and x, y are the coordinates of any other point on the line.

This formula is given in the *Formulae and Tables* booklet.

$y - y_1 = m(x - x_1)$

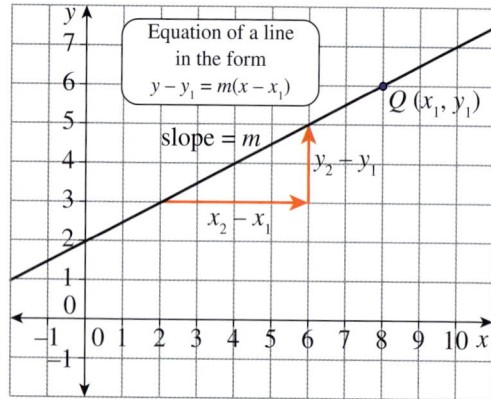

To form the equation of a given line, we need two pieces of information about the line:

    1 the slope, m

    2 the coordinates of a point on the line, (x_1, y_1).

Then the value for the slope and the point coordinates can be substituted into the formula $y - y_1 = m(x - x_1)$, and the result simplified.

Example

Given the points $A(2, -3)$ and $B(5, -2)$, find the equation of the line AB.

Solution

$$(x_1, y_1) \qquad (x_2, y_2)$$
$$\Updownarrow \Updownarrow \qquad \Updownarrow \Updownarrow$$
$$A(2, -3) \qquad B(5, -2)$$

We need two pieces of information about the line: (1) its slope, m, and (2) the coordinates of a point on the line.

  1 $m = \dfrac{y_2 - y_1}{x_2 - x_1}$

$$= \frac{(-2) - (-3)}{5 - 2} = \frac{-2 + 3}{3} = \frac{1}{3}$$

  2   A point on the line $= A(2, -3)$

Substitute the value for the slope and the point coordinates into the formula $y - y_1 = m(x - x_1)$ and simplify.

$$y - (-3) = \frac{1}{3}(x - 2)$$
$$3(y + 3) = (x - 2)$$
$$3y + 9 = x - 2$$
$$-x + 3y + 9 + 2 = 0$$
$$-x + 3y + 11 = 0$$
$$\text{or}$$
$$x - 3y - 11 = 0$$

The equation of a line in the form $ax + by + c = 0$

In this form of the equation of a line, a, b and $c \in \mathbb{Z}$. The slope of the line, m, can be found by rearranging the equation $ax + by + c = 0$ to make y the subject of the equation in the form $y = mx + c$.

$ax + by + c = 0$

$by = -ax - c$

$y = -\dfrac{a}{b}x - \dfrac{c}{b}$

The coefficient of x is the slope of the line. So $m = -\dfrac{a}{b}$.

Example

The table below gives the equations of three lines and the slope of each line. Match each of the equations with its corresponding slope.

Line 1	Slope (m_A) $= -\dfrac{1}{3}$
$2x + 3y + 6 = 0$	
Line 2	Slope (m_B) $= -\dfrac{2}{3}$
$-3x + 2y - 6 = 0$	
Line 3	Slope (m_C) $= \dfrac{3}{2}$
$x + 3y + 2 = 0$	

Solution

To find the slope, we can rearrange the equation $ax + by + c = 0$ to make y the subject of the equation in the form $y = mx + c$.

Line 1	Line 2	Line 3
$2x + 3y + 6 = 0$	$-3x + 2y - 6 = 0$	$x + 3y + 2 = 0$
$3y = -2x - 6$	$2y = 3x + 6$	$3y = -x - 2$
$\dfrac{3y}{3} = \dfrac{-2}{3}x - \dfrac{6}{3}$	$\dfrac{2y}{2} = \dfrac{3}{2}x + \dfrac{6}{2}$	$\dfrac{3y}{3} = \dfrac{-1}{3}x - \dfrac{2}{3}$
$y = -\dfrac{2}{3}x - 2$	$y = \dfrac{3}{2}x + 3$	$y = -\dfrac{1}{3}x - \dfrac{2}{3}$
$\therefore$ Slope (m_B) $= -\dfrac{2}{3}$	$\therefore$ Slope (m_C) $= \dfrac{3}{2}$	$\therefore$ Slope (m_A) $= -\dfrac{1}{3}$

How to verify if a point is on a line

To verify if a point is on a line, substitute the coordinates of the given point into the equation of the line and if it satisfies the equation then it is on the line.

Example

Investigate whether or not the point (2, 3) is on either of the given lines s and t.

$s : 2x + y - 6 = 0$

$t : y = 2x - 5$

Solution

Line s

Substitute the point (2, 3) into the equation for line s.

$s : 2x + y - 6 = 0$

$2(2) + (3) - 6 = 1 \neq 0$

Therefore, the point (2, 3) is not on the line.

Line t

Substitute the point (2, 3) into the equation for line t.

$t : y = 2x - 5 = 2(2) - 1 = 3$

Therefore, the point (2, 3) is on the line.

Parallel lines

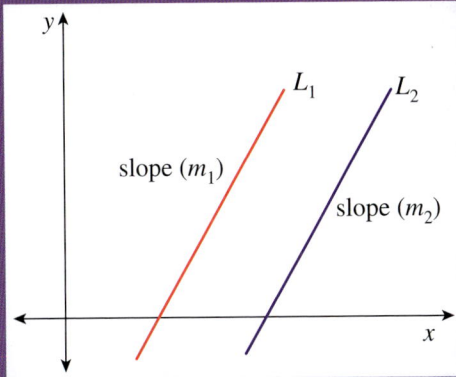

Example

Find the equation of the line p which is parallel to $q : 3x + y - 2 = 0$ and contains the point $(1, -2)$.

Solution

Step 1: To find the slope of q, we can rearrange the equation $ax + by + c = 0$ to make y the subject of the equation in the form $y = mx + c$.

$q : 3x + y - 2 = 0$

$q : y = -3x + 2$

$\therefore$ Slope $(m_q) = -3$

Alternatively find the slope by finding the value of $\dfrac{-a}{b} = \dfrac{-3}{1} = -3$

Step 2: As $p \parallel q$, slope m_p = slope m_q = −3

A point on line p is given as $(1, -2)$.

Now substitute the slope and the point into the formula $y - y_1 = m(x - x_1)$.

(x_1, y_1)

$\Updownarrow \ \Updownarrow$

$(1, -2)$

$p : y - y_1 = m(x - x_1)$

$y - (-2) = -3(x - 1)$

$y + 2 = -3x + 3$

$y + 3x + 2 - 3 = 0$

$p : y + 3x - 1 = 0$

or

$p : -y - 3x + 1 = 0$

Perpendicular lines

Points to note

If two lines are perpendicular to each other, when their slopes are multiplied together the answer will always be −1.

$m_1 \times m_2 = -1$.

To form the equation of a line perpendicular to a given line, we can follow these steps:

Step 1 : Identify the slope of the given line.

Step 2 : To find the slope of the perpendicular line, just turn the known slope upside down and change its sign.

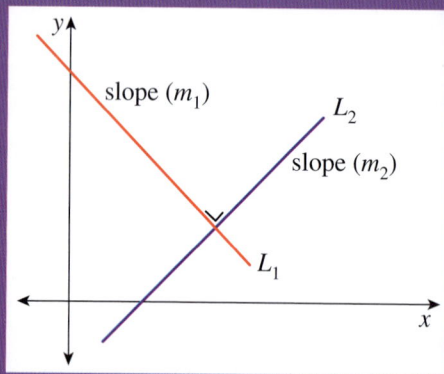

Step 3 : To form the equation of the perpendicular line we need two pieces of information:

1 the slope, m

2 the coordinates of a point on the line, (x_1, y_1).

Substitute the value of the slope and the point coordinates into the formula $y - y_1 = m(x - x_1)$

Quick rule

To find the slope of the perpendicular line, just turn the known slope upside down and change its sign. Here are some examples.

Slope (m_1)	Parallel lines (m_2) $m_1 = m_2$	Perpendicular lines (m_2) $m_1 \times m_2 = -1$
$\dfrac{2}{5}$	$\dfrac{2}{5}$	$-\dfrac{5}{2}$
2	2	$-\dfrac{1}{2}$
-2	-2	$\dfrac{1}{2}$
$-\dfrac{2}{5}$	$-\dfrac{2}{5}$	$\dfrac{5}{2}$

Example

Find the equation of the line a which is perpendicular to $b : 2x - 4y - 8 = 0$ and contains the point $(-2, 7)$.

Solution

Step 1: To find the slope of b, we can rearrange the equation $ax + by + c = 0$ to make y the subject of the equation in the form $y = mx + c$.

$b : 2x - 4y - 8 = 0$

$b : -4y = -2x + 8$

$b : \dfrac{-4y}{-4} = \dfrac{-2}{-4}x + \dfrac{8}{-4}$

$b : y = \dfrac{1}{2}x - 2$

$\therefore$ Slope $(m_b) = \dfrac{1}{2}$

Alternatively find the slope by finding the value of $\dfrac{-a}{b} = \dfrac{-2}{-4} = \dfrac{1}{2}$

Step 2: To find the slope of the perpendicular line, just turn the known slope upside down and change its sign.

Slope (m_b)	Perpendicular lines (m_a) $m_b \times m_a = -1$
$\dfrac{1}{2}$	-2

Step 3: To form the equation of the perpendicular line we need two pieces of information:

1 the slope of a: as $a \perp b$, $m_a = -2$.

2 a point on the line is given as $(-2, 7)$.

Now substitute the slope and the point into the formula $y - y_1 = m(x - x_1)$.

$(x_1, \ y_1)$

$\Updownarrow \quad \Updownarrow$

$(-2, \ 7)$

$a : y - y_1 = m(x - x_1)$

$y - 7 = -2(x - (-2))$

$y - 7 = -2x - 4$

$y + 2x - 7 + 4 = 0$

$a : y + 2x - 3 = 0$

or

$a : -y - 2x + 3 = 0$

Points of intersection

A line may intersect with the x-axis, the y-axis, or with another line.

> ## Points to note
>
> Points of intersection of a given line with the x-axis and y-axis
>
>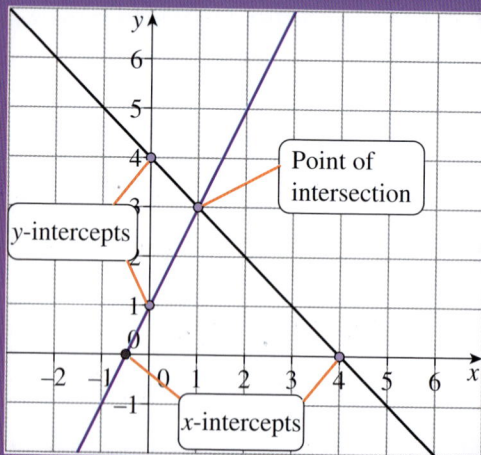
>
> - The line intersects the x-axis at the coordinate $(x, 0)$
> - The line intersect the y-axis at the coordinate $(0, y)$

Point of intersection of two given lines

Example

Two lines are given by $3x - 6y - 24 = 0$ and $2x + 4y - 8 = 0$.

(a) Find the point of intersection of the two lines using the graphical method.

(b) Verify your answer using algebra.

Solution

(a) Find the points where the lines intersect the axes.

Line $3x - 6y - 24 = 0$

Let $x = 0$ and find the corresponding y value. Point is written as $(x, y) = (0, y \text{ value})$.	Let $y = 0$ and find the corresponding x value. Point is written as $(x, y) = (x \text{ value}, 0)$.
$3x - 6y - 24 = 0$	$3x - 6y - 24 = 0$
$3(0) - 6y - 24 = 0$	$3x - 6(0) - 24 = 0$
$-6y - 24 = 0$	$3x - 24 = 0$
$-6y = 24$	$3x = 24$
$\dfrac{-6y}{-6} = \dfrac{24}{-6}$	$\dfrac{3x}{3} = \dfrac{24}{3}$
$\therefore y = -4$	$\therefore x = 8$
Therefore the line intersects the y-axis at $(0, -4)$.	Therefore the line intersects the x-axis at $(8, 0)$.

Line $2x + 4y - 8 = 0$

Let $x = 0$ and find the corresponding y value. Point is written as $(x, y) = (0, y$ value$)$.

$$2x + 4y - 8 = 0$$
$$2(0) + 4y - 8 = 0$$
$$4y - 8 = 0$$
$$4y = 8$$
$$\frac{4y}{4} = \frac{8}{4}$$
$$\therefore y = 2$$

Therefore the line intersects the y-axis at $(0, 2)$.

Let $y = 0$ and find the corresponding x value. Point is written as $(x, y) = (x$ value$, 0)$.

$$2x + 4y - 8 = 0$$
$$2x + 4(0) - 8 = 0$$
$$2x - 8 = 0$$
$$2x = 8$$
$$\frac{2x}{2} = \frac{8}{2}$$
$$\therefore x = 4$$

Therefore the line intersects the x-axis at $(4, 0)$.

Using these four points, the two lines can be drawn and their point of intersection determined. By visual inspection, the point is $(6, -1)$.

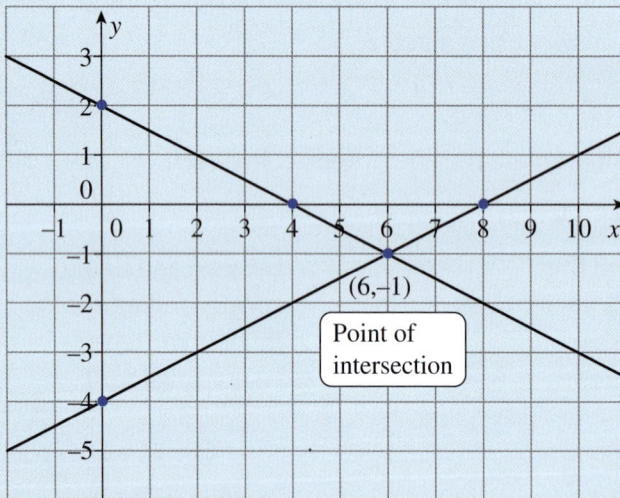

(b) $3x - 6y - 24 = 0$ (1)

     $2x + 4y - 8 = 0$ (2)

Multiply (1) by 2 and (2) by –3 and add the results to eliminate x.

$$2 \times (1) \Rightarrow 6x - 12y - 48 = 0$$
$$(-3) \times (2) \Rightarrow -6x - 12y + 24 = 0$$
$$\overline{ -24y - 24 = 0}$$
$$-24y = 24$$
$$\therefore y = -1$$

Substitute $y = -1$ into (1) to find x.

$$3x - 6y - 24 = 0$$
$$3x - 6(-1) - 24 = 0$$
$$3x + 6 - 24 = 0$$
$$3x - 18 = 0$$
$$3x = 18$$
$$x = \frac{18}{3} = 6$$

Therefore, the point of intersection is $(6, -1)$.

Exercise

Q1 Given the points $A(-2, 3)$ and $B(7, -5)$:

    (a) plot the points A and B,

    (b) find $|AB|$, and

    (c) find the midpoint of $[AB]$.

Q2 Given the points $X(2, -4)$ and $Y(6, 8)$:

    (a) find the slope of the line XY, and

    (b) find the equation of the line XY.

Q3 (a) The coordinate diagram represents the lines l_1, l_2 and l_3, and the table contains the equation of each line. Match each of the lines to its correct equation.

Equation
$y = 2x + 3$
$2y = -x + 8$
$y = -x - 2$

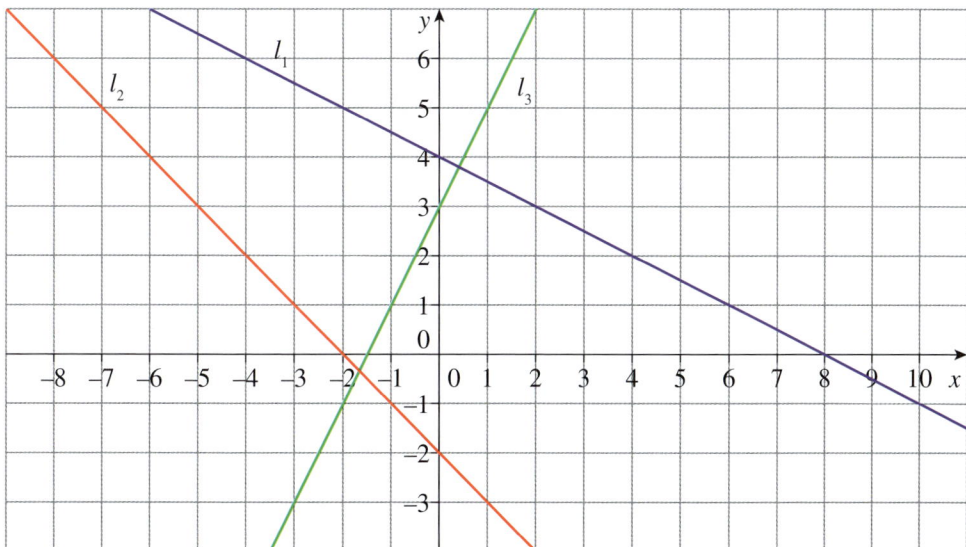

(b) Identify the line with the greatest slope. Explain your answer.

(c) Identify which two lines are perpendicular to each other. Explain your answer.

Q4 (a) The table below gives the equations of three lines and the slope of each line. Match the correct equation with its corresponding slope.

Line 1 $-x + 2y - 3 = 0$	Slope $(m_A) = -2$
Line 2 $4x + 2y - 3 = 0$	Slope $(m_B) = 3$
Line 3 $-6x + 2y + 3 = 0$	Slope $(m_C) = \dfrac{1}{2}$

(b) State whether each statement below is true or false.

   (i) The point $(-1, 4)$ is on the line $y = 3x + 7$.

   (ii) The point $(-3, 3)$ is not on the line $-3x - y - 6 = 0$.

   (iii) The point $(0, -2)$ is on the line $x + 4y = 10$.

Q5 Given the points $A(2, 2)$, $B(-2, -2)$ and $C(4, -4)$:

(a) plot the points A, B and C,

(b) find the lengths of $|AB|$, $|AC|$ and $|BC|$, and

(c) hence, or otherwise, identify whether the triangle $\triangle ABC$ is:

- equilateral,

- isosceles, or

- scalene.

Q6 (a) $a : -5x - 10y - 5 = 0$

   $b : 4x - 2y - 8 = 0$

   Investigate whether the two given lines are perpendicular to each other. Explain your answer.

(b) $p : x - 3y + 12 = 0$

   $q : x + 3y - 12 = 0$

   Investigate whether the two given lines are parallel to each other. Explain your answer.

(c) Find the point of intersection between the following two lines, using algebra.

   $s : 61 - 6y = 5x$

   $t : 3y + 2x = 25$

Q7 $A(2, 3)$, $B(10, 4)$, $C(12, 9)$, and $D(4, 8)$ are four points.

(a) Plot the points on a coordinate plane and join them to form the quadrilateral $ABCD$.

(b) Verify that one pair of opposite sides of $ABCD$ are equal in length.

(c) By finding E and F, the midpoints of $[AC]$ and $[BD]$ respectively, verify that the diagonals of $ABCD$ bisect each other.

Q8 The equation of the line l is $5 + y - 2x = 0$.

(a) Using algebra, find the co-ordinates of the x-intercept and y-intercept of the line l.

(b) Find the slope of the line l.

The line j goes through the point $(11, 6)$ and is perpendicular to the line l.

(c) **(i)** Write down the slope of the line j.

(ii) Find the equation of the line j.

(SEC 2015)

Q9 The table below gives the equations of six lines.

Line 1	$y = 3x - 6$
Line 2	$y = 3x + 12$
Line 3	$y = 5x + 20$
Line 4	$y = x - 7$
Line 5	$y = -2x + 4$
Line 6	$y = 4x - 16$

(a) Which line has the greatest slope? Give a reason for your answer.

(b) Which lines are parallel? Give a reason for your answer.

(c) Draw a sketch of Line 1.

(d) The diagram given represents one of the given lines. Which line does it represent?

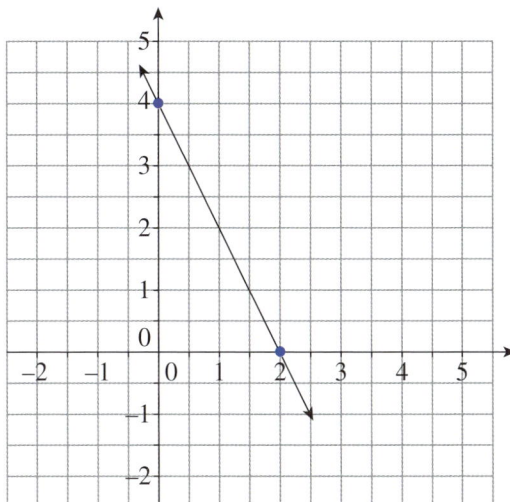

(e) The table shows some values of x and y for the equation of one of the lines. Which line's equation do they satisfy?

x	y
7	12
9	20
10	24

(f) There is one value of x which will give the same value of y for Line 4 as it will for Line 6. Find, using algebra, this value of x and the corresponding value of y.

(g) Verify your answer to **(f)** above.

(SEC 2012)

Solutions

Q1 (a)

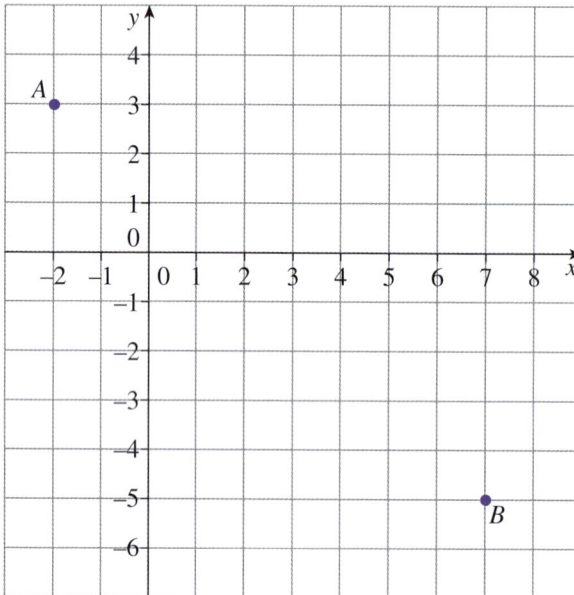

(b) Label one of the points, say A, as (x_1, y_1) and the other as $B(x_2, y_2)$.

$$(x_1, y_1) \qquad (x_2, y_2)$$
$$\Updownarrow \Updownarrow \qquad \Updownarrow \Updownarrow$$
$$A(-2,\ 3) \qquad B(7, -5)$$

Substituting this information into the distance formula and simplifying:

$$|AB| = \sqrt{(x_2 - x_1)^2 + (y_2 - y_1)^2}$$
$$= \sqrt{(7 - (-2))^2 + (-5 - 3)^2}$$
$$= \sqrt{(9)^2 + (-8)^2} = \sqrt{81 + 64} = \sqrt{145}$$

(c) Label one of the points, say A, as (x_1, y_1) and the other as $B(x_2, y_2)$.
Call the midpoint point P.

$$(x_1, y_1) \qquad (x_2, y_2)$$
$$\Updownarrow \;\; \Updownarrow \qquad \Updownarrow \;\; \Updownarrow$$
$$A(-2,\ 3) \qquad B(7, -5)$$

Substituting this information into the midpoint formula:

$$P = \left(\frac{x_1 + x_2}{2}, \frac{y_1 + y_2}{2} \right)$$
$$= \left(\frac{-2 + 7}{2}, \frac{3 + (-5)}{2} \right)$$
$$= \left(\frac{5}{2}, \frac{-2}{2} \right)$$
$$= (2{\cdot}5, -1)$$

Q2 (a) Label one of the points, say X, as (x_1, y_1) and the other as $Y(x_2, y_2)$.

$$(x_1,\ y_1) \qquad (x_2, y_2)$$
$$\Updownarrow,\ \Updownarrow \qquad \Updownarrow, \Updownarrow$$
$$X(2, -4) \qquad Y(6, 8)$$

Substituting this information into the slope formula:

$$m = \frac{y_2 - y_1}{x_2 - x_1}$$
$$= \frac{8 - (-4)}{6 - 2}$$
$$= \frac{12}{4} = 3$$

(b) The slope of the line, m, is 3.

A point on the line is, say, $X = (2, -4)$.

Substitute the value of the slope and the point coordinates into the formula $y - y_1 = m(x - x_1)$.

$$y - (-4) = 3(x - 2)$$
$$y + 4 = 3x - 6$$
$$-3x + y + 4 + 6 = 0$$
$$-3x + y + 10 = 0$$

or

$$3x - y - 10 = 0$$

Q3 (a) The graph can be used to find the 'rise' and 'run' figures and the y-intercepts. Then in each case the values for m and c can be substituted into the equation $y = mx + c$ to obtain the equation of the line.

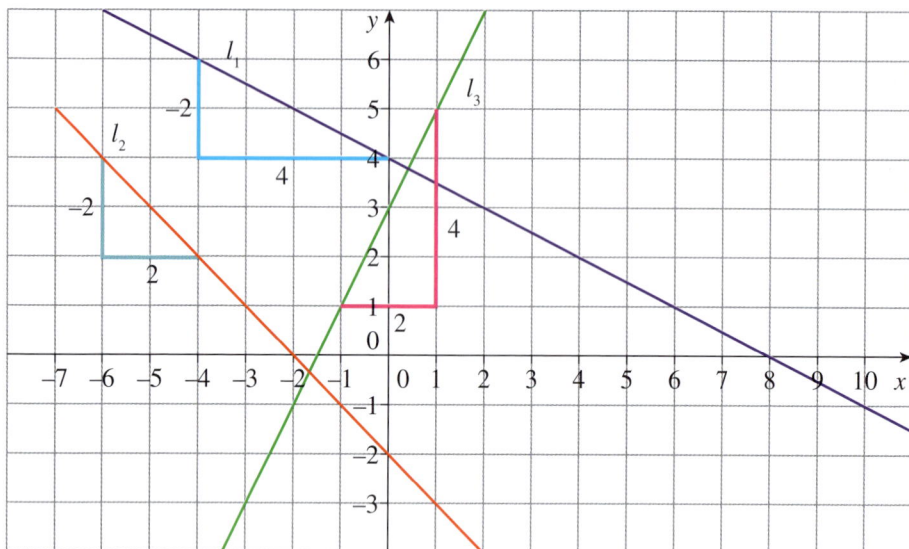

Line l_1

Slope $m = \dfrac{\text{rise}}{\text{run}} = \dfrac{-2}{4} = -\dfrac{1}{2}$ and y-intercept $(0, 4)$.

Substituting into the equation of a line in the form $y = mx + c$

$\Rightarrow l_1 : y = -\dfrac{1}{2}x + 4$

$\Rightarrow l_1 : 2y = -x + 8$

Line l_2

Slope $m = \dfrac{\text{rise}}{\text{run}} = \dfrac{-2}{2} = -1$ and y-intercept $(0, -2)$.

Substituting into the equation of a line in the form $y = mx + c$

$\Rightarrow l_2 : y = -x - 2$

Line l_3

Slope $m = \dfrac{\text{rise}}{\text{run}} = \dfrac{4}{2} = 2$ and y-intercept $(0, 3)$.

Substituting into the equation of a line in the form $y = mx + c$

$\Rightarrow l_3 : y = 2x + 3$

(b) The line with the greatest slope is $l_3 : y = 2x + 3$ as 2 represents the greatest slope.

(c) $l_1 : y = -\dfrac{1}{2}x + 4$ and $l_3 : y = 2x + 3$ are perpendicular, because when their slopes are multiplied together, the result is -1.

$$m_{l_1} \times m_{l_2} = \left(-\dfrac{1}{2}\right) \times (2) = \dfrac{-2}{2} = -1$$

Q4 (a) To find the slope, we can rearrange the equation $ax + by + c = 0$ to make y the subject of the equation in the form $y = mx + c$.

Line 1	Line 2	Line 3
$-x + 2y - 3 = 0$	$4x + 2y - 3 = 0$	$-6x + 2y + 3 = 0$
$2y = x + 3$	$2y = -4x + 3$	$2y = 6x - 3$
$\dfrac{2y}{2} = \dfrac{1}{2}x + \dfrac{3}{2}$	$\dfrac{2y}{2} = \dfrac{-4}{2}x + \dfrac{3}{2}$	$\dfrac{2y}{2} = \dfrac{6}{2}x - \dfrac{3}{2}$
$y = \dfrac{1}{2}x + \dfrac{3}{2}$	$y = -2x + \dfrac{3}{2}$	$y = 3x - \dfrac{3}{2}$
$\therefore$ Slope $m_C = \dfrac{1}{2}$	$\therefore$ Slope $m_A = -2$	$\therefore$ Slope $m_B = 3$

(b) (i) Statement: the point $(-1, 4)$ is on the line $y = 3x + 7$.

Substitute the point $(-1, 4)$ into the line $y = 3x + 7$.

$(4) = 3(-1) + 7$

$(4) = -3 + 7$

$\quad 4 = 4$

Therefore the statement is true.

(ii) Statement : the point $(-3, 3)$ is not on the line $-3x - y - 6 = 0$.

Substitute the point $(-3, 3)$ into the line $-3x - y - 6 = 0$.

$-3(-3) - (3) - 6 = 0$

$\quad 9 - 3 - 6 = 0$

$\quad\quad\quad 0 = 0$

Therefore the statement is false, as the point is on the line.

(iii) Statement: the point $(0, -2)$ is on the line $x + 4y = 10$.

Substitute the point $(0, -2)$ into the line $x + 4y = 10$.

$(0) + 4(-2) = 10$

$\quad 0 - 8 = 10$

$\quad\quad -8 \neq 10$

Therefore the statement is false.

Q5 (a)

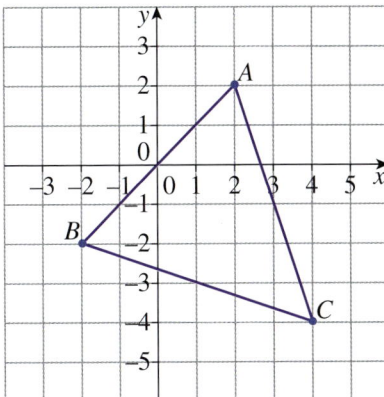

(b) To find the length of $|AB|$, label one of the points, say A, as (x_1, y_1) and the other as $B(x_2, y_2)$.

$$(x_1, y_1) \qquad (x_2, y_2)$$
$$\updownarrow \updownarrow \qquad\qquad \updownarrow \updownarrow$$
$$A(2,\ 2) \qquad B(-2, -2)$$

Substituting this information into the distance formula and simplifying:

$$|AB| = \sqrt{(x_2 - x_1)^2 + (y_2 - y_1)^2}$$
$$= \sqrt{(-2 - 2)^2 + (-2 - 2)^2}$$
$$= \sqrt{(-4)^2 + (-4)^2}$$
$$= \sqrt{16 + 16}$$
$$= \sqrt{32} = 4\sqrt{2}$$

To find the length of $|AC|$, label one of the points, say A, as (x_1, y_1) and the other as $B(x_2, y_2)$.

$$(x_1,\ y_1) \qquad (x_2,\ y_2)$$
$$\updownarrow \updownarrow \qquad\qquad \updownarrow \updownarrow$$
$$A(2,\ 2) \qquad C(4,\ -4)$$

Substituting this information into the distance formula and simplifying:

$$|AC| = \sqrt{(x_2 - x_1)^2 + (y_2 - y_1)^2}$$
$$= \sqrt{(4 - 2)^2 + (-4 - 2)^2}$$
$$= \sqrt{(2)^2 + (-6)^2}$$
$$= \sqrt{4 + 36}$$
$$= \sqrt{40} = 2\sqrt{10}$$

To find the length of $|BC|$, label one of the points, say B, as (x_1, y_1) and the other as $C(x_2, y_2)$.

$$(x_1, y_1) \qquad (x_2, y_2)$$
$$\updownarrow \updownarrow \qquad\qquad \updownarrow \updownarrow$$
$$B(-2, -2) \qquad C(4, -4)$$

Substituting this information into the distance formula and simplifying:

$$|BC| = \sqrt{(x_2 - x_1)^2 + (y_2 - y_1)^2}$$
$$= \sqrt{(4 - (-2))^2 + (-4 - (-2))^2}$$
$$= \sqrt{(6)^2 + (-2)^2}$$
$$= \sqrt{36 + 4}$$
$$= \sqrt{40} = 2\sqrt{10}$$

(c) The triangle $\triangle ABC$ is an isosceles triangle as two of the sides are the same length but the third is different.

Q6 (a) $a : -5x - 10y - 5 = 0$

$b : 4x - 2y - 8 = 0$

To find the slope of these lines, we can rearrange each equation $ax + by + c = 0$ to make y the subject of the equation in the form $y = mx + c$.

$a : -5x - 10y - 5 = 0$

$-10y = 5x + 5$

$\dfrac{-10}{-10}y = \dfrac{5x}{-10} + \dfrac{5}{-10}$

$y = -\dfrac{1}{2}x - \dfrac{1}{2}$

$\therefore$ Slope $m_a = -\dfrac{1}{2}$

$b : 4x - 2y - 8 = 0$

$-2y = -4x + 8$

$\dfrac{-2}{-2}y = \dfrac{-4}{-2}x + \dfrac{8}{-2}$

$y = 2x - 4$

$\therefore$ Slope $m_b = 2$

If the lines are perpendicular, then $m_a \times m_b = -1$

$\left(-\dfrac{1}{2}\right) \times (2) = -1$

Therefore the lines a and b are perpendicular to each other.

(b) $p : x - 3y + 12 = 0$

$q : x + 3y - 12 = 0$

To find the slope of these lines, we can rearrange each equation $ax + by + c = 0$ to make y the subject of the equation in the form $y = mx + c$.

$p : x - 3y + 12 = 0$

$-3y = -x - 12$

$\dfrac{-3}{-3}y = \dfrac{-1}{-3}x - \dfrac{12}{-3}$

$y = \dfrac{1}{3}x + 4$

$\therefore$ Slope $m_p = \dfrac{1}{3}$

$q : x + 3y - 12 = 0$

$3y = -x + 12$

$\dfrac{3}{3}y = \dfrac{-1}{3}x + \dfrac{12}{3}$

$y = -\dfrac{1}{3}x + 4$

$\therefore$ Slope $m_q = -\dfrac{1}{3}$

If the two lines are parallel, then $m_p = m_q$.

But $\dfrac{1}{3} \neq -\dfrac{1}{3}$.

Therefore the lines p and q are not parallel to each other.

(c) $s : 61 - 6y = 5x$

$t : 3y + 2x = 25$

Rearrange in the form $ax + by = c$

$s : 5x + 6y = 61$

$t : 2x + 3y = 25$

Multiply (s) by 2 and (t) by -5 and add the results, to eliminate x.

$2 \times (s) \Rightarrow 10x + 12y = 122$

$-5 \times (t) \Rightarrow \underline{-10x - 15y = -125}$

$-3y = -3$

$\therefore y = 1$

Substitute $y = 1$ in the equation for line t.

$t : 2x + 3y = 25$

$\quad 2x + 3(1) = 25$

$\quad\quad 2x + 3 = 25$

$\quad\quad\quad 2x = 22$

$\quad\quad\quad x = \dfrac{22}{2} = 11$

Therefore, the point of intersection is $(11, 1)$.

Q7 (a)

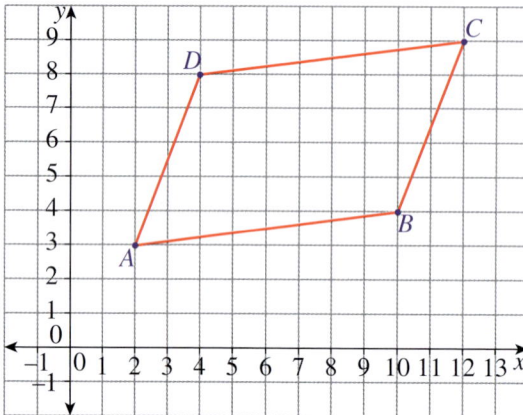

(b) Prove that $|AB| = |CD|$.

To calculate $|AB|$:

Label the points (x_1, y_1) and (x_2, y_2).

$$\begin{array}{cc} (x_1, y_1) & (x_2, y_2) \\ \Updownarrow\Updownarrow & \Updownarrow\Updownarrow \\ A(2, 3) & B(10, 4) \end{array}$$

Substitute this information into the distance formula and simplify.

$|AB| = \sqrt{(x_2 - x_1)^2 + (y_2 - y_1)^2}$

$\quad = \sqrt{(10 - 2)^2 + (4 - 3)^2}$

$\quad = \sqrt{(8)^2 + (1)^2}$

$\quad = \sqrt{64 + 1}$

$\quad = \sqrt{65}$

To calculate $|CD|$:

Label the points (x_1, y_1) and (x_2, y_2).

$$\begin{array}{cc} (x_1, y_1) & (x_2, y_2) \\ \Updownarrow\Updownarrow & \Updownarrow\Updownarrow \\ C(12, 9) & D(4, 8) \end{array}$$

Substitute this information into the distance formula and simplify.

$|CD| = \sqrt{(x_2 - x_1)^2 + (y_2 - y_1)^2}$

$\quad = \sqrt{(4 - 12)^2 + (8 - 9)^2}$

$\quad = \sqrt{(-8)^2 + (-1)^2}$

$\quad = \sqrt{64 + 1}$

$\quad = \sqrt{65}$

Therefore, $|AB| = |CD|$.

(Alternatively, work through the same process to prove that $|AD| = |BC|$.)

(c) To find the midpoint E of $[AC]$, label the points (x_1, y_1) and (x_2, y_2).

$$(x_1, y_1) \qquad (x_2, y_2)$$
$$\Updownarrow \, \Updownarrow \qquad \Updownarrow \, \Updownarrow$$
$$A(2, 3) \qquad C(12, 9)$$

Substitute this information into the midpoint formula:

$$E = \left(\frac{x_1 + x_2}{2}, \frac{y_1 + y_2}{2} \right)$$
$$= \left(\frac{2 + 12}{2}, \frac{3 + 9}{2} \right)$$
$$= \left(\frac{14}{2}, \frac{12}{2} \right)$$
$$= (7, 6)$$

To find the midpoint F of $[BD]$, label the points (x_1, y_1) and (x_2, y_2).

$$(x_1, y_1) \qquad (x_2, y_2)$$
$$\Updownarrow \, \Updownarrow \qquad \Updownarrow \, \Updownarrow$$
$$B(10, 4) \qquad D(4, 8)$$

Substitute this information into the midpoint formula:

$$F = \left(\frac{x_1 + x_2}{2}, \frac{y_1 + y_2}{2} \right)$$
$$= \left(\frac{10 + 4}{2}, \frac{4 + 8}{2} \right)$$
$$= \left(\frac{14}{2}, \frac{12}{2} \right)$$
$$= (7, 6)$$

As both the midpoints of $[AC]$ and $[BD]$ lie at $(7, 6)$, the diagonals must bisect each other.

Q8 (a) Let $x = 0$ and find the corresponding y value.

Point is written as $(x, y) = (0, y \text{ value})$.

$5 + y - 2x = 0$

$5 + y - 2(0) = 0$

$5 + y = 0$

$\therefore y = -5$

Therefore, the line intersects the y-axis at $(0, -5)$.

Let $y = 0$ and find the corresponding x value.

Point is written as $(x, y) = (x \text{ value}, 0)$.

$5 + y - 2x = 0$

$5 + (0) - 2x = 0$

$5 = 2x$

$$\therefore \frac{5}{2} = 2{\cdot}5 = x$$

Therefore, the line intersects the x-axis at $(2{\cdot}5, 0)$.

(b) Rearrange the equation to be in the form $y = mx + c$:

$$y = 2x - 5$$

$$\therefore \text{Slope} = 2$$

(c) **(i)** To calculate the slope of j, given that $m_l \perp m_j$.

$$m_l \times m_j = -1$$

$$\therefore \text{Slope of } j = -\frac{1}{2}$$

(ii) The line j goes through the point $(11, 6)$ and is perpendicular to the line l.

$$\therefore \text{Slope of } j = -\frac{1}{2}$$

To work out the equation of j, use equation of a line in the form $y - y_1 = m(x - x_1)$.

$$y - 6 = -\frac{1}{2}(x - 11)$$

$$2(y - 6) = -1(x - 11)$$

$$2y - 12 = -x + 11$$

$$x + 2y - 12 - 11 = 0$$

$$x + 2y - 23 = 0$$

Q9 (a) Line 3, because 5 is the biggest number in front of x for any of the lines.

(b) Line 1 and Line 2, because they have the same slope (3).

(c) Work out the points of intersection of Line 1 with the x-axis and y-axis.

$$y = 3x - 6$$

Let $x = 0$ and solve for the y coordinate:

$$y = 3(0) - 6$$

$$y = -6$$

$\therefore$ Point of intersection on y-axis is $(0, -6)$

Now let $y = 0$ and solve for the x coordinate:

$$0 = 3x - 6$$

$$6 = 3x$$

$$\frac{6}{3} = \frac{3x}{3}$$

$$2 = x$$

$\therefore$ Point of intersection with the x-axis is $(2, 0)$.

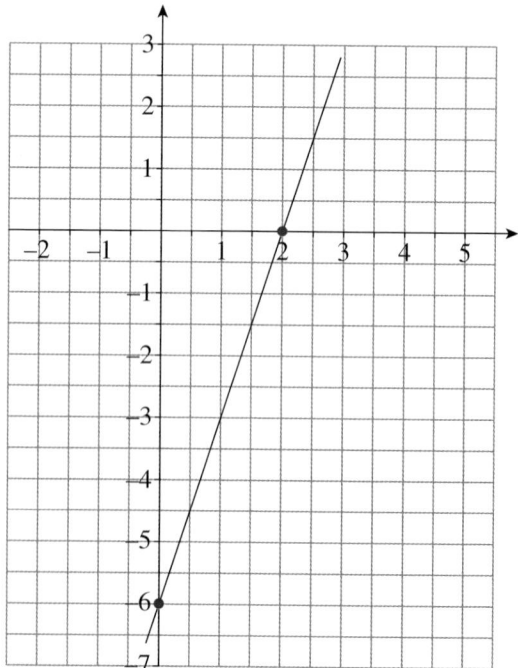

(d) The points of intersection on the axes are $(0, 4)$, $(2, 0)$.

Use the formula $m = \dfrac{y_2 - y_1}{x_2 - x_1}$ to work out the slope of the line.

$$m = \frac{0 - 4}{2 - 0} = -\frac{4}{2} = -2$$

Hence, given that the y-intercept is 4, the equation of the line is:

$$y = -2x + 4$$

Answer: Line 5

(e) Use two of the given points, say $(7, 12)$ and $(9, 20)$, to work out the slope of the line:

$$m = \frac{y_2 - y_1}{x_2 - x_1}$$

$$m = \frac{20 - 12}{9 - 7} = \frac{8}{2} = 4$$

Now work out the equation of the line using the form $y - y_1 = m(x - x_1)$:

$$y - 12 = 4(x - 7)$$
$$y - 12 = 4x - 28$$
$$y = 4x - 28 + 12$$
$$y = 4x - 16$$

To check this answer, substitute the given x values into the equation and check that the results are the given values of y.

$$y = 4(7) - 16 = 12$$
$$y = 4(9) - 16 = 20$$
$$y = 4(10) - 16 = 24$$

(f) Solve using simultaneous equations, by subtracting Line 4 from Line 6:

Line 6: $y = 4x - 16$

Line 4: $y = x - 7$

$$\overline{0 = 3x - 9}$$
$$9 = 3x$$
$$3 = x$$
$$\therefore\ y = 3 - 7 = -4$$

Point of intersection $= (3, -4)$.

(g) Substitute the x value from part **(f)** into the equations for Line 4 and Line 6 and work out the corresponding y value.

Line 4	Line 6
$y = x - 7$	$y = 4x - 16$
$y = (3) - 7 = -4$	$y = 4(3) - 16 = 12 - 16 = -4$

Both answers give the value of y as -4. This verifies the solution to part **(f)**.

10 Transformation Geometry

Learning objectives

In this chapter you will learn about:

- How to recognise images of points and objects under:
  - Translations
  - Central symmetry
  - Axial symmetry
  - Rotation
- How to locate axes of symmetry and centres of symmetry in simple objects.

Transformations

In geometry, a **transformation** is just a way to change the position of a figure or shape. A transformation never changes the size of a shape.

The four types of transformation which we will focus on for the Junior Certificate course are shown below.

1 Translations

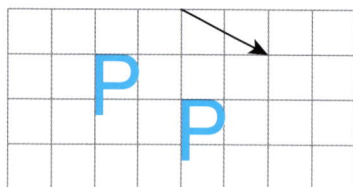

2 Axial symmetry

3 Central symmetry

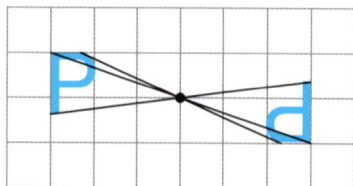

4 Rotation

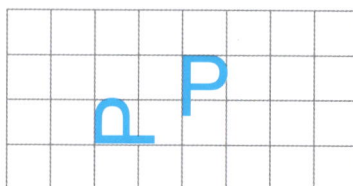

How to label a transformation

The original object generally has each point or vertex labelled with a capital letter. Then a little dash is used to indicate each new point or vertex (corner) of the image. For example, in the diagram, ABC is the **object** and $A'B'C'$ is the **image** of ABC under axial symmetry of the y-axis.

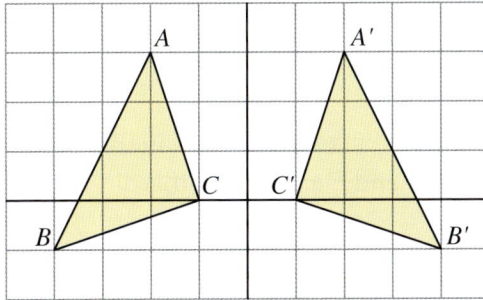

Translations

When an object undergoes a translation it is simply moved to a new position. This movement can be described in terms of how far horizontally and vertically it has moved.

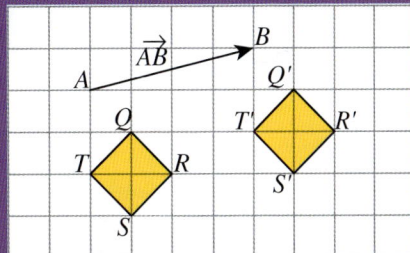

Example

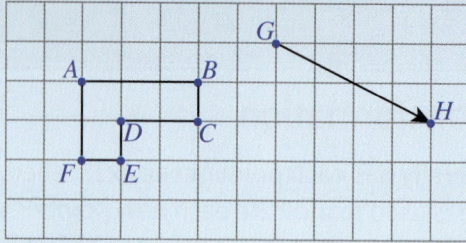

(a) Describe the translation $\overrightarrow{GH}$ in the given diagram.

(b) Copy and draw the image of the object under the translation $\overrightarrow{GH}$.

Solution

(a) The translation $\overrightarrow{GH}$ moves every point 4 units to the right and 2 units down.

(b) So the points A, B, C, D, E and F all move in this direction and this distance.

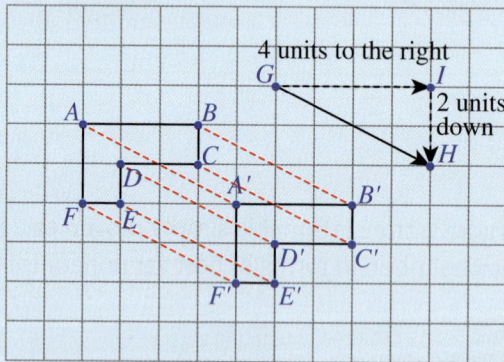

Example

Identify the correct image of the object shown under the given translation.

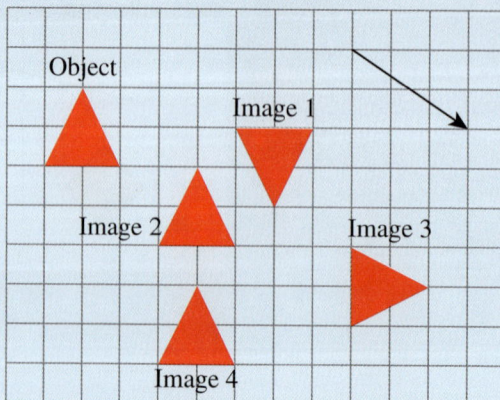

Solution

Under the given translation of 2 units down and 3 units to the right, the correct image is Image 2.

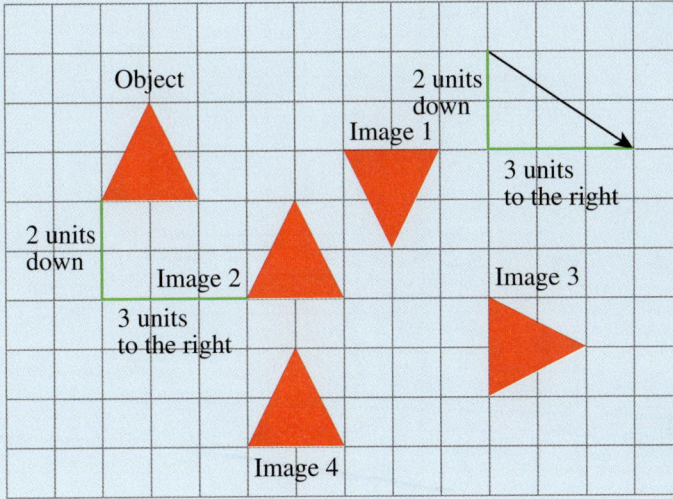

Central symmetry

Central symmetry is the reflection of an object through a given point where the image is the same distance on the other side of the given point.

Points to note

1 All points are projected through the point that the central symmetry is constructed about.

2 The image points are the **same distance** from the point that central symmetry is constructed about as the object points.

3 The image is always upside down and back to front compared to the object.

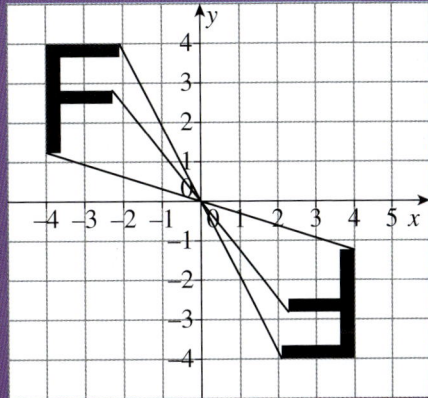

Example

Copy the triangle and construct the image of the triangle under central symmetry through the origin.

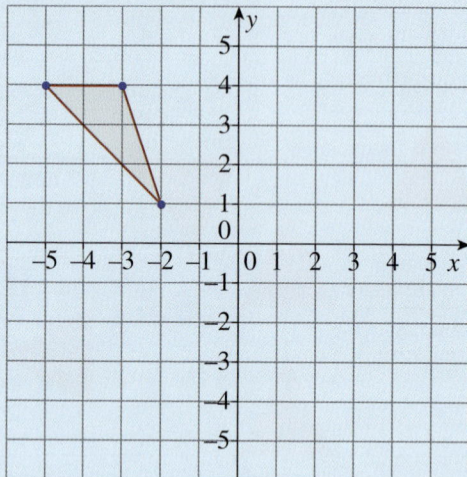

Solution

Note the typical features of central symmetry shown by this solution:

- All points are **projected through the origin**.

- The image points are the **same distance** from the origin.

- The image is **always upside down** and **back to front** compared to the object.

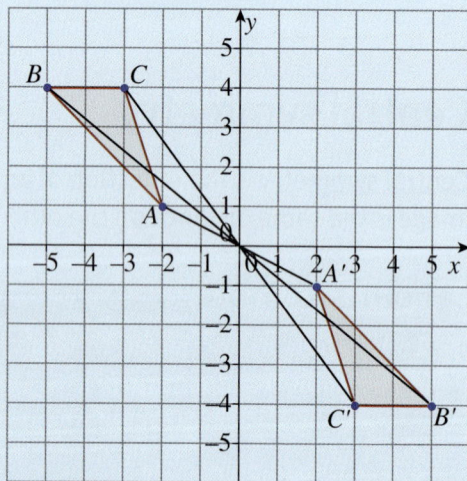

Example

Identify the correct image of the object shown under central symmetry through the point *A*.

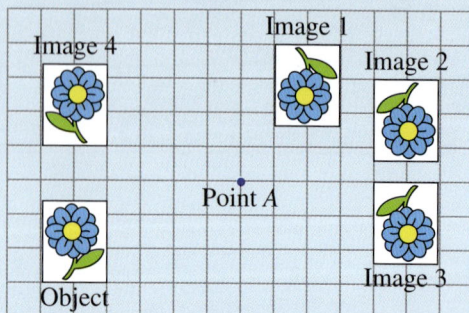

Solution

The image of the object given under central symmetry in the point A, is Image 2, as shown in the diagram.

Note: we only needed to find two image points to identify the image of the object.

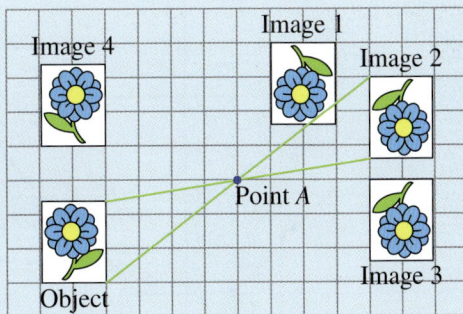

Axial symmetry

Axial symmetry is a reflection which **flips the object over a line when compared to the image**. This image is also called **a mirror image**.

Points to note

1 The new image stays the same size as the object.

2 The points of the new image are the same distance from the axis as the object points.

3 The new image is a mirror image of the object.

4 A reflection can be thought of as 'flipping' an object over the line of reflection.

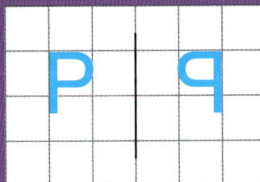

Axial symmetry across the x-axis

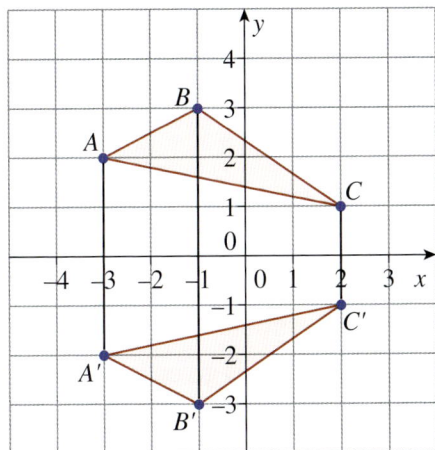

The x values stay the same and the y values change sign.

$$ABC \rightarrow A'B'C'$$

$$(x, y) \rightarrow (x, -y)$$

$$A(-3, 2) \rightarrow A'(-3, -2)$$

$$B(-1, 3) \rightarrow B'(-1, -3)$$

$$C(2, 1) \rightarrow C'(2, -1)$$

Axial symmetry across the *y*-axis

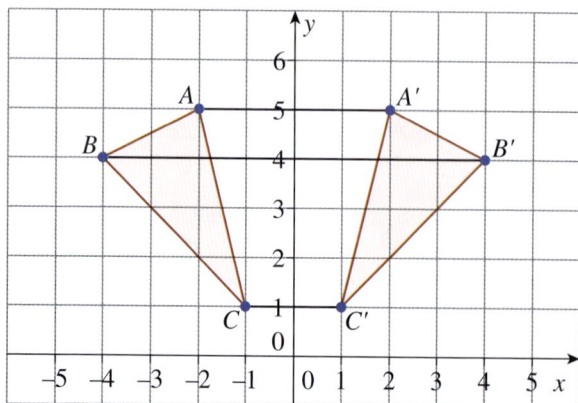

The *y* values stay the same and the *x* values change sign.

$$ABC \rightarrow A'B'C'$$

$$(x, y) \rightarrow (-x, y)$$

$$A(-2, 5) \rightarrow A'(2, 5)$$

$$B(-4, 4) \rightarrow B'(4, 4)$$

$$C(-1, 1) \rightarrow C'(1, 1)$$

Example

Draw the image of the given triangle under axial symmetry in the given axis.

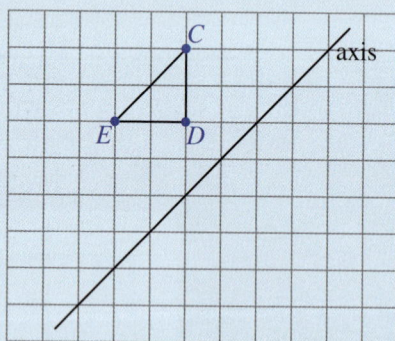

Solution

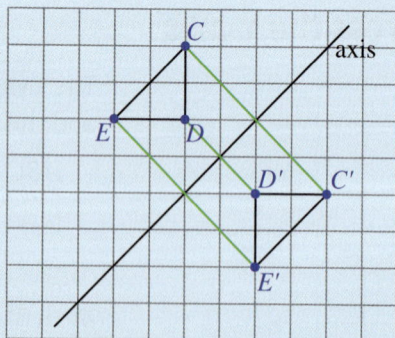

Note the typical features of axial symmetry shown by this solution:

1 All points are **projected perpendicularly over the line of axis given.**

2 The image points are the **same distance** from the given axis.

Rotations

A **rotation** is a transformation that turns an object about a fixed point called the centre of rotation. The object and its rotation are the **same shape and size**, but the **object and image may be turned in different directions**.

Clockwise rotation

Anti-clockwise rotation

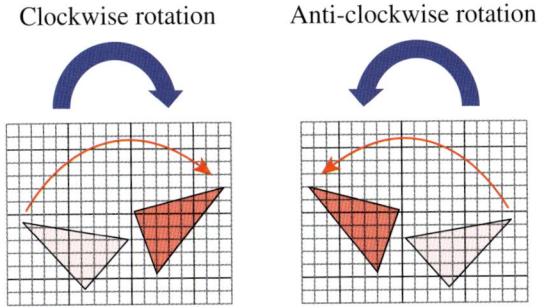

Points to note

1 The image remains the same size as the object.

2 The points of the image are the same distance from the point of rotation as the object points.

3 The image rotates clockwise or anti-clockwise but doesn't change the size or shape of the object.

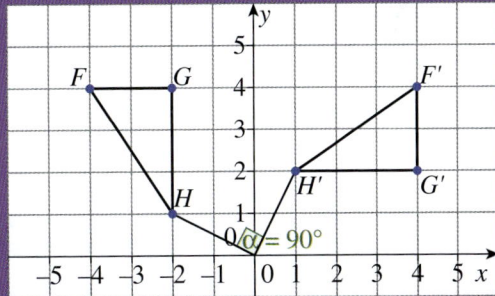

Example

Copy the coordinate diagram and construct the image of the given object by a 90° clockwise rotation about the origin.

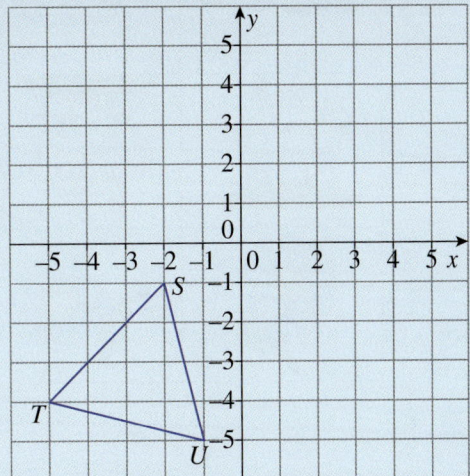

Solution

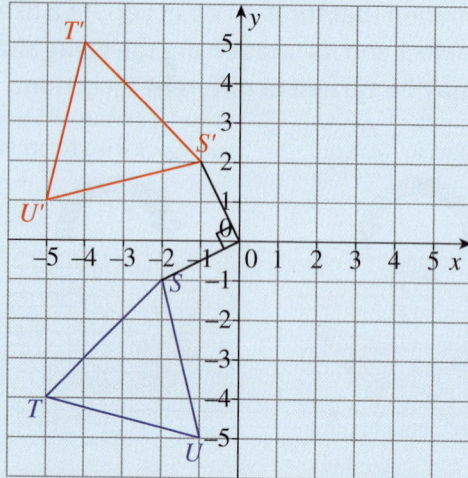

Note the typical features of rotation shown by this solution:

1 The points of the image are **the same distance from the origin (point of rotation) as the object points.**

2 The image is **rotated 90° clockwise about the origin.**

Example

A, B and C are images of the object given under a set transformation. For each image state if the transformation is central symmetry, axial symmetry or a 90° rotation.

Object	A	B	C

Solution

Object	A	B	C
	Central symmetry	90° rotation	Axial symmetry
	Central symmetry	Axial symmetry	90° rotation
	90° rotation	Axial symmetry	Central symmetry

How to locate axes of symmetry and centres of symmetry in simple shapes

Axes of symmetry

An axis of symmetry is a line that divides the object or image into two symmetrical parts in such a way that the image on one side of the line is the mirror image of the image on the other side of the line. Some examples are shown in the table below.

Image with no axes of symmetry	Image with 1 axis of symmetry	Image with 2 axes of symmetry	Image with 4 axes of symmetry

When the shape is folded in half along the **axis of symmetry**, then the two halves will match up exactly.

Example

Copy each of the shapes given and draw in all axes of symmetry on each shape.

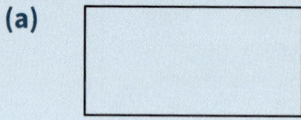

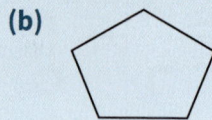

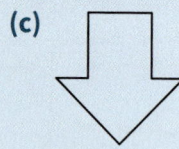

(a)

(b)

(c)

Solution

(a)

(b)

(c)

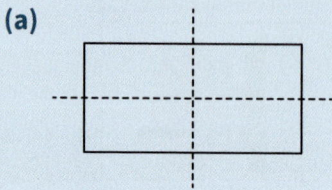

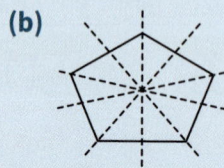

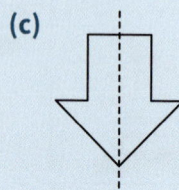

Note that a shape may have one, two, or more axes of symmetry, or of course none at all.

Centre of symmetry

The centre of symmetry is a point, within an object or image, such that when the image is rotated 180° about this point, the image will be identical to the image in its original position.

Test for centre of symmetry

To check if an object or image has a centre of symmetry:

1 Pick the point which you think is the centre of symmetry.

2 Rotate the image clockwise or anti-clockwise about the point by 180°.

3 If the image is exactly the same after rotation, then the object has a centre of symmetry.

Example of an image with a centre of symmetry

Original position
of the card

Position of the
card after rotation
of 180°

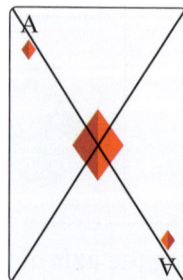

When the Ace of diamonds is rotated 180°, the resulting image is identical to the image before rotation.

Therefore the Ace of diamonds **has** a centre of symmetry.

Example of an image with NO centre of symmetry

Original position of the card

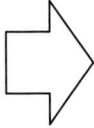

Position of the card after rotation of 180°

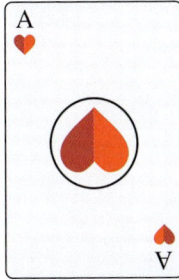

When the Ace of hearts is rotated 180°, the resulting image is not identical to the image before rotation.

Therefore the Ace of hearts **does not** have a centre of symmetry.

Example

Identify which of the following images has a centre of symmetry.

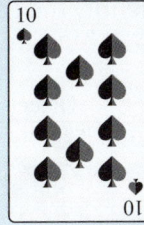

Solution

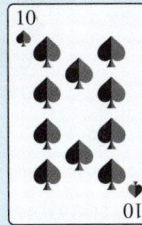

1. Pick the point which you think is the centre of symmetry.
2. Rotate the image clockwise or anti-clockwise about the point by 180° degrees.
3. If the image is exactly the same after rotation, then the object has a centre of symmetry.

The image is not identical to the object before rotation. Therefore the six of spades **does not** have a centre of symmetry.

The image is not identical to the object before rotation. Therefore the seven of diamonds **does not** have a centre of symmetry.

The image is identical to the object before rotation. Therefore the nine of diamonds **does have** a centre of symmetry.

The image is not identical to the object before rotation. Therefore the ten of spades **does not** have a centre of symmetry.

Exercise

Q1 (a) Describe the translation $\vec{AB}$ in the given diagram.

(b) Copy and draw the image of the object under the translation $\vec{AB}$.

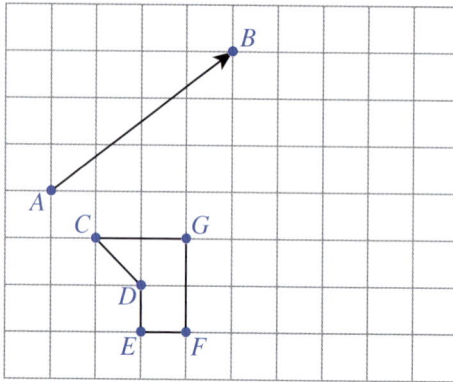

Q2 Identify the correct image of the object shown under the given translation.

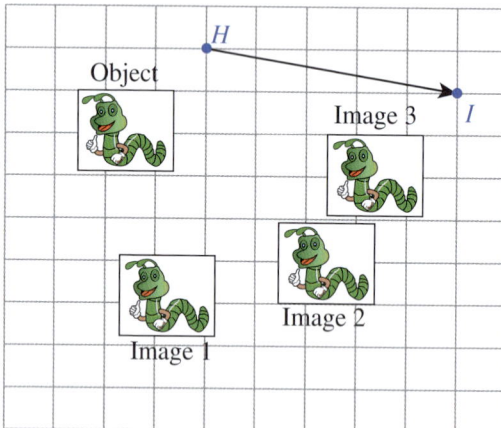

Q3 Copy the object and construct the image of the object under central symmetry in the origin.

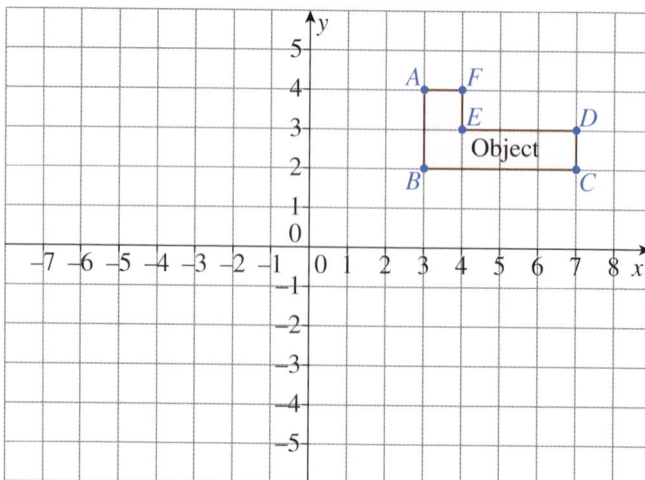

Q4 Draw the image of the capital letter F under axial symmetry in the axis shown.

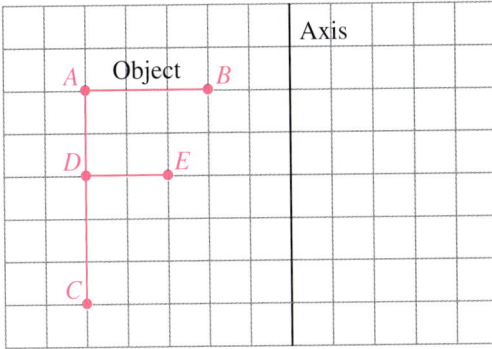

Q5 Identify the correct image of the object shown under central symmetry in the point H.

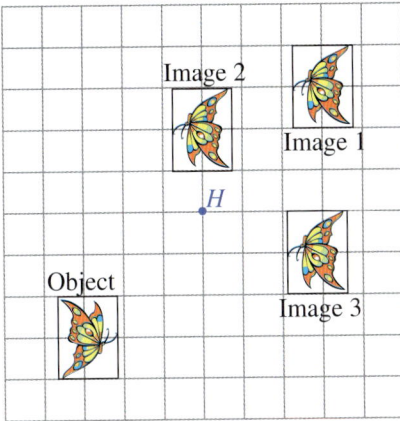

Q6 **(a)** Copy the coordinate diagram and construct the image of the given object by a rotation of 180° clockwise about the origin.

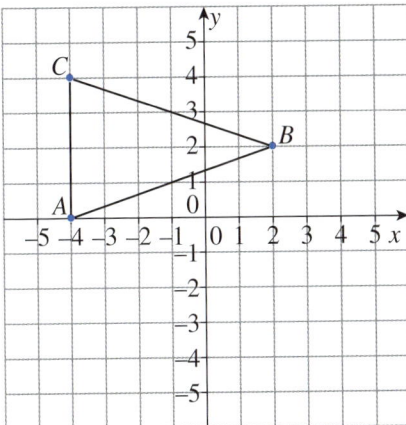

(b) Copy the coordinate diagram and construct the image of the given object by a rotation of 90° in an anticlockwise motion about the origin.

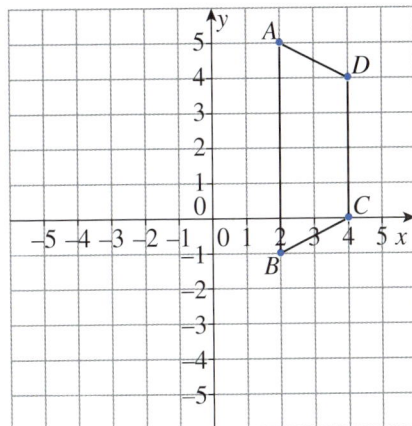

Q7 State the number of axes of symmetry for each shape given. Bear in mind that a shape does not necessarily have an axis of symmetry.

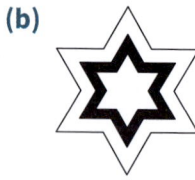

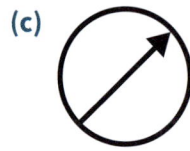

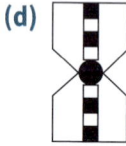

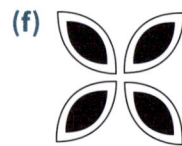

(a)

(b)

(c)

(d)

(e)

(f)

Q8 Each of the three figures labelled A, B and C are an image of the figure shown in the box on the left under a transformation. For each of A, B and C, state what the transformation is (translation, central symmetry, axial symmetry or rotation) and, in the case of a rotation, state the angle.

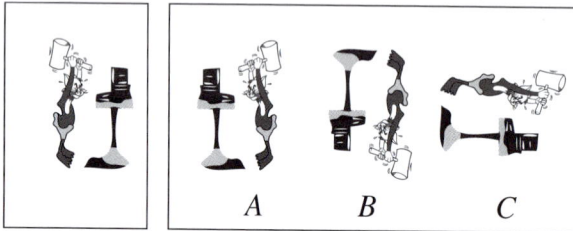

A B C

(SEC 2007)

Q9 The coordinate diagram below shows the lines n, p, r and s.

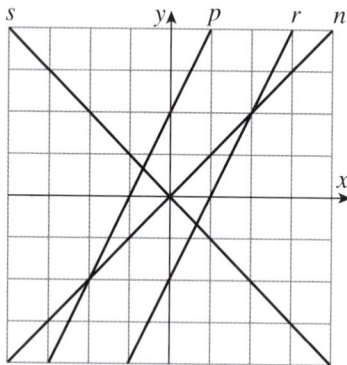

Complete the following sentences. Write one of the letters n, p, r or s in each box.

(a) You can use a translation to map the line ☐ onto the line ☐.

(b) You can use an axial symmetry in the y-axis to map the line ☐ onto the line ☐.

(c) The line ☐ is mapped onto itself under central symmetry in the point $(0, 0)$.

(SEC 2015)

Q10 Each of the three figures labelled A, B and C shown below is the image of the figure X under a transformation. For each of A, B and C, state what the transformation is (translation, central symmetry, axial symmetry or rotation) and in the case of a rotation, state the angle.

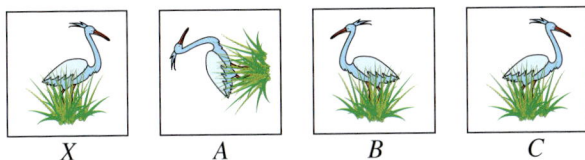

X A B C

(SEC 2009)

Solutions

Q1 (a) The translation $\overrightarrow{AB}$ moves every point 4 units to the right and 3 units up.

(b) The points C, D, E, F and G all move in this direction and this distance.

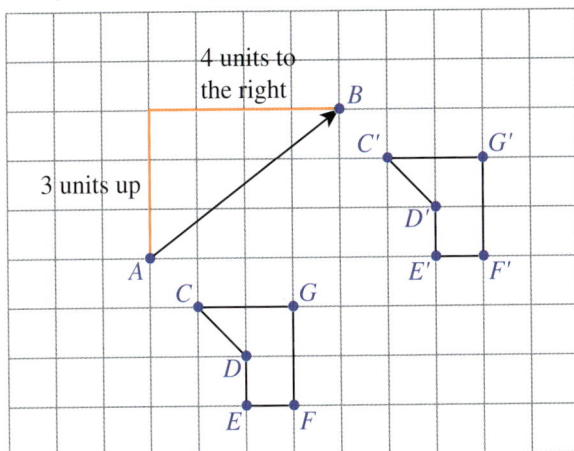

Q2 Under the given translation of 1 unit down and 5 units to the right, the correct image is Image 3.

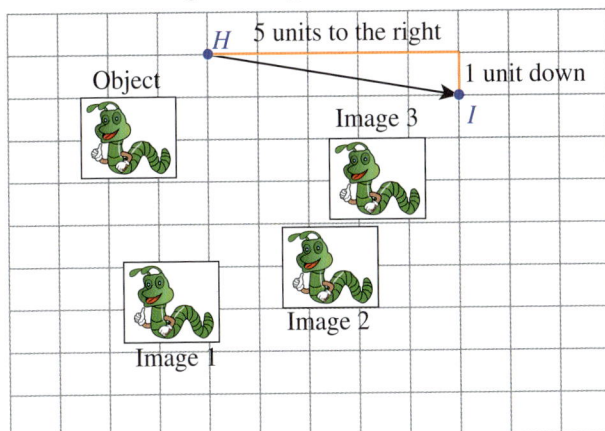

Q3

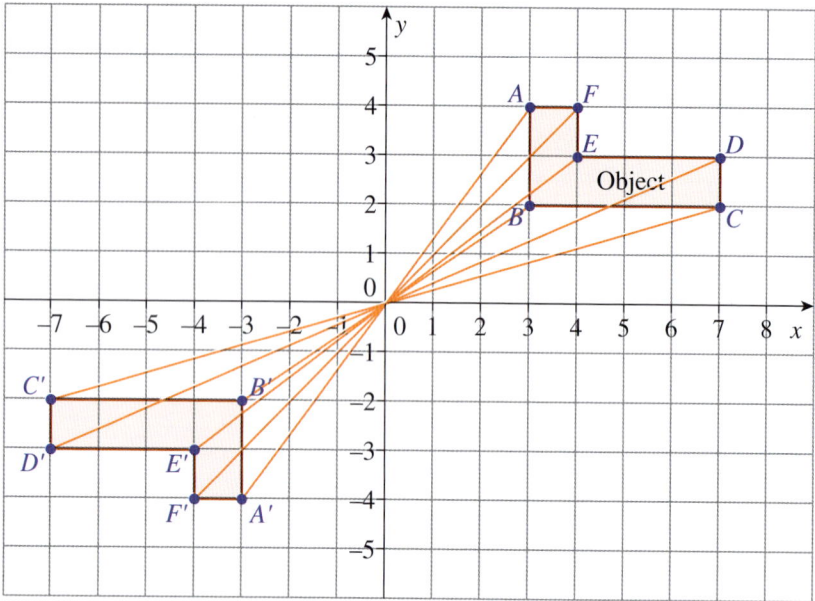

Q4

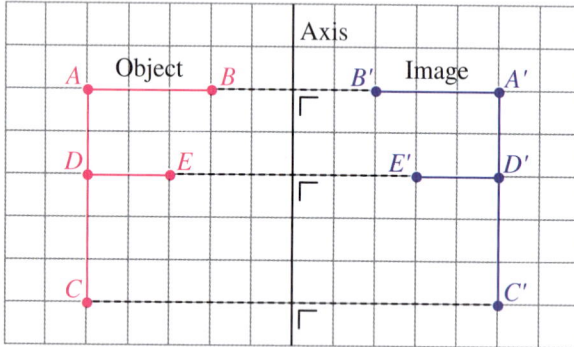

Q5 The Image of the object given under central symmetry in the point H is Image 1, as shown in the diagram.

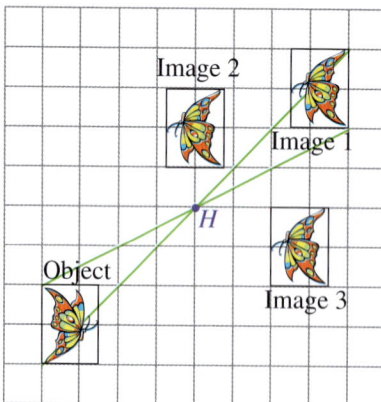

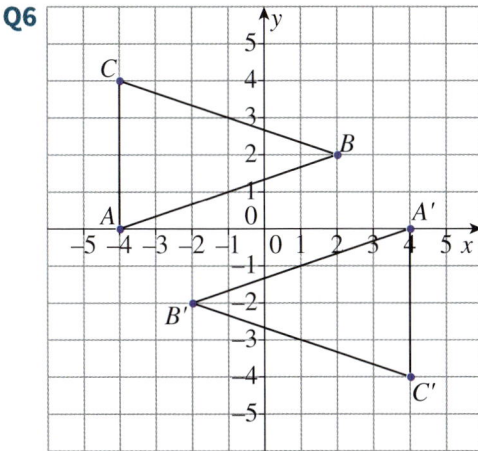

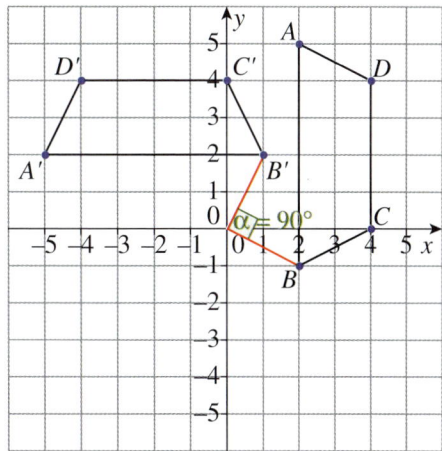

Q6

Q7 (a) 3 axes of symmetry

(b) 6 axes of symmetry

(c) 1 axis of symmetry

(d) 2 axes of symmetry

(e) No axis of symmetry

(f) 4 axes of symmetry

Q8

Object	A	B	C
	Axial symmetry	Central symmetry or 180° rotation	90 degree rotation clockwise

Q9 (a) A translation can be used to map the line $\boxed{p \text{ or } r}$ onto the line $\boxed{r \text{ or } p.}$

(b) Axial symmetry in the y-axis can be used to map the line $\boxed{n \text{ or } s}$ onto the line $\boxed{s \text{ or } n.}$

(c) The line $\boxed{s \text{ or } n}$ is mapped onto itself under central symmetry in the point $(0, 0)$.

Q10 A: Rotation of 90°[anti-clockwise] or Rotation of 270°[clockwise]

B: Axial symmetry

C: Translation or Rotation of 360°

11 Trigonometry 1: Theory of Trigonometry

Learning objectives

In this chapter, you will learn about:

- Problem solving using Pythagoras' Theorem

- Trigonometric ratios: sine, cosine and tangent

- Finding an unknown side or angle, in a right-angled triangle, using trigonometric ratios

- Angle measure in degrees, minutes and seconds

- Working with the angles 30°, 45° and 60°.

Key terminology and information

Key Terminology

Word(s)	Meaning
Pythagoras' Theorem	The theorem states that, in a right-angled triangle, the square of the hypotenuse equals the sum of the squares of the other two sides.
Adjacent	Beside or alongside
Opposite	Across from
Trigonometric ratios	• Ratios that identify the relationship between a given angle and the sides of a right-angled triangle. • The trigonometric ratios are called sine, cosine and tangent from Greek words. They are usually shortened to sin, cos and tan.

Problem solving using Pythagoras' Theorem

Points to note

- Pythagoras' Theorem states that, in a right-angled triangle, the square of the hypotenuse equals the sum of the squares of the other two sides.

- Pythagoras' Theorem is given in the *Formulae and Tables* booklet as:

$$c^2 = a^2 + b^2$$

  c = **hypotenuse** side, as it is **opposite** the **right-angle** (90°)

  a = **opposite** side, as it is **across from** angle A

  b = **adjacent** side, as it is **beside/alongside** angle A

- The hypotenuse side is always the longest side, as it is always opposite the biggest angle (the 90° angle).

- Pythagoras' Theorem is used to solve trigonometry problems when:

  1 We know the length of two sides and wish to find the value of the third length.

  2 We wish to verify/check that a triangle is right-angled.

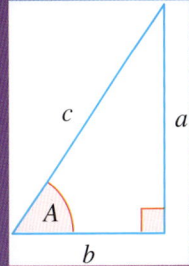

Example

ABC is a triangle such that $|\angle ABC| = 90°$, $|AB| = 12$ and $|AC| = 13$. Find $|BC|$.

Solution

Note: as an angle is not labelled on the diagram, the length 12 can be labelled as either a or b. In this case let $b = 12$.

So c = hypotenuse = 13, $a = |BC|$ and $b = 12$.

First substitute all known values for a, b and c into $c^2 = a^2 + b^2$.

$13^2 = |BC|^2 + 12^2$

Then swap sides so the unknown value is on the left.

$|BC|^2 + 12^2 = 13^2$

$\Rightarrow |BC|^2 + 144 = 169$

$\Rightarrow |BC|^2 = 169 - 144$

$\Rightarrow |BC| = \sqrt{25}$

Finally, write down the positive value for $\sqrt{25}$ only, as length is positive. $|BC| = 5$ units

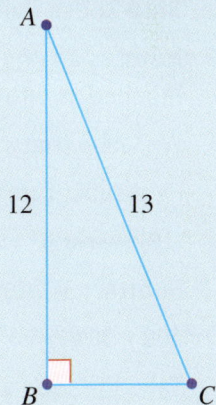

Example

The isosceles triangle shown in the diagram has a base of length 12 cm and the other two sides are each 10 cm in length.

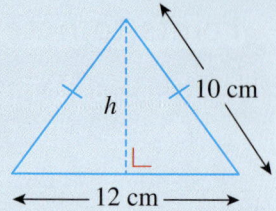

(a) Prove that the perpendicular line divides the isosceles triangle into two congruent triangles.

(b) Find h, the perpendicular height of the triangle.

(SEC 2007)

Solution

(a) The perpendicular line divides the isosceles triangle into two smaller right-angled triangles. Comparing these two triangles:

$10 = 10$	... (Property of isosceles triangle)
$h = h$	... (Common side)
$90° = 90°$	... (Right angles because h is a perpendicular line)

This proves by SAS that the perpendicular line divides the isosceles triangle into two congruent triangles.

(b) To find h, the perpendicular height, follow the steps below.

Step 1: Draw a right-angled triangle using the information given. The length of half the base is 6 cm, as the triangle is an isosceles triangle.

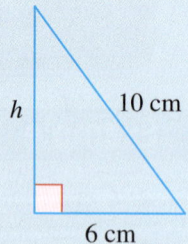

Step 2: Use Pythagoras' Theorem to find the length $|h|$.

Note: as an angle is not labelled on the diagram, the length 6 cm can be labelled as either a or b. In this case let $b = 6$ cm.

We know that c = hypotenuse = 10 cm, $a = |h|$ and $b = 6$ cm.

First substitute all known values in for a, b and c into $c^2 = a^2 + b^2$.

$(10)^2 = h^2 + 6^2 \Rightarrow 100 = h^2 + 36$

Subtract 36 from both sides.

$100 - 36 = h^2 \Rightarrow 64 = h^2$

Take the square root of both sides, swap sides and write down the positive value for the result only, as length is positive.

$h^2 = \sqrt{64} \Rightarrow h = 8$ cm

Trigonometric ratios

1 Trigonometric ratios identify the relationship between a given angle and the sides of a right-angled triangle.

2 The trigonometric ratios are called sine, cosine and tangent from Greek words. They are usually shortened to sin, cos and tan for ease of use.

3 The trigonometric ratios are given in the *Formulae and Tables* book as:

$$\sin A = \frac{a}{c}$$

$$\cos A = \frac{b}{c}$$

$$\tan A = \frac{a}{b}$$

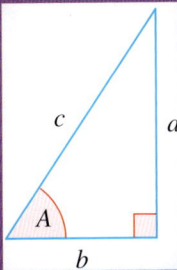

Note:

c = **hypotenuse side**, as it is **opposite the right-angle** (90°)

a = **opposite side**, as it is **across from** angle A

b = **adjacent** side, as it is **beside** angle A

* This information is not in the formulae and tables booklet.

4 However, the trigonometric ratios are usually taught using the diagram below:

$$\sin \theta = \frac{\text{opposite}}{\text{hypotenuse}}$$

$$\cos \theta = \frac{\text{adjacent}}{\text{hypotenuse}}$$

$$\tan \theta = \frac{\text{opposite}}{\text{adjacent}}$$

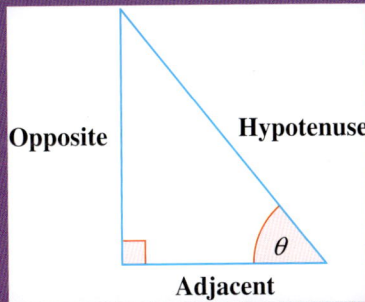

Where θ = theta (a Greek letter)

5 The trigonometric ratios are usually learned using one of these acronyms:

- **O** Hell, **A**nother **H**our, **O**f **A**lgebra
- **S**illy = $\dfrac{\text{Old}}{\text{Harry}}$, **C**aught = $\dfrac{\text{A}}{\text{Herring}}$, **T**rawling = $\dfrac{\text{Over}}{\text{America}}$
- **SOH–CAH–TOA**

6 Never write 'sin' or 'cos' or 'tan' **without an angle**, as they mean nothing unless the angle is specified.

7 The sin, cos and tan buttons are on the calculator. Because for the Junior Certificate Course all angles must be measured in degrees, the calculator must be in Degrees mode (usually denoted by a D at the top of the screen).

To make sure the calculator is in Degrees mode:

- Look for D on the top right-hand corner of the display screen.
- If the calculator is not in Degrees mode, follow these steps:
  - Press ⬭ (SHIFT) then the ⬭ (MODE SETUP) button.
  - The list

1:MthIO	2:LineIO
3:Deg	4:Rad
5:Gra	6:Fix
7:Sci	8:Norm

    will appear on the screen.
  - Press (3) to choose degrees for the angle setting.

8 In some cases, it may be easier to find the value of the trigonometric ratios using the table shown below. This table can be found in the *Formulae and Tables* booklet. Note that a dash in the table means that the value is not defined.

A (degrees)	0°	90°	180°	270°	30°	45°	60°
A (radians)	0	$\dfrac{\pi}{2}$	π	$\dfrac{3\pi}{2}$	$\dfrac{\pi}{6}$	$\dfrac{\pi}{4}$	$\dfrac{\pi}{3}$
cos A	1	0	−1	0	$\dfrac{\sqrt{3}}{2}$	$\dfrac{1}{\sqrt{2}}$	$\dfrac{1}{2}$
sin A	0	1	0	−1	$\dfrac{1}{2}$	$\dfrac{1}{\sqrt{2}}$	$\dfrac{\sqrt{3}}{2}$
tan A	0	–	0	–	$\dfrac{1}{\sqrt{3}}$	1	$\sqrt{3}$

Example

Show that $\cos 90° \neq \cos 60° + \cos 30°$, using the table in the *Formulae and Tables* booklet.

Solution

Substitute in the values from the table.

LHS = 0

RHS = $\dfrac{1}{2} + \dfrac{\sqrt{3}}{2} = \dfrac{1 + \sqrt{3}}{2}$

$\Rightarrow$ LHS $\neq$ RHS

Therefore, $\cos 90° \neq \cos 60° + \cos 30°$.

Remember

The symbol (≠) means 'is not equal to'.

Example

Show that tan 95° ≠ tan 60° + tan 35°, using the calculator. Round all values to two decimal places.

Solution

Make sure that your calculator is in Degrees mode!

From the calculator: $\tan 95° = -11·43$, $\tan 60° = \sqrt{3} = 1·73$ and $\tan 35° = 0·70$, to 2 d.p.

Substitute in these values from your calculator:

LHS = −11·43

RHS = 1·73 + 0·70 = 2·43

⇒ LHS ≠ RHS

Therefore, tan 95° ≠ tan 60° + tan 35°

Example

(a) In the table given, write down the values of cos θ and sin θ for the angles listed. Give your answers correct to three significant figures.

(b) What can you conclude from these results? Give a reason for your answer.

(c) During an examination Katie notices that her calculator is not working properly. The cos θ gives an error message. Assuming all other functions are working correctly, explain how she might use her calculator to calculate the value of cos 35°.

θ	Cosθ	Sinθ
0°		
10°		
20°		
30°		
40°		
50°		
60°		
70°		
80°		
90°		

Solution

(a)

θ	Cosθ	Sinθ
0°	1	0
10°	0·985	0·174
20°	0·940	0·342
30°	0·866	0·5
40°	0·766	0·643
50°	0·643	0·766
60°	0·5	0·866
70°	0·342	0·940
80°	0·174	0·985
90°	0	1

(b) The value for $\cos\theta = \sin(90° - \theta)$ or $\sin\theta = \cos(90° - \theta)$.

For example: $\cos 10° = \sin 80° = 0·985$, $\cos 20° = \sin 70° = 0·940$, etc.

This is because θ and $(90° - \theta)$ are complementary angles in a right-angled triangle.

(c) As the cos function is not working properly on Katie's calculator she could find the complementary sin value. To do this, she would use the fact that $\cos\theta = \sin(90° - \theta)$:

$\cos 35° = \sin(90° - 35°)$

$\Rightarrow \cos 35° = \sin 55°$

$\Rightarrow \sin 55° = 0·819$

> **Points to note**
>
> From the examples shown above, we have found that:
>
> - The value of $\cos A + \cos B \neq \cos(A + B)$, $\tan A + \tan B \neq \tan(A + B)$. We can further extend this to include $\sin A + \sin B \neq \sin(A + B)$.
>
> - The value of $\cos\theta$ and $\sin\theta$ for acute angles is always ≤ 1.
>
> - The value of $\tan\theta$, for an acute angle, can be any value.
>
> This information can be used to check that the values for $\cos\theta$, $\sin\theta$ and $\tan\theta$ are correct, when solving right-angled triangle problems using trigonometric ratios.

Example

(a) Construct a right-angled triangle containing an angle A such that $\cos A = \dfrac{4}{7}$.

(b) Find $\tan A$ and $\sin A$, giving your answer in surd form.

Solution

(a) First set the cosine trigonometric ratio equal to its value:

$\cos A = \dfrac{4}{7} = \dfrac{\text{adjacent}}{\text{hypotenuse}}$

Therefore hypotenuse = 7 and the adjacent = 4.

Construct the right-angled triangle using the construction techniques learned in Chapter 8.

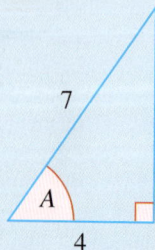

(b) Use Pythagoras' Theorem to find the length of the opposite side:

$\text{Opposite}^2 + 4^2 = 7^2$

$\Rightarrow \text{Opposite}^2 = 49 - 16$

$\Rightarrow \text{Opposite} = \sqrt{33}$

Hence opposite = $\sqrt{33}$, adjacent = 4 and hypotenuse = 7.

To find tan A, use the trigonometric ratio:	To find sin A, use the trigonometric ratio:
$\tan A = \dfrac{\text{opposite}}{\text{adjacent}}$	$\sin A = \dfrac{\text{opposite}}{\text{hypotenuse}}$
$\Rightarrow \tan A = \dfrac{\sqrt{33}}{4}$	$\Rightarrow \sin A = \dfrac{\sqrt{33}}{7}$

Finding an unknown side or angle, in a right-angled triangle, using trigonometric ratios

Points to note

Trigonometric ratios can be used for a right-angled triangle, to find:

- an unknown angle, given the lengths of two sides; or
- an unknown length, given an angle and the length of one side.

Top Tip

To use the trigonometric formulae, we must:

1 Label all three sides of the triangle.

2 Write down the known information.

3 Write down the required information.

4 Identify the trigonometric ratio which connects this information.

5 Substitute the relevant information into this ratio.

6 Solve to find the unknown information.

Examples

(a) *ABC* is a right-angled triangle. $|\angle ACB| = 60°$ and $|AC| = 10$ cm.
Calculate the length of $[AB]$, correct to two decimal places.

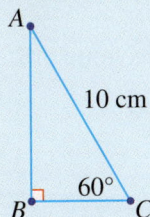

(b) *MNO* is a triangle with [*OP*] perpendicular to [*MN*]. $|MP| = 10$ cm, $|ON| = 30$ cm and $|\angle PMO| = 65°$.

Calculate:

(i) $|OP|$, correct to one decimal place.

(ii) $|MON|$, correct to one decimal place.

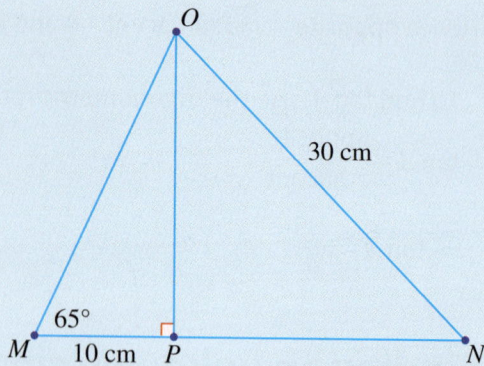

(SEC 2011)

Solutions

(a) To calculate the length of [*AB*], use the sine trigonometric ratio, as $|\angle ACB| = 60°$ and $|AC| = $ hypotenuse $= 10$ cm are known and we need to find $|AB| = $ opposite.

$$\sin|\angle ACB| = \frac{\text{opposite}}{\text{hypotenuse}}$$

$$\Rightarrow \sin|\angle ACB| = \frac{|AB|}{|AC|}$$

Substituting in the known values and solving for $|AB|$:

$$\sin 60° = \frac{|AB|}{10}$$

$$\Rightarrow |AB| = 10 \sin 60°$$

$$\Rightarrow |AB| = 10\left(\frac{\sqrt{3}}{2}\right) = 5\sqrt{3} \text{ cm}$$

$$\Rightarrow |AB| = 8.66025 \text{ cm} = 8.66 \text{ cm to 2 d.p.}$$

(b) (i) To calculate $|OP|$, use the tan ratio as the adjacent length $= |MP| = 30$ cm and $|\angle PMO| = 65°$ are known and we need to find $|OP| = $ opposite length.

$$\tan|\angle PMO| = \frac{\text{opposite}}{\text{adjacent}}$$

$$\Rightarrow \tan|\angle PMO| = \frac{|OP|}{|ON|}$$

Substituting in the known values and solving for $|OP|$:

$$\tan 65° = \frac{|OP|}{10}$$

$$\Rightarrow |OP| = 10 \tan 65°$$

Use your calculator to find the value of $10\tan(65°)$

$|OP| = 21.445$ cm $= 21.4$ to 1 d.p.

(ii) Step 1: Find $|\angle ONP|$, using the sine ratio, $|OP| = 21 \cdot 4$ cm and $|ON| = 30$ cm

$$\sin|\angle ONP| = \frac{\text{opposite}}{\text{hypotenuse}}$$

$$\Rightarrow \sin|\angle ONP| = \frac{|OP|}{|ON|} = \frac{21 \cdot 4}{30} = 0 \cdot 71\dot{3}$$

$$|\angle ONP| = \sin^{-1}(0 \cdot 71\dot{3})$$

$$\Rightarrow |\angle ONP| = 45 \cdot 50677577°$$

Give the answer correct to two decimal places, as the final answer must be rounded to one decimal place.

$$\Rightarrow |\angle ONP| = 45 \cdot 51°$$

Step 2: Find $|\angle MON|$.

$|\angle MON| = 180° - 65° - |\angle ONP|$, as the sum of angles in a triangle add up to 180°.

$$\therefore |\angle MON| = 180° - 65° - 45 \cdot 51°$$

$$\Rightarrow |\angle MON| = 69 \cdot 49° = 69 \cdot 5° \text{ to 1 d.p.}$$

Top Tip!

To find the value of $|\angle ONP|$, we must carry out the opposite operation of sine. This is the inverse function of sine. To do this we press SHIFT, sin⁻¹, then type in the value.

Angle measure in degrees, minutes and seconds

Points to note

Sometimes a question may ask you to convert the value of an angle from decimal form into DMS form, or vice versa.

- These are both methods of expressing fractions of degrees.

- **Decimal form** states the fraction as a decimal of a degree. For example, 37·7047°.

- **DMS** stands for degrees, minutes and seconds. The symbol for degrees is °, for minutes is ′, and for seconds is ″. This method divides each degree into **60 minutes** (1° = 60′), then each minute into **60 seconds** (1′ = 60″). For example, 37° 42′ 17″.

- To convert from DMS to decimal form, (or vice versa), we use the ° ′ ″ button on a Casio calculator. Other calculators may use a DMS button.

Examples

(a) Convert 13° 23′ 16″ to decimal form, correct to two decimal places.

(b) Convert 78·36° to DMS form.

Solutions

(a) **Step 1:** Make sure the calculator is in Degrees mode.

Step 2: Type 13° 23′ 16″ into the calculator. This is called the DMS (degrees, minutes and seconds) form.

- Press 1 3 then the °′″ button

- Press 2 3 then the °′″ button

- Press 1 6 then the °′″ button

- Press = button

- Press the °′″ button

- Round to two decimal places
  Answer = 13·39° in decimal form.

(b) **Step 1:** Make sure the calculator is in Degrees mode.

Step 2: Type 7 8 · 3 6 into the calculator (this is called the decimal form)

Press the = button

Press the °′″ button

Step 3: Write down the solution in DMS form.

Answer: 78·36° = 78° 21′ 36″, pronounced 78 degrees, 21 minutes and 36 seconds.

Working with the angles 30°, 45° and 60°

- Trigonometric ratios for 45°

  The sine, cosine and tangent ratios can be determined from the isosceles triangle shown.

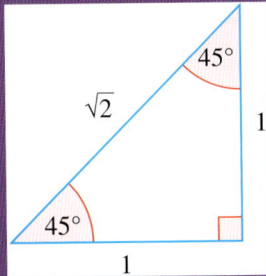

$$\sin 45° = \frac{1}{\sqrt{2}}$$

$$\cos 45° = \frac{1}{\sqrt{2}}$$

$$\tan 45° = \frac{1}{1} = 1$$

- Trigonometric ratios for 30° and 60°

  The sine, cosine and tangent ratios can be determined from the right-angled triangle shown.

- Note that you do not need to learn the values of these trigonometric ratios, as they are given in the *Formulae and Tables* booklet.

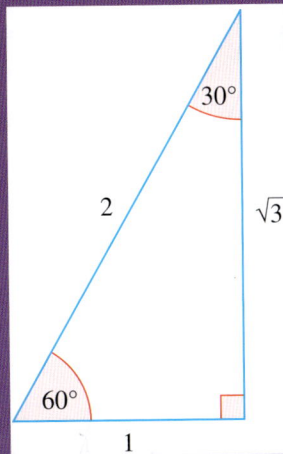

$$\sin 30° = \frac{O}{H} = \frac{1}{2}$$

$$\cos 30° = \frac{A}{H} = \frac{\sqrt{3}}{2}$$

$$\tan 30° = \frac{O}{A} = \frac{1}{\sqrt{3}}$$

$$\sin 60° = \frac{O}{H} = \frac{\sqrt{3}}{2}$$

$$\cos 60° = \frac{A}{H} = \frac{1}{2}$$

$$\tan 60° = \frac{O}{A} = \frac{\sqrt{3}}{1} = \sqrt{3}$$

Example

Without using a calculator, find the values of x and y in the right-angled triangle shown.

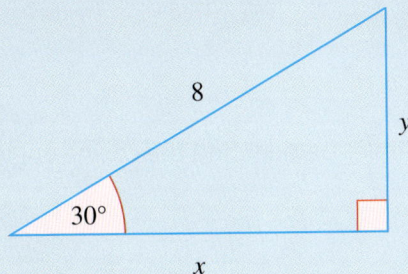

Solution

To find x:

Use $\cos \theta = \dfrac{A}{H}$ and $\cos 30° = \dfrac{\sqrt{3}}{2}$ from the tables.

$$\Rightarrow \frac{\sqrt{3}}{2} = \frac{x}{8}$$

$$\Rightarrow \frac{8\sqrt{3}}{2} = x$$

$$\Rightarrow 4\sqrt{3} = x$$

To find y:

Use $\sin \theta = \dfrac{O}{H}$ and $\sin 30° = \dfrac{1}{2}$ from the tables.

$$\Rightarrow \frac{1}{2} = \frac{y}{8}$$

$$\Rightarrow \frac{8}{2} = y$$

$$\Rightarrow 4 = y$$

Example

Without using a calculator, find the value of the angle B, in the right-angled triangle shown.

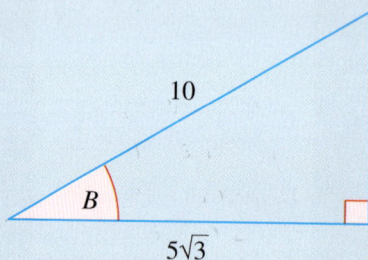

Solution

Use $\cos B = \dfrac{A}{H}$, $A = 5\sqrt{3}$ and $H = 10$.

$$\Rightarrow \cos B = \frac{5\sqrt{3}}{10}$$

$$\cos B = \frac{\sqrt{3}}{2}$$

Using the *Formulae and Tables* booklet find the cosine angle for $\dfrac{\sqrt{3}}{2}$:

$$\Rightarrow B = 30°$$

Exercise

Q1 The triangle ABC is shown below. Find $|BC|$.

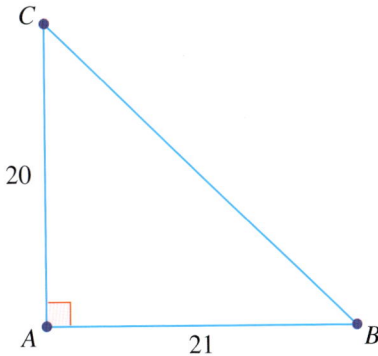

Q2 The triangle PQR is shown below. Find $|PQ|$.

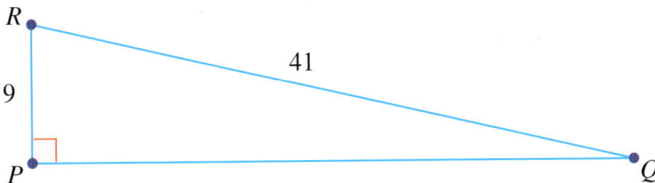

Q3 Show that $\sin 155° \neq \sin 90° + \sin 65°$, using the calculator.

Round all values to two decimal places, where necessary.

Q4 During a trigonometry lesson, a group of students made some predictions about what they expected to find for the values of the trigonometric functions of some angles. They then found the sine, cosine and tangent of 25° and 50°.

(a) In the table given, show, correct to three decimal places, the values they found.

sin 25° =	cos 25° =	tan 25° =
sin 50° =	cos 50° =	tan 50° =

(b) (i) Maria had said, 'The value from any of these trigonometric functions will always be less than 1.' Was Maria correct? Give a reason for your answer.

  (ii) Sharon had said, 'If the size of the angle is doubled, then the value from any of these trigonometric functions will also double.' Was Sharon correct? Give a reason for your answer.

  (iii) James had said, 'The value for all of these trigonometric functions will increase if the size of the angle is increased.' Was James correct? Give a reason for your answer.

(SEC 2014)

Q5 If $\tan A = \dfrac{1}{7}$, find the value of $\sin^2 A + \cos^2 A$.

Q6 (a) The diagram below shows the angle A in a right-angled triangle. Indicate which side is adjacent and which is opposite in relation to the angle A, and which side is the hypotenuse.

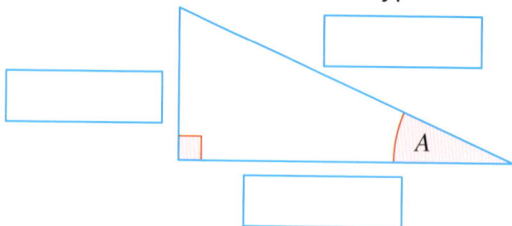

(b) Fill in the appropriate ratios in the table below.

Trigonometric ratio	Ratio
$\sin A$	
$\cos A$	
$\tan A$	

(c) In the right-angled triangle here, $B = 35°$ and the opposite side is 12 cm. Find the length of the hypotenuse correct to the nearest centimetre.

(SEC 2012)

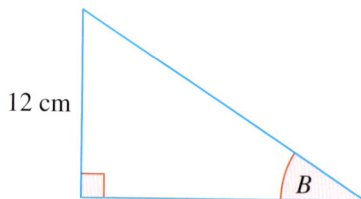

12 cm

B

Q7 (a) For the right-angled triangle shown:

(i) Calculate the ratios $\sin A$, $\cos A$ and $\tan A$.

(ii) Find the measure of the angle A.

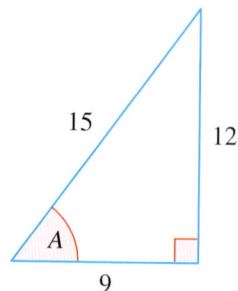

15

12

A

9

(b) In the right-angled triangle XYZ, $|XZ| = 13$ and $|\angle YXZ| = 60°$.

(i) Find $|XY|$.

(ii) Find $|YZ|$.

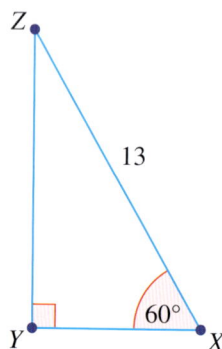

Z

13

$60°$

Y X

Q8 (a) Convert 67° 28′ 13″ to decimal form, correct to two decimal places.

(b) Convert 38·93° to DMS form.

Q9 Without using a calculator, find the value of x in the right-angled triangle shown.

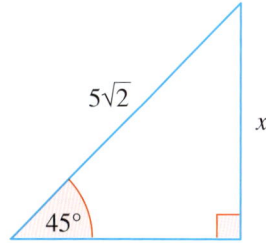

$5\sqrt{2}$

x

$45°$

Q10 Without using a calculator, find the value of the angle A, in the right-angled triangle shown.

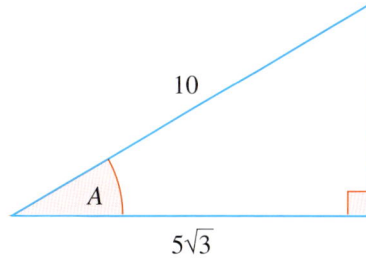

10

A

$5\sqrt{3}$

Q11 (a) (i) Write 2° 43′ 5″ in degrees in decimal form, correct to two decimal places.

(ii) Write 3·14° in DMS (i.e. degrees, minutes, and seconds).

(b) The diagram shows a right-angled triangle, with the angle A marked. Given that $\cos A = \sin A$, show that this triangle must be isosceles.

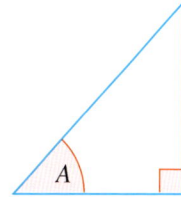

A

(c) A right-angled triangle has sides of length 7 cm, 24 cm and 25 cm. Find the size of the smallest angle in this triangle. Give your answer correct to one decimal place.

(SEC 2016)

Q12 (a) The triangle PQR has sides of length 8, 11, and y. Write down **one** value of y for which $\triangle PQR$ is an **isosceles** triangle.

(b) The triangle STU has sides of length 4, 7, and x. Find the **two** values of x for which $\triangle STU$ is a **right-angled** triangle. Give each answer in surd form.

(SEC 2015)

Q13 (a) Use the diagram shown to calculate the value of x. Give your answer in surd form.

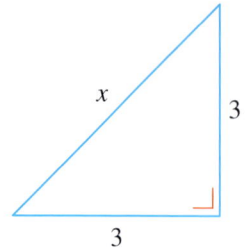

(b) Use the diagram shown to calculate the value of y. Give your answer in surd form.

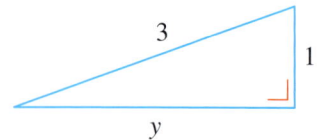

(c) A rectangle with sides of length x and y is drawn using the values of x and y from parts **(a)** and **(b)**, as shown.

Write the **perimeter** of this rectangle in the form $a\sqrt{2}$, where $a \in \mathbb{N}$.

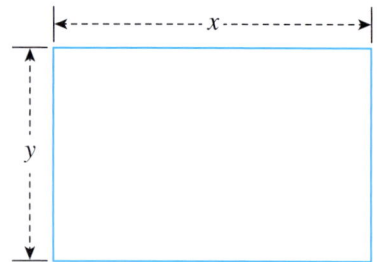

(SEC 2014)

Q14 During a trigonometry lesson a group of students wrote down some statements about what they expected to happen when they looked at the values of trigonometric functions of some angles. Here are some of the things they wrote down.

(a) The value from any of these trigonometric functions will always be less than 1.

(b) If the size of the angle is doubled then the value from the trigonometric functions will not double.

(c) The value from all the trigonometric functions will increase if the size of the angle is increased.

(d) I do not need to use a calculator to find sin 60°. I can do it by drawing an equilateral triangle. The answer will be in surd form.

They then found the sin, cos and tan of some angles, correct to three decimal places, to test their ideas.

(i) Do you think that **(a)** is correct? Give an example to justify your answer.

(ii) Do you think that **(b)** is correct? Give an example to justify your answer.

(iii) Do you think that **(c)** is correct? Give an example to justify your answer.

(iv) Show how an equilateral triangle of side 2 cm can be used to find sin 60° in surd form.

(SEC 2014)

Q15 In the right-angled triangle shown in the diagram, one of the acute angles is four times as large as the other acute angle.

(a) Find the measures of the two acute angles in the triangle.

(b) The triangle in part (a) is placed on a coordinate diagram. The base is parallel to the x-axis.

Find the slope of the line l that contains the hypotenuse of the triangle. Give your answer correct to three decimal places.

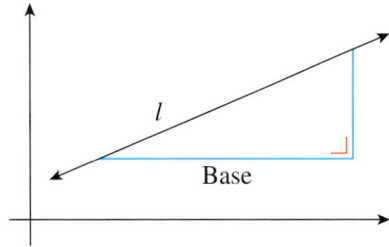

(SEC 2014)

Q16 In the right-angled triangle ABC, $|AB| = 2$ and $|BC| = 1$.

(a) Find $|AC|$, giving your answer in surd form.

(b) Write $\cos |\angle BAC|$ and hence find $|\angle BAC|$.

(c) Sketch a right-angled isosceles triangle in which the equal sides are 1 unit each and use it to write $\cos 45°$ in surd form.

(d) Show that $\cos 75° \neq \cos 45° + \cos 30°$.

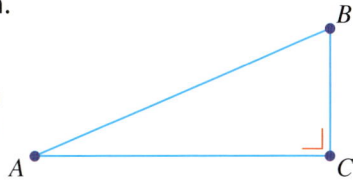

(SEC 2013)

Q17 (a) Construct a right-angled triangle containing an angle A such that $\sin A = 0{\cdot}4$.

(b) Find, from your triangle, $\cos A$ in surd form.

(SEC 2012)

Q18 In the diagram ABC is a right-angled triangle, with AC perpendicular to BC. $|AC| = 2\sqrt{2}$ and $|BC| = 3\sqrt{3}$.

Calculate:

(a) $|AB|$, leaving your answer in surd form.

(b) $|\angle ABC|$, correct to the nearest degree.

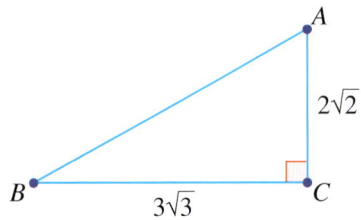

(SEC 2012)

Q19 Without using a calculator, construct the angle A such that $6 \tan A = 8$, $0° \leq A < 90°$.

(SEC 2010)

Q20 abc is an isosceles triangle with $|ac| = |bc|$, $|ab| = \sqrt{50}$ and $|\angle acb| = 90°$.

Find $|bc|$.

(SEC 2009)

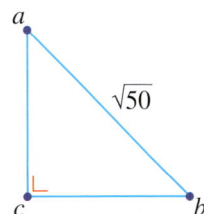

Q21 Given that $\tan A = 4$, write $\cos A$ in the form $\dfrac{1}{\sqrt{x}}$, $x \in \mathbb{N}$.

(SEC 2008)

Q22 Given that $\cos C = \dfrac{2}{3}$, find the value of x.

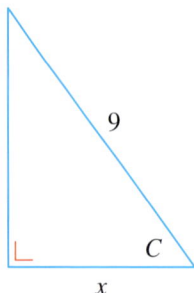

(SEC 2005)

Solutions

Q1 As an angle is not labelled on the diagram, the lengths 20 or 21 can be labelled a and b or b and a. In this case let $a = 21$ and $b = 20$.

So $c = |BC|$, $a = 21$ and $b = 20$.

First substitute all known values in for a, b and c into $c^2 = a^2 + b^2$.

$|BC|^2 = 20^2 + 21^2 = 400 + 441 = 841$

$\Rightarrow BC = \sqrt{841}$

Write down the positive value for $\sqrt{841}$ only, as length is positive.

$|BC| = 29$ units

Q2 Let $c = 41$, $a = |PQ|$ and $b = 9$.

First, substitute all known values in for a, b and c into $c^2 = a^2 + b^2$.

$(41)^2 = |PQ|^2 + (9)^2$

Then solve for $|PQ|$ by squaring both sides and simplifying.

$1681 - 81 = |PQ|^2$

$\Rightarrow |PQ|^2 = 1600$

$\Rightarrow |PQ| = \sqrt{1600}$

Write down the positive value for $\sqrt{1600}$ only, as length is positive.

$|PQ| = 40$ units

Q3 Make sure that your calculator is in Degrees mode. Then, from the calculator:

$\sin(155°) = 0.42$, $\sin(90°) = 1$ and $\sin(65°) = 0.91$, to two decimal places.

LHS $= \sin 155° = 0.42$

RHS $= \sin 90° + \sin 65° = 1 + 0.91 = 1.91$

So RHS $\neq$ LHS

Therefore, $\sin 155° \neq \sin 90° + \sin 65°$

Q4 (a)

$\sin 25° = 0.423$	$\cos 25° = 0.906$	$\tan 25° = 0.466$
$\sin 50° = 0.766$	$\cos 50° = 0.643$	$\tan 50° = 1.192$

(b) **(i)** Maria was not correct. Values for the trigonometric ratios are not always less than 1. For example, $\tan 50° = 1.192$.

(ii) Sharon was not correct, as doubling the angles did not result in the values for the trigonometric ratios doubling.

(iii) James was not correct, as the values for the trigonometric ratios did not always increase when the angle increased. For example, $\cos 25° = 0.906$ and $\cos 50° = 0.643$. In this case the angle increased and the value for the ratio decreased.

Q5 Step 1 Construct the right-angled triangle.

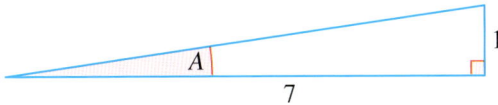

$\tan A = \dfrac{1}{7} = \dfrac{\text{opposite}}{\text{adjacent}}$

Step 2 Use Pythagoras' Theorem to find the length of the hypotenuse, by substituting $opp = 1$ and $adj = 7$ into the formula $(hyp)^2 = (opp)^2 + (adj)^2$

$(hyp)^2 = (1)^2 + (7)^2$

$\Rightarrow (hyp)^2 = 1 + 49$

$\Rightarrow hyp = \sqrt{50}$

Step 3 Find the value of the trigonometric ratios $\sin A$ and $\cos A$.

$\sin A = \dfrac{opp}{hyp} = \dfrac{1}{\sqrt{50}}$ and $\cos A = \dfrac{adj}{hyp} = \dfrac{7}{\sqrt{50}}$

Step 4 Substitute both values of the ratios into the expression $\sin^2 A + \cos^2 A$. Note that $\sin^2 A$ is another way of writing $(\sin A)^2$, from algebra.

$(\sin A)^2 + (\cos A)^2 = \left(\dfrac{1}{\sqrt{50}}\right)^2 + \left(\dfrac{7}{\sqrt{50}}\right)^2 = \dfrac{1}{50} + \dfrac{49}{50} = \dfrac{50}{50} = 1$

From this we can conclude that $\sin^2 A + \cos^2 A = 1$. This formula is also given in the *Formulae and Tables* booklet.

Q6 (a)

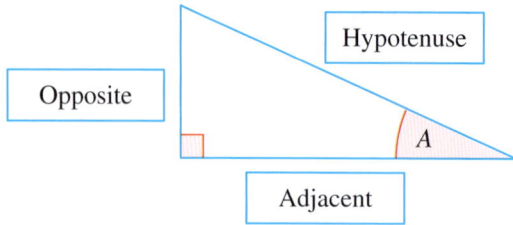

(b)

Trigonometric ratio	Ratio
sin A	$\dfrac{\text{opposite}}{\text{hypotenuse}}$
cos A	$\dfrac{\text{adjacent}}{\text{hypotenuse}}$
tan A	$\dfrac{\text{opposite}}{\text{adjacent}}$

(c) $B = 35°$ and the opposite side is 12 cm. So to find the hypotenuse, use the sine ratio.

$$\sin A = \frac{\text{opposite}}{\text{hypotenuse}}$$

$$\Rightarrow \sin 35° = \frac{12}{\text{hypotenuse}}$$

$$\Rightarrow \text{hypotenuse} \times (\sin 35°) = 12$$

$$\Rightarrow \text{hypotenuse} = \frac{12}{\sin 35°}$$

$\Rightarrow$ hypotenuse = 20·92 cm = 21 cm to the nearest centimetre.

Q7 (a) Opposite = 12, adjacent = 9 and the hypotenuse = 15.

(i) $\sin A = \dfrac{\text{opposite}}{\text{hypotenuse}} = \dfrac{12}{15} = \dfrac{4}{5}$

$\cos A = \dfrac{\text{adjacent}}{\text{hypotenuse}} = \dfrac{9}{15} = \dfrac{3}{5}$

$\tan A = \dfrac{\text{opposite}}{\text{adjacent}} = \dfrac{12}{9} = \dfrac{4}{3}$

(ii) Any of the ratios found in part (i) can be used to find the measure (size) of the angle. They will all give the same value for A, as shown below.

$\sin A = \dfrac{4}{5} \Rightarrow A = \sin^{-1}\left(\dfrac{4}{5}\right) = 53·13°$

$\cos A = \dfrac{3}{5} \Rightarrow A = \cos^{-1}\left(\dfrac{3}{5}\right) = 53·13°$

$\tan A = \dfrac{4}{3} \Rightarrow A = \tan^{-1}\left(\dfrac{4}{3}\right) = 53·13°$

(b) Opposite = $|YZ|$, adjacent = $|XY|$, hypotenuse = 13 and $|\angle YXZ| = 60°$.

   (i) To find $|XY|$, use the cosine ratio.

$$\cos 60° = \frac{\text{adjacent}}{\text{hypotenuse}} = \frac{|XY|}{13}$$

$$\Rightarrow 13\,(\cos 60°) = |XY|$$
$$\Rightarrow 6 \cdot 5 = |XY|$$
$$\Rightarrow |XY| = 6 \cdot 5 \text{ units}$$

   (ii) To find $|YZ|$, use the sine ratio.

$$\sin 60° = \frac{\text{opposite}}{\text{hypotenuse}} = \frac{|YZ|}{13}$$

$$\Rightarrow 13\,(\sin 60°) = |YZ|$$
$$\Rightarrow \frac{13\sqrt{3}}{2} = |YZ|$$
$$\Rightarrow |YZ| = 11 \cdot 26 \text{ units, correct to 2 decimal places.}$$

An alternative way of reaching the same solution is to use Pythagoras' Theorem and the result from part **(i)**.

Q8 (a) **Step 1:** Make sure the calculator is in Degrees mode.

Step 2: Type 67° 28′ 13″ into the calculator. This is called DMS (degrees, minutes and seconds) form.

- Press **6** **7** then the °‚„ button
- Press **2** **8** then the °‚„ button
- Press **1** **3** then the °‚„ button
- Press **=**
- Press the °‚„ button
- Round to two decimal places

Answer = 67·47°

(b) **Step 1:** Make sure the calculator is in Degrees mode.

Step 2: Type **3** **8** **.** **9** **3** into the calculator (this is called decimal form)

Press the **=** button

Press the °‚„ button

Step 3: Write down the solution in DMS form.

Answer: $38{\cdot}93° = 38° \, 55' \, 48''$, pronounced 38 degrees, 55 minutes and 48 seconds.

Q9 Opposite $= x$ and the hypotenuse $= 5\sqrt{2}$.

So, use the sine ratio $\sin\theta = \dfrac{O}{H}$.

From the *Formulae and Tables* booklet, $\sin 45° = \dfrac{1}{\sqrt{2}}$.

Substitute all known information into the ratio and solve for x.

$$\dfrac{1}{\sqrt{2}} = \dfrac{x}{5\sqrt{2}}$$

$$\Rightarrow \dfrac{5\sqrt{2}}{\sqrt{2}} = x$$

$$\Rightarrow x = 5$$

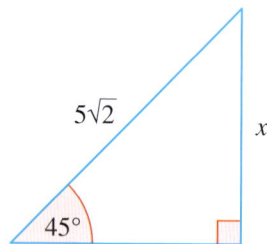

Q10 To find the value of the angle A in the right-angled triangle shown (without using a calculator) follow these steps.

Write down all known information:

The hypotenuse $= 10$ and the adjacent side $= 5\sqrt{3}$.

Therefore, we must use the trigonometric ratio: $\cos A = \dfrac{adj}{hyp}$

$$\Rightarrow \cos A = \dfrac{5\sqrt{3}}{10}$$

$$\Rightarrow \cos A = \dfrac{\sqrt{3}}{2}$$

$$\Rightarrow A = \cos^{-1}\left(\dfrac{\sqrt{3}}{2}\right) = 30°$$

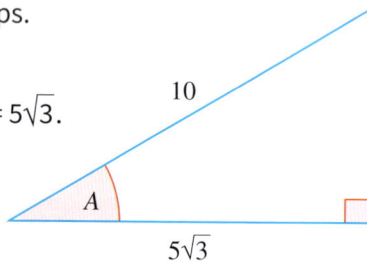

Q11 (a) (i) Step 1: Make sure the calculator is in Degrees mode.

- To check: look for D on the top right hand corner of the screen.
- If it is not in Degrees mode, follow these steps:
- Press ⬤ (SHIFT) then the ⬤ (SETUP) button.
- The list

1:MthIO	2:LineIO
3:Deg	4:Rad
5:Gra	6:Fix
7:Sci	8:Norm

will appear on the screen.

- Press **3** to choose Degrees for the angle setting.

Step 2: Type 2° 43′ 5″ into the calculator. This is called DMS (degrees, minutes and seconds) form.

- Press **2** then the ◦,,, button
- Press **4** **3** then the ◦,,, button
- Press **5** then the ◦,,, button
- Press **=**
- Press ◦,,,

Answer = 2·718055556, in decimal form.

Step 3: Answer: 2° 43′ 5″ = 2·72, correct to two decimal places

(ii) **Step 1:** Make sure the calculator is in Degrees mode.

Step 2: Type **3** **.** **1** **4** into the calculator (this is called decimal form)

Press **=**

Press ◦,,,

Step 3: Answer: 3·14° = 3° 8′ 24″, pronounced 3 degrees, 8 minutes and 24 seconds.

(b) We know that $\cos A = \sin A$ and the longest side is always the hypotenuse length.

Hence, to show that the triangle is isosceles, we must show that the lengths of the adjacent and opposite sides are the same.

Step 1: Label the sides of the triangle.

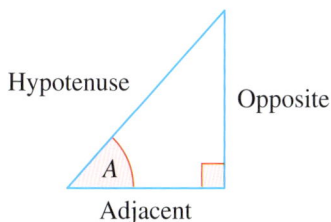

Step 2: It is given that $\cos A = \sin A$

But $\cos A = \dfrac{\text{adjacent}}{\text{hypotenuse}}$ and $\sin A = \dfrac{\text{opposite}}{\text{hypotenuse}}$

$\therefore \dfrac{\text{adjacent}}{\text{hypotenuse}} = \dfrac{\text{opposite}}{\text{hypotenuse}}$

$\Rightarrow$ adjacent = opposite, as the denominator is the same on both sides.

As the adjacent length equals the opposite length, then the triangle is isosceles.

(c) Step 1: Label the angle (smallest) opposite the smallest length A, the hypotenuse length 25 cm (it is the longest side) and then label the other two sides of the triangle:

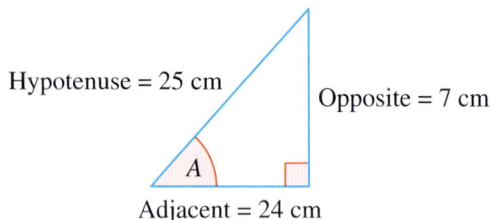

Hypotenuse = 25 cm
Opposite = 7 cm
A
Adjacent = 24 cm

Step 2: Use any of the three trigonometric ratios to find the angle A.

Option 1:	Option 2:	Option 3:
$\tan A = \dfrac{\text{opposite}}{\text{adjacent}}$	$\sin A = \dfrac{\text{opposite}}{\text{hypotenuse}}$	$\cos A = \dfrac{\text{adjacent}}{\text{hypotenuse}}$
$\tan A = \dfrac{7}{24}$	$\sin A = \dfrac{7}{25}$	$\cos A = \dfrac{24}{25}$
$A = \tan^{-1}\left(\dfrac{7}{24}\right)$	$A = \sin^{-1}\left(\dfrac{7}{25}\right)$	$A = \cos^{-1}\left(\dfrac{24}{25}\right)$
$A = 16{\cdot}26°$	$A = 16{\cdot}26°$	$A = 16{\cdot}26°$

Step 3: Answer: $A = 16{\cdot}3°$ to 1 d.p.

Q12 (a) As the triangle $\triangle PQR$ is an isosceles triangle then two of the sides are the same length.

Therefore the value of y can be either 8 or 11.

(b)

Case 1: x lies on either the opposite or adjacent side.	Case 2: x lies on the hypotenuse side.
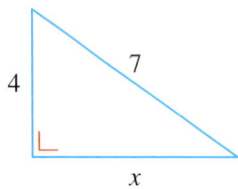 4, 7, x	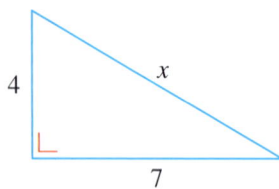 4, x, 7
$4^2 + x^2 = 7^2$	$4^2 + 7^2 = x^2$
$\Rightarrow x^2 = 49 - 16$	$\Rightarrow x^2 = 49 + 16$
$\Rightarrow x^2 = 33$	$\Rightarrow x^2 = 65$
$\Rightarrow x = \sqrt{33}$	$\Rightarrow x = \sqrt{65}$

Q13 (a) Method 1: Use Pythagoras' Theorem to solve for x.

$x^2 = 3^2 + 3^2 = 9 + 9$

$\Rightarrow x = \sqrt{18}$

As lengths are positive, write down the positive value of $\sqrt{18}$ only.

$x = 3\sqrt{2}$

Method 2: Use trigonometric ratios to solve for x.

The triangle is isosceles, as the adjacent and opposite sides are the same length. Therefore, the angles opposite both sides are 45°.

We know: x = hypotenuse, opposite = 3, adjacent = 3 and $\angle A = 45°$.

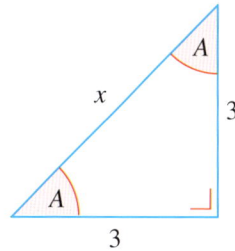

Use the sine trigonometric ratio to find the value of x:

$\sin A = \dfrac{\text{opposite}}{\text{hypotenuse}}$

$\Rightarrow \sin 45° = \dfrac{3}{x}$

$\Rightarrow x = \dfrac{3}{\sin 45°}$

Find $\sin 45°$ using a calculator the *Formulae and Tables* booklet.

$x = \dfrac{3}{\left(\dfrac{1}{\sqrt{2}}\right)} = 3\sqrt{2}$

(b) $y^2 + 1^2 = 3^2$

$\Rightarrow y^2 = 9 - 1$

$\Rightarrow y = \sqrt{8}$

As lengths are positive, write down the positive value of $\sqrt{8}$ only.

$y = 2\sqrt{2}$

(c) Let P = perimeter.

$P = 2x + 2y \Rightarrow 2\left(3\sqrt{2}\right) + 2\left(2\sqrt{2}\right) \Rightarrow 6\sqrt{2} + 4\sqrt{2} = 10\sqrt{2}$

For more about the perimeter, see Chapter 13, Applied Measure.

Q14 (i) (a) is not true. For example, $\tan(250°) = 2\cdot727$. In this case the value of the trigonometric function is more than 1.

(ii) (b) is true. For example, $\sin(90°) = 0$ but $\sin(180°) = -1$. In this case the value of the trigonometric function did not double.

(iii) (c) is not true. For example, as $\cos(45°) = 0\cdot7071$, but $\cos(90°) = 0$. In this case the value decreases as the angle increases.

(iv) Step 1: Construct an equilateral triangle with sides of length 2 cm, and then bisect (cut in two) the triangle to form two right-angled triangles.

Step 2: Find the length of the perpendicular height of the triangle.

Let x denote the length of the perpendicular height.

Since both triangles are right-angled, they must satisfy Pythagoras' Theorem.

Thus, $1^2 + x^2 = 2^2$

$\Rightarrow x^2 = 4 - 1$

$\Rightarrow x = \sqrt{3}$

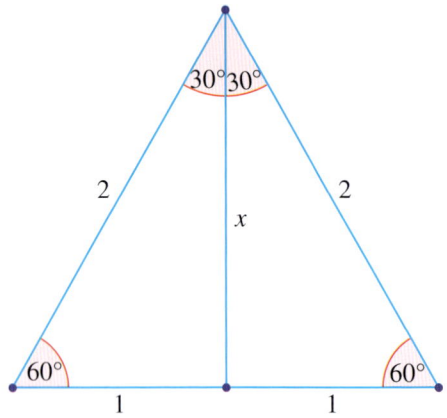

Step 3: In an equilateral triangle, the three angles are all 60°.

Using the result from Step 2:

In a right-angled triangle:

$$\sin 60° = \frac{\text{opposite}}{\text{hypotenuse}}$$

$$\Rightarrow \sin 60° = \frac{\sqrt{3}}{2}$$

Q15 (a) Let x denote the smallest angle in the triangle; then the other acute angle is equal to $4x$.

Since all angles must sum to 180°:

$x + 4x + 90° = 180°$

$\Rightarrow 5x = 90°$

$\Rightarrow x = 18°$

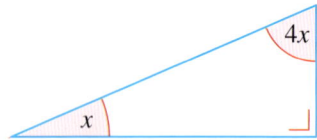

(b) The slope of the line will be the change in y-values divided by the change in x-values.

In relation to the triangle, this will be $\dfrac{\text{opposite}}{\text{adjacent}}$, which we know is equal to the tangent of the angle to the left of the triangle.

Part **(a)** proved that the size of the angle $x = 18°$.

So the slope equals $\tan(18°) = 0{\cdot}325$, correct to three decimal places.

For more on this topic see Chapter 9: Coordinate Geometry of the Line.

Q16 (a) To find $|AC|$, in surd form, use Pythagoras' Theorem.

$|AB| = 2$ and $|BC| = 1$, and AB is the hypotenuse of the triangle.

$\therefore 2^2 = |AC|^2 + 1^2$

$\Rightarrow |AC|^2 = 2^2 - 1^2$

$\Rightarrow AC = \sqrt{4 - 1}$

As lengths are positive, write down the positive value of $\sqrt{3}$ only.

$|AC| = \sqrt{3}$

(b) To find $|\angle BAC|$, use the trigonometric ratio $\cos\theta = \dfrac{\text{adjacent}}{\text{hypotenuse}}$.

$\cos|\angle BAC| = \dfrac{\sqrt{3}}{2}$

$\Rightarrow |\angle BAC| = \cos^{-1}\left(\dfrac{\sqrt{3}}{2}\right)$

$\Rightarrow |\angle BAC| = 30°$

(c) To write $\cos 45°$ in surd form, sketch a right-angled isosceles triangle in which the equal sides are 1 unit each and use it.

Hypotenuse $= \sqrt{1^2 + 1^2} = \sqrt{2}$

$\cos 45° = \dfrac{\text{adjacent}}{\text{hypotenuse}} = \dfrac{1}{\sqrt{2}}$

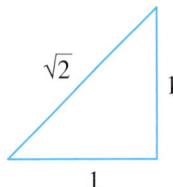

(d) $\cos 75° = 0\cdot 2588$

$\cos 45° + \cos 30° = \dfrac{1}{\sqrt{2}} + \dfrac{\sqrt{3}}{2} = 0\cdot 7071 + 0\cdot 8660 = 1\cdot 5731$

$\therefore \cos 45° + \cos 30° \neq \cos 75°$

Q17 (a) $\sin A = 0\cdot 4$

Convert $0\cdot 4$ into a fraction using the S $\Leftrightarrow$ D button on your calculator.

$\Rightarrow \sin A = \dfrac{4}{10} = \dfrac{\text{opposite}}{\text{hypotenuse}}$

From the ratio, the hypotenuse length is 10 and the opposite side is 4.

Construct the right-angled triangle using the construction techniques learned in Chapter 8.

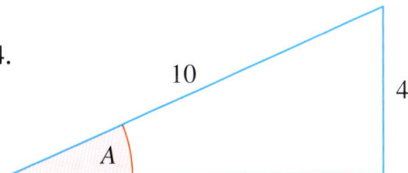

(b) First find the length of the adjacent side, using Pythagoras' Theorem.

adjacent$^2 + 4^2 = 10^2$

$\Rightarrow$ adjacent$^2 = 100 - 16 = \sqrt{84} = 2\sqrt{21}$

To find $\cos A$, use the trigonometric ratio $\cos A = \dfrac{\text{adjacent}}{\text{hypotenuse}}$.

$\cos A = \dfrac{2\sqrt{21}}{10} = \dfrac{\sqrt{21}}{5}$

Q18 (a) To find $|AB|$, in surd form, use Pythagoras' Theorem.

$|AC| = 2\sqrt{2}$ and $|BC| = 3\sqrt{3}$, and AB is the hypotenuse.

$|AB|^2 = |BC|^2 + |AC|^2$

$\Rightarrow |AB|^2 = \left(3\sqrt{3}\right)^2 + \left(2\sqrt{2}\right)^2 \Rightarrow 9(3) + 4(2) \Rightarrow 27 + 8 = 35$

The positive value is the only solution, as it is a length.

$|AB| = \sqrt{35}$ units

(b) Opposite = $2\sqrt{2}$, adjacent = $3\sqrt{3}$ and hypotenuse = $\sqrt{35}$.

To find $|\angle ABC|$, correct to the nearest degree, any of the three trigonometric ratios can be used.

Option 1:	Option 2:	Option 3:
$\tan |\angle ABC| = \dfrac{\text{opposite}}{\text{adjacent}}$	$\sin |\angle ABC| = \dfrac{\text{opposite}}{\text{hypotenuse}}$	$\cos |\angle ABC| = \dfrac{\text{adjacent}}{\text{hypotenuse}}$
$\Rightarrow \tan |\angle ABC| = \dfrac{2\sqrt{2}}{3\sqrt{3}}$	$\sin |\angle ABC| = \dfrac{2\sqrt{2}}{\sqrt{35}}$	$\cos |\angle ABC| = \dfrac{3\sqrt{3}}{\sqrt{35}}$
$|\angle ABC| = \tan^{-1}\left(\dfrac{2\sqrt{2}}{3\sqrt{3}}\right)$	$|\angle ABC| = \sin^{-1}\left(\dfrac{2\sqrt{2}}{\sqrt{35}}\right)$	$|\angle ABC| = \cos^{-1}\left(\dfrac{3\sqrt{3}}{\sqrt{35}}\right)$
$|\angle ABC| = 28 \cdot 56°$	$|\angle ABC| = 28 \cdot 56°$	$|\angle ABC| = 28 \cdot 56°$

Hence $|\angle ABC| = 29°$ to the nearest degree.

Q19 $6 \tan A = 8$

$$\Rightarrow \tan A = \frac{8}{6} = \frac{4}{3}$$

But $\tan A = \dfrac{4}{3} = \dfrac{\text{opposite}}{\text{adjacent}}$

Hence, construct a triangle with the opposite length = 4 units and the adjacent side = 3 units, using techniques shown in Chapter 8.

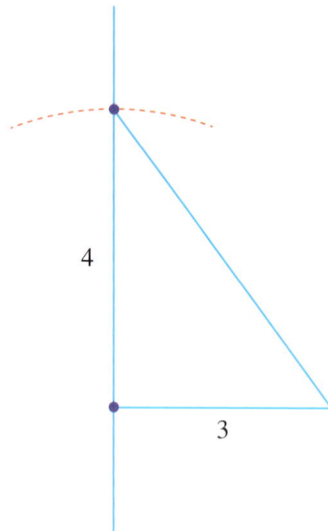

Q20

Method 1: Use Pythagoras' Theorem.	**Method 2:** Use the sine (or cosine) ratio.
Let $\lvert bc\rvert = \lvert ac\rvert = x$. Then: $$\left(\sqrt{50}\right)^2 = x^2 + x^2$$ $$\Rightarrow 50 = 2x^2$$ $$\Rightarrow \frac{50}{2} = x^2$$ $$\Rightarrow x = \sqrt{25}$$ $$\Rightarrow x = 5$$ 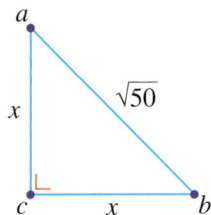	Let $\lvert bc\rvert = \lvert ac\rvert = x$. Know $\lvert \angle abc\rvert = \lvert \angle cab\rvert = 45°$. Then: $$\sin(45°) = \frac{x}{\sqrt{50}}$$ $$\Rightarrow \sin(45°)\sqrt{50} = x$$ $$\Rightarrow \left(\frac{1}{\sqrt{2}}\right)\left(\sqrt{50}\right) = x$$ Simplify using $\sqrt{a}\sqrt{b} = \sqrt{ab}$ $$\left(\sqrt{\frac{50}{2}}\right) = x \Rightarrow \sqrt{25} = x$$ As length is a positive value, write down the positive value of $\sqrt{25}$ only $$\Rightarrow x = 5$$

Q21 To find $\cos A$ in the form $\dfrac{1}{\sqrt{x}}, x \in \mathbb{N}$, we must follow the steps shown.

Step 1: Sketch the right-angled triangle using the fact that $\tan A = 4$.

$$\tan A = 4 = \frac{4}{1} = \frac{\text{opposite}}{\text{adjacent}}$$

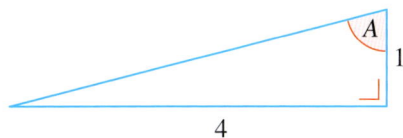

Step 2: Use Pythagoras' Theorem to find the hypotenuse length.

Let hypotenuse $= h$. Then: $h^2 = 4^2 + 1^2 = 16 + 1 = 17$

$$\Rightarrow h = \sqrt{17}$$

Step 3: Use the cosine trigonometric ratio to find $\cos A$ in the form $\dfrac{1}{\sqrt{x}}, x \in \mathbb{N}$.

$$\cos A = \frac{\text{adjacent}}{\text{hypotenuse}}$$

$$\Rightarrow \cos A = \frac{1}{\sqrt{17}}$$

Q22 $\cos C = \dfrac{2}{3}$.

From the right-angled triangle:

$$\cos C = \frac{\text{adjacent}}{\text{hypotenuse}} = \frac{x}{9}$$

$$\Rightarrow \frac{x}{9} = \frac{2}{3} \Rightarrow 9\left(\frac{x}{9}\right) = 9\left(\frac{2}{3}\right) \Rightarrow x = 6$$

For more on this topic see Revise Wise 1 Chapter 2, Applied Arithmetic: ratios.

12 Trigonometry 2: Applications of Trigonometry

Learning objectives

In this chapter you will learn about:

- Angles of elevation and depression
- Using a clinometer
- Solving real-life problems using trigonometry rules.

Key information required when solving problems using trigonometry

Points to note

Rule	Formulae	Diagram
Pythagoras' Theorem	$c^2 = a^2 + b^2$, given in the *Formulae and Tables* booklet c = **hypotenuse** side, as it is **opposite the right-angle** (90°) a = **opposite** side, as it is **across from** angle A b = **adjacent** side, as it is **beside** angle A	

Rule	Formulae	Diagram
Sine ratio	$\sin \theta = \dfrac{\text{opposite}}{\text{hypotenuse}}$	Opposite, Hypotenuse, Adjacent, θ
Cosine ratio	$\cos \theta = \dfrac{\text{adjacent}}{\text{hypotenuse}}$	
Tangent ratio	$\tan \theta = \dfrac{\text{opposite}}{\text{adjacent}}$	θ = theta (a Greek letter)
Compass directions		A is N 30° E (or E 60° N) B is N 60° W (or W 30° N) C is S 70° E (or E 20° S) D is S 80° W (or W 10° S) Note: N 30° E means start at North and turn 30° East.

When solving problems using trigonometry follow the steps below:

1 Draw and label a diagram to represent the problem.

2 Write down all the information provided.

3 Identify the information required.

4 Identify whether a trigonometric ratio or Pythagoras' Theorem can be used to help solve the problem.

5 Solve the problem and check the solution.

Angles of elevation and depression

Points to note

Word	Meaning	Diagram
Angle of elevation	The angle between the horizontal and the line of sight **up** to an object. Note: An angle of elevation has an equal angle of depression, from alternate angles.	Object, angle of elevation, horizontal, θ
Angle of depression	The angle between the horizontal and the line of sight **down** to an object. Note: An angle of depression has an equal angle of elevation, from alternate angles.	horizontal, angle of depression, Object, θ

Example

A boat approches a 300 m high cliff. An observer on the top of the cliff calculates that the angle of depression from the top of the cliff to the boat is 15°. Calculate how far the boat is from the base of the cliff, to the nearest metre.

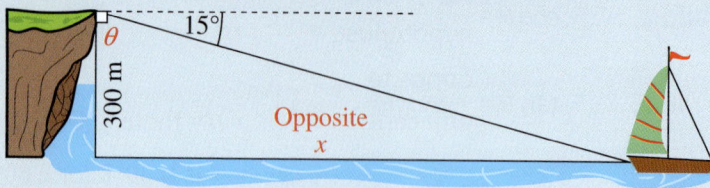

Solution

Method 1

1 Draw and label a diagram.

2 Write down all the information given.

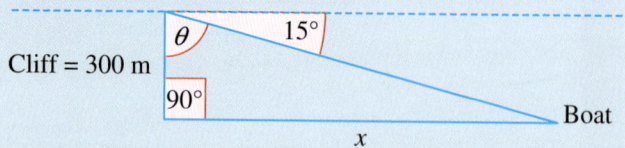

$\theta = 90° - 15° = 75°$

Adjacent side length = 300 m

3 Identify the information required.

We want to find the opposite length = x m

4 Use the tangent ratio to solve the problem.

$\tan \theta = \dfrac{\text{opposite}}{\text{adjacent}}$ $\Rightarrow \tan 75° = \dfrac{x}{300}$

5 Solve the problem.

$\tan 75° = \dfrac{x}{300} \Rightarrow x = 300 \tan 75° = 1119 \cdot 615... = 1120$ m

Method 2

1 Draw and label a diagram.

2 Write down all the information given.

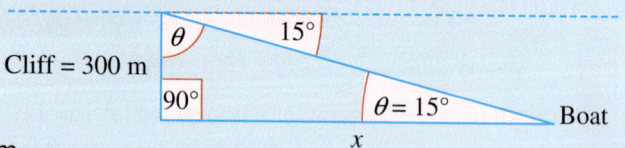

Opposite side length = 300 m

$\theta = 15°$, from alternate angles.

3 Identify the information you need.

We want to find the adjacent length = x m

4 Use the tangent ratio to solve the problem.

$\tan \theta = \dfrac{\text{opposite}}{\text{adjacent}}$ $\Rightarrow \tan 15° = \dfrac{300}{x}$

5 Solve the problem.

$\tan 15° = \dfrac{300}{x} \Rightarrow x = \dfrac{300}{\tan 15°} = 1119 \cdot 615... = 1120$ m

Therefore, the boat is 1120 m from the base of the cliff, to the nearest metre.

Using a clinometer to solve trigonometry problems

Point to note

A clinometer is a tool that is used to measure the angle of elevation, or angle from the ground, in a right-angled triangle. You can use a clinometer to measure the height of tall things where the top is out of reach, for example flag poles, buildings, or trees.

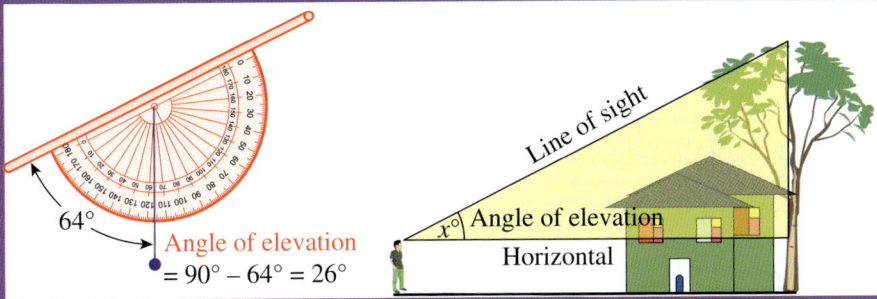

64°

Angle of elevation
= 90° − 64° = 26°

Line of sight

$x°$ Angle of elevation

Horizontal

Example

Seán has made a clinometer using a protractor, a straw, a piece of thread and a piece of plasticine (used as a weight). He stands 10 m from a tree and uses his clinometer to measure the angle of elevation to the top of the tree as shown. Seán is 1·75 m in height.

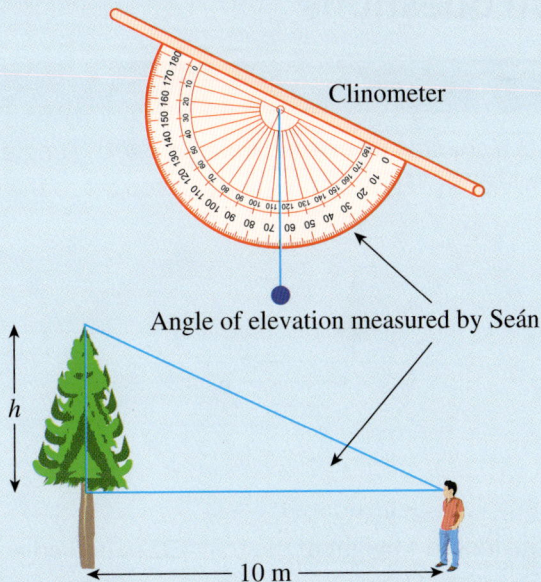

Clinometer

Angle of elevation measured by Seán

h

10 m

(a) Find the angle of elevation by reading the clinometer above.

(b) Calculate the height h, as shown in the diagram. Give your answer correct to two decimal places.

(c) Find the total height of the tree.

(d) Another student uses the same method as Seán and finds the height of the tree to be 23·1 m. Seán did not get this answer. Give one possible reason why the answer might be different.

Solution

(a) Each sector is equal to 10°. The angle on the clinometer is in the middle of the 6th and 7th sector, which is 65°. Therefore, the angle of elevation is the angle complementary to this angle which 90° – 65° = 25°.

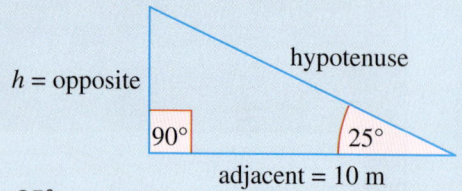

h = opposite

hypotenuse

90°   25°

adjacent = 10 m

(b) Adjacent side length = 10 m and $\theta = 25°$. h is the length of the opposite side. So use the trigonometric formula: $\tan \theta = \dfrac{\text{opposite}}{\text{adjacent}}$

$\tan 25° = \dfrac{h}{10} \Rightarrow h = 10 \tan 25° = 4{\cdot}66307 \simeq 4{\cdot}66$ m

(c) The total height of the tree,

H = Seán's measurement + Seán's height

$H = 4{\cdot}66 + 1{\cdot}75 = 6{\cdot}41$ m

(d) Another student might have used a different angle, for example of 24° or 26°.

Application questions

Example

A tree 32 m high casts a shadow 63 m long. Calculate θ, the angle of elevation of the sun. Give your answer in degrees and minutes (correct to the nearest minute).

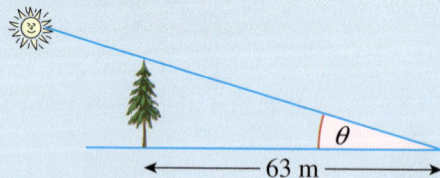

θ

63 m

(SEC 2013)

Solution

We know that opposite length = height of the tree = 32 m and adjacent length = 63 m.

We want to find the angle θ.

Use the trigonometric formula: $\tan \theta = \dfrac{\text{opposite}}{\text{adjacent}}$.

$\tan \theta = \dfrac{32}{63} \Rightarrow \theta = \tan^{-1}\left(\dfrac{32}{63}\right)$

To find the inverse function of tangent, press [shift], [tan] and the value.

$\Rightarrow \theta = 26 \cdot 92767785°$

To convert to DMS form press the ⌐°,,, button.

$\theta = 26°\ 55'\ 39\cdot64''$, pronounced 26 degrees, 55 minutes, and 39·64 seconds.

Example

The angle of elevation of the top of a
building, as viewed from a point a, 81 m
from the base of the building, is 27°.

(a) Find the height of the building correct to
the nearest metre.

The bottom of a balloon is 62 m above the top
of the building, as shown.

(b) Find the angle of elevation of the
bottom of the balloon as viewed from the point a.
Give your answer correct to the nearest degree.

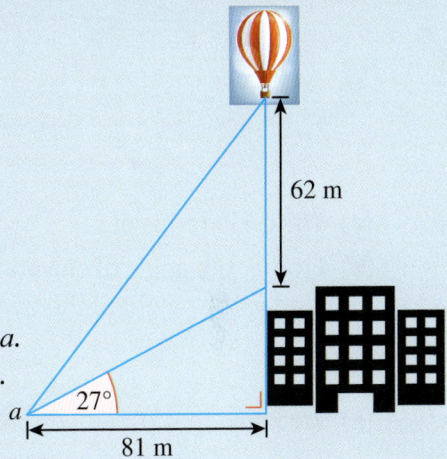

62 m

27°

a

81 m

(SEC 2009)

Solution

(a) We know that adjacent side = 81 m and $\theta = 27°$.

Let h = height of the building = opposite side.

Use the trigonometric formula: $\tan\theta = \dfrac{\text{opposite}}{\text{adjacent}}$.

$\tan 27° = \dfrac{\text{opposite}}{\text{adjacent}} = \dfrac{h}{81} \Rightarrow \tan 27° = \dfrac{h}{81}$

$\Rightarrow h = 81 \tan 27°$

$\Rightarrow h = 41\cdot27156141 = 41$ m, correct to the nearest metre.

(b) The distance from the base of the building to the bottom of the balloon is
the opposite side = 62 + 41 = 103 m and adjacent side = 81 m.

Let the angle of elevation be θ.

Use the trigonometric formula: $\tan\theta = \dfrac{\text{opposite}}{\text{adjacent}}$.

$\tan\theta = \dfrac{103}{81}$

$\Rightarrow \theta = \tan^{-1}\left(\dfrac{103}{81}\right) = 51\cdot81824157° = 52°$, correct to the nearest degree.

Example

Two vertical poles A and B, each of height h, are standing on opposite sides of a level road. They are 24 m apart. The point P, on the road directly between the two poles, is a distance x from pole A. The angle of elevation from P to the top of pole A is 60°.

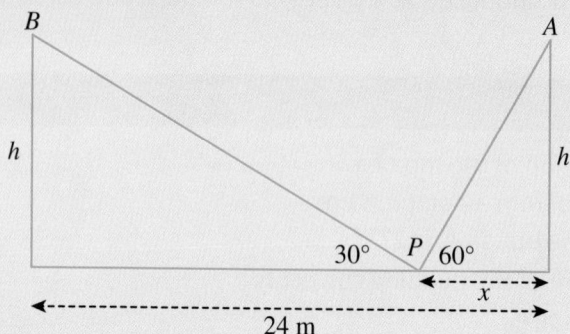

(a) Write h in terms of x.

(b) From P the angle of elevation to the top of pole B is 30°.
Find h, the height of the two poles.

(SEC 2012)

Solution

(a) We know that $\theta = 60°$, opposite $= h$ and adjacent $= x$ m.

Also, we know that $\theta = 30°$, opposite $= h$ and adjacent $= 24 - x$ m.

Right side triangle	Left side triangle
$\tan 60° = \dfrac{h}{x}$	$\tan 30° = \dfrac{h}{24 - x}$
$\Rightarrow \sqrt{3} = \dfrac{h}{x}$	$\Rightarrow \dfrac{1}{\sqrt{3}} = \dfrac{h}{24 - x}$
$\Rightarrow h = \sqrt{3}x$	$\Rightarrow h = \dfrac{24 - x}{\sqrt{3}}$

(b) Since the height h is the same for both poles:

$$\sqrt{3}x = \frac{24 - x}{\sqrt{3}}$$

$$\Rightarrow \sqrt{3} \cdot \sqrt{3}x = 24 - x$$

$$\Rightarrow 3x = 24 - x$$

$$\Rightarrow 4x = 24$$

$$\Rightarrow x = 6$$

Then substitute this value for x in either equation for h.

$$\Rightarrow h = 6\sqrt{3} \approx 10{\cdot}39 \text{ m}$$

Two height of the two poles is 10·39 m

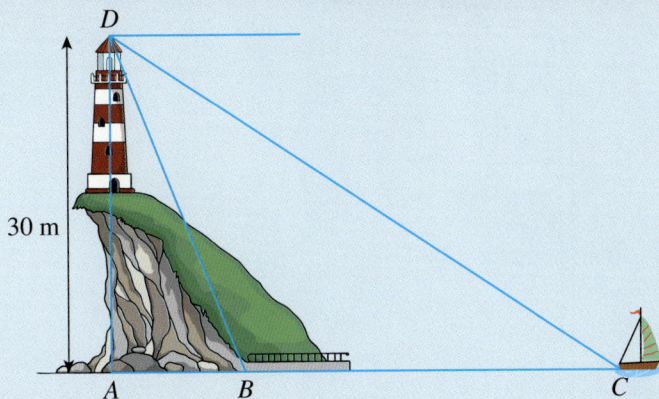

A boat sails due east from the base A of a 30 m high lighthouse, $[AD]$. At the point B the angle of depression of the boat from the top of the lighthouse is 68°. Ten seconds later the boat is at the point C and the angle of depression is now 33°.

(a) Find $|BC|$, the distance the boat has travelled in this time, correct to two decimal places.

(b) Calculate the average speed at which the boat is sailing between B and C. Give your answer in metres per second, correct to one decimal place.

(SEC 2011)

Solution

(a) At point B, the angle of depression of the boat from the top of the lighthouse is 68°, so $\theta = 68°$ from alternate angles.

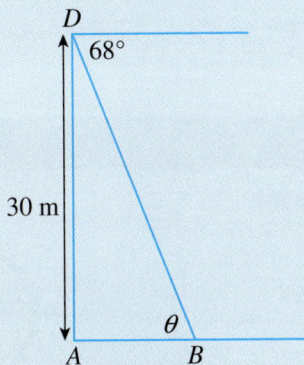

We know that opposite side = 30 m and $\theta = 68°$.

We want to find the adjacent length $|AB|$.

Use the trigonometric formula $\tan \theta = \dfrac{\text{opposite}}{\text{adjacent}}$.

$\tan 68° = \dfrac{30}{|AB|} \Rightarrow |AB| = \dfrac{30}{\tan 68°} = 12{\cdot}12078\ldots$

$\Rightarrow |AB| = 12{\cdot}12$ m, correct to 2 d.p.

At point C, the angle of depression of the boat from the top of the lighthouse is 33°, so $\theta = 33°$ from alternate angles.

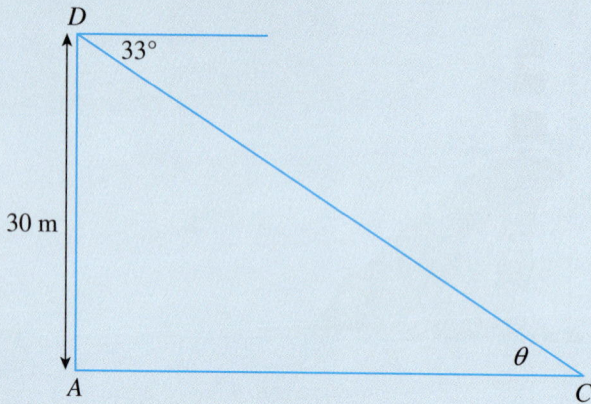

We know that:

Opposite side = 30 m and $\theta = 33°$.

We want to find the adjacent length $|AC|$.

Use the trigonometric formula: $\tan \theta = \dfrac{\text{opposite}}{\text{adjacent}}$

$\Rightarrow \tan 33° = \dfrac{30}{|AC|} \Rightarrow |AC| = \dfrac{30}{\tan 33°} = 46.19594...$

$\Rightarrow |AC| = 46.2$ m, correct to 1 d.p.

Hence, the distance the boat has sailed from point B to point C is:

$|BC| = |AC| - |AB| = 46.2 - 12.12 = 34.08$ m, correct to 2 d.p.

(b) Average speed $= \dfrac{\text{distance}}{\text{time}} = \dfrac{34.1}{10} = 3.41 = 3.4$ m/s, correct to 1 d.p.

> **Key-note**
>
> The formula is:
>
> $\text{Speed} = \dfrac{\text{distance}}{\text{time}}$

Example

A boat travels due north from A for 30 minutes at 20 km/h.

It reaches B and then travels due east for 24 minutes at 10 km/h.

It is then at C.

(a) How many kilometres has the boat travelled?

(b) On the diagram, draw a line segment that shows the shortest distance from C back to A.

(c) Find the shortest distance $|AC|$, correct to the nearest metre.

olution

a) First find the distance from A to B.

We know:

Speed = 20 km/h

Time = 30 minutes = $\dfrac{30}{60}$ = 0·5 hr

Distance = Speed × Time

Therefore $|AB|$ = 20 × 0·5 = 10 km

Next find the distance from B to C.

We know:

Speed = 10 km/h

Time = 24 minutes = $\dfrac{24}{60}$ = 0·4 hr

Distance = Speed × Time

Therefore $|BC|$ = 10 × 0·4 = 4 km

Total distance travelled = $|AB| + |BC|$ = 10 + 4 = 14 km

b)

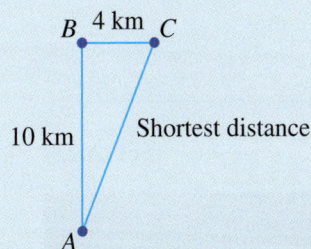

(c) To find the shortest distance $|AC|$ use Pythagoras' Theorem, given in the *Formulae and Tables* booklet as $c^2 = a^2 + b^2$.

$c^2 = 10^2 + 4^2 = 100 + 16$

$\Rightarrow c = \sqrt{116} = 10·77032961$ km

To change km to m, multiply by 1000.

The shortest distance $|AC|$ = 10 770 m, correct to the nearest metre.

Key note

Use the formula:

Distance = Speed × Time

Exercise

Q1 A sailing boat is taking part in a race. During the race, the boat sails towards a lighthouse which stands on a vertical cliff face. The top of the lighthouse is 214 m above sea level. At point A, the angle of elevation from the top of the lighthouse to the boat is 16°. When the boat reaches point B the angle of elevation from the lighthouse to the boat is 28°. Calculate $|AB|$, the distance the boat has sailed towards the cliff. Give your answer correct to the nearest metre.

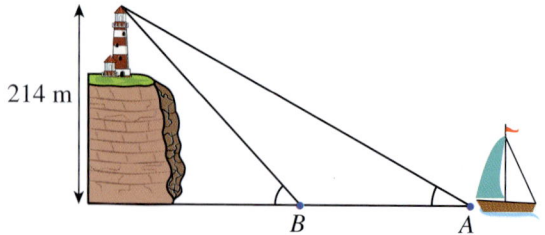

214 m

B   *A*

(SEC 2013)

Q2 A homeowner wishes to replace the three identical steps leading to her front door with a ramp. Each step is 10 cm high and 35 cm long. Find the length of the ramp. Give your answer correct to one decimal place.

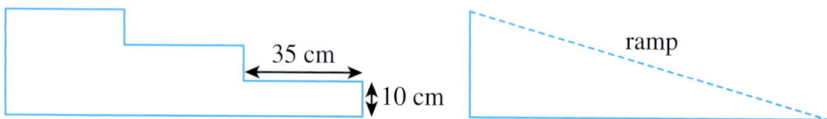

35 cm

10 cm

ramp

(SEC 2012)

Q3 A group of students wish to calculate the height of the Millennium Spire in Dublin. The spire stands on flat level ground. Maria, who is 1·72 m tall, looks up at the top of the spire using a clinometer and records an angle of elevation of 60°. Her feet are 70 m from the base of the spire. Ultan measures the circumference of the base of the spire as 7·07 m.

(a) Explain how Ultan's measurement will be used in the calculation of the height of the spire.

(b) Draw a suitable diagram and calculate the height of the spire, to the nearest metre, using the measurements obtained by the students.

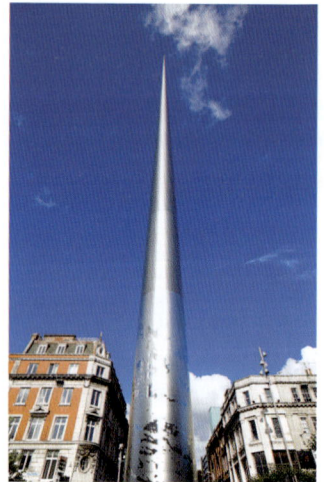

(SEC 2011)

Q4 A builder wants to construct a roof with a pitch of 30°. The height of the apex above the ceiling level is 2 m, as shown in the diagram.

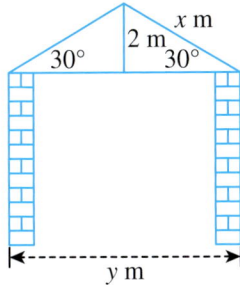

(a) Calculate x, the length of the rafter.

(b) Calculate y, the length of the ceiling joist, correct to two decimal places.

(SEC 2010)

Q5 The diagram shows an equilateral triangle and the incircle of the triangle with centre o.

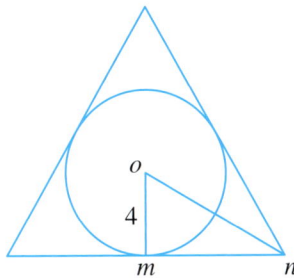

(a) Given that $|om| = 4$, find $|mn|$, giving your answer in surd form.

(b) Find $|on|$.

(c) Write down the height of the equilateral triangle.

(d) Calculate the area of the equilateral triangle, giving your answer in surd form.

(SEC 2008)

Q6 In the diagram shown, *abcd* represents the course in a triathlon.

Competitors must swim the 9 km from *a* to *b*, then run the 12 km from *b* to *c* and cycle from *c* to *d* and back to *a*.

$|\angle adc| = 36\cdot87°$

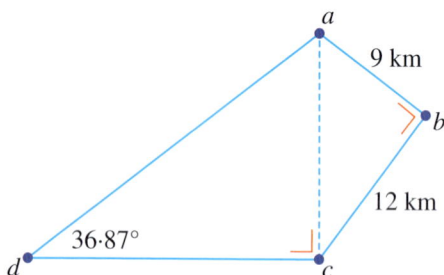

(a) Find the distance from *a* to *c*.

(b) Find the distance from *c* to *d*, correct to the nearest km.

(c) Find the total length of the course.

(SEC 2007)

Q7 Some students wish to estimate the height of a tree standing on level ground. One of them stands so that the end of his shadow coincides with the end of the shadow of the tree, as shown in the diagram. This student is 1·6 m tall. His friend then measures the distances shown in the diagram. *A* is the angle of elevation of the sun.

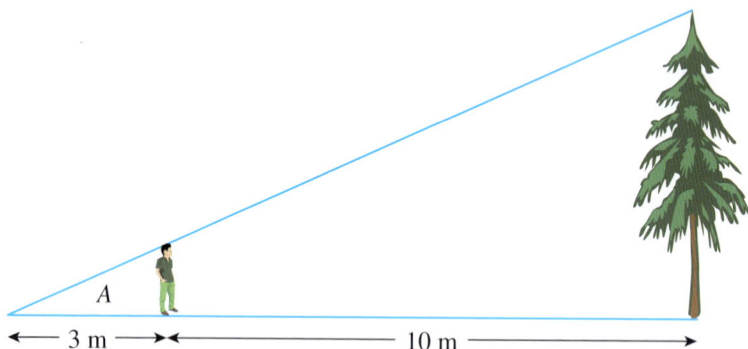

(a) Find *A*, correct to the nearest degree.

(b) Find the height of the tree correct to one decimal place.

(SEC 2005)

Solutions

Q1 First find the distance from the boat at point A to the cliff.

Label triangle A as shown.

Opposite side = 214 m and $\theta = 16°$.

Required: the adjacent length x.

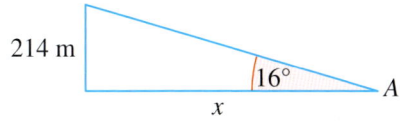

Use the trigonometric formula: $\tan \theta = \dfrac{\text{opposite}}{\text{adjacent}}$.

$\tan 16° = \dfrac{214}{x} \Rightarrow x = \dfrac{214}{\tan 16°} = 746{\cdot}306691$

$\Rightarrow x = 746{\cdot}31$ m

Then find how far it is from the boat at point B to the cliff.

Label triangle B as shown:

Opposite side = 214 m and $\theta = 28°$.

Required: the adjacent length y.

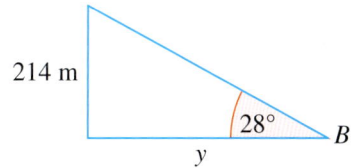

Use the trigonometric formula: $\tan \theta = \dfrac{\text{opposite}}{\text{adjacent}}$.

$\tan 28° = \dfrac{214}{y} \Rightarrow y = \dfrac{214}{\tan 28°} = 402{\cdot}475...$

$\Rightarrow y = 402{\cdot}48$ m

Hence, the distance the boat has sailed towards the cliff is:

$|AB| = x - y = 746{\cdot}31 - 402{\cdot}48 = 343{\cdot}83$ m = 344 m to the nearest metre.

Q2 The three steps are 10 cm high and 35 cm long. So the total height is 30 cm and the total length is 105 cm.

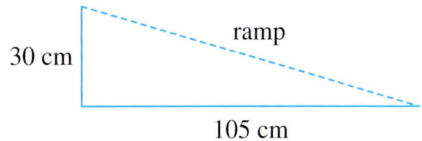

Use Pythagoras' Theorem to find the hypotenuse side.

$\text{hypotenuse}^2 = 30^2 + 105^2$

$= \sqrt{900 + 11\,025}$

$= \sqrt{11\,925}$

$= 109{\cdot}2$ cm, correct to one decimal place.

The ramp must have a length of 109·2 cm, correct to one decimal place.

Q3 (a) Ultan's measurement of the circumference of the base of the spire can be used in the calculation of the height of the spire, as the circumference can be used to calculate the radius, which will give the full distance that Maria is from the centre of the base of the spire.

$$2\pi r = 7{\cdot}07 \Rightarrow r = \frac{7{\cdot}07}{2\pi} = 1{\cdot}125 \text{ m}$$

(b) Using the diagram:

$$\tan 60° = \frac{x}{71{\cdot}13}$$

$$\Rightarrow x = 71{\cdot}13 \times (\tan 60°)$$

$$\Rightarrow x = 123{\cdot}2$$

$\therefore$ Height of the spire= 123·2 + 1·72
= 124·92 = 125 m

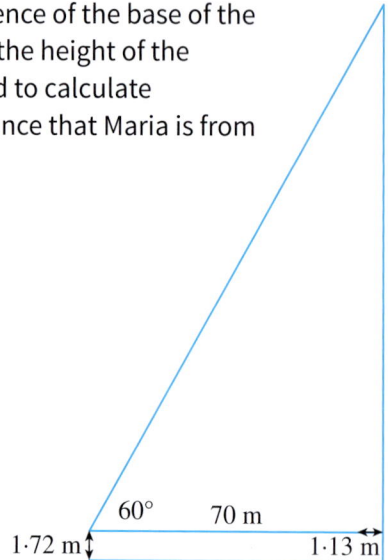

Q4 (a) $\theta = 30°$, opposite = 2 m
and hypotenuse = x m.

$$\sin 30° = \frac{\text{opposite}}{\text{hypotenuse}} = \frac{2}{x} \Rightarrow \frac{1}{2} = \frac{2}{x} \Rightarrow x = 4 \text{ m}$$

(b) $\theta = 30°$, opposite = 2 m and adjacent = $\frac{y}{2}$ m.

$$\tan 30° = \frac{\text{opposite}}{\text{adjacent}} = \frac{2}{\left(\dfrac{y}{2}\right)} \Rightarrow y = 4\sqrt{3} = 6{\cdot}928... = 6{\cdot}93 \text{ m}$$

The length of the ceiling joist, correct to two decimal places is 6·93 m.

Q5 (a) As this is an equilateral triangle, each angle is 60°.

$\theta = 30°$ and opposite = $|om| = 4$.

Required: the adjacent = $|mn|$

$$\tan 30° = \frac{\text{opposite}}{\text{adjacent}} = \frac{|om|}{|mn|} = \frac{4}{|mn|} \Rightarrow \frac{1}{\sqrt{3}} = \frac{4}{|mn|} \Rightarrow |mn| = 4\sqrt{3}$$

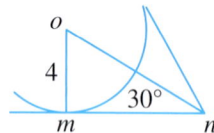

(b) Use Pythagoras' Theorem to find the hypotenuse side $|on|$:

$$\text{hypotenuse}^2 = 4^2 + \left(4\sqrt{3}\right)^2 \Rightarrow |on| = \sqrt{16 + 48} \Rightarrow |on| = \sqrt{64} \Rightarrow |on| = 8$$

(c) The height of the equilateral triangle = $|on| + |om| = 8 + 4 = 12$.

(d) Total area = 6(area of the triangle $\triangle mon$)

$$= 6 \times \frac{1}{2} \times \text{base} \times \text{perpendicular height}$$

Area of the equilateral triangle = $6 \times \dfrac{1}{2} \times 4\sqrt{3} \times 4 = 48\sqrt{3}$ units^2

Q6 (a) Use Pythagoras' Theorem to find the distance from a to c.

$$\text{hypotenuse}^2 = 12^2 + 9^2$$

$$\Rightarrow |ac| = \sqrt{144 + 81}$$

$$\Rightarrow |ac| = \sqrt{225}$$

$$\therefore |ac| = 15 \text{ km}$$

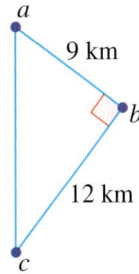

(b) $\theta = 36{\cdot}87°$ and opposite = 15 km.

Required: the adjacent = $|cd|$

$$\tan 36{\cdot}87° = \frac{\text{opposite}}{\text{adjacent}} = \frac{15}{|cd|}$$

$$\Rightarrow |cd| = \frac{15}{\tan 36{\cdot}87°}$$

$$\Rightarrow |cd| = 19{\cdot}999... = 20 \text{ km}$$

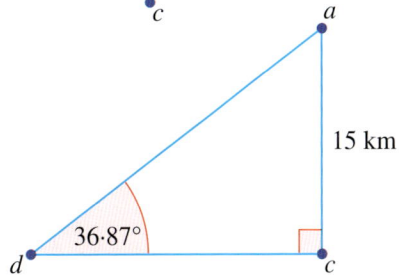

(c) Use Pythagoras' Theorem to find the distance $|ad|$.

$$|ad|^2 = 20^2 + 15^2 = 400 + 225 = 625$$

$$\Rightarrow |ad| = \sqrt{625} = 25 \text{ km}$$

Therefore total length of the course = $|ab| + |bc| + |cd| + |da|$
$= 9 + 12 + 20 + 25 = 66$ km

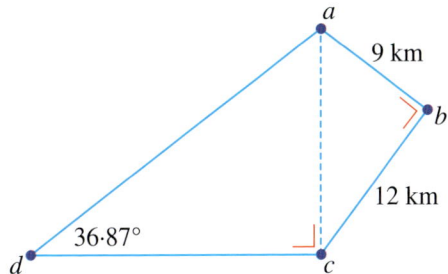

Q7 This student is 1·6 m tall.

(a) Opposite = 1·6 m and adjacent = 3 m.

Required: angle A

$$\tan A = \frac{\text{opposite}}{\text{adjacent}} = \frac{1{\cdot}6}{3} = 0{\cdot}533... \Rightarrow A = \sin^{-1}(0{\cdot}5333) = 28{\cdot}07° = 28°$$

(b) $A = 28°$ and adjacent = 13 m.

Required: opposite = h

$$\tan A = \frac{\text{opposite}}{\text{adjacent}} \Rightarrow \tan 28° = \frac{h}{13} \Rightarrow h = 13 \tan 28° = 6{\cdot}9329 = 6{\cdot}9 \text{ m}$$

The height of the tree, correct to one decimal place is 6·9 m.

13 Applied Measure

Learning objectives

In this chapter you will learn about:

- 2D Shapes: Perimeter and area
- 3D Shapes: Nets, volume and surface area
- Problems involving:
  - Combined 3D shapes
  - Displacement of liquid
  - Recasting
  - Flow of liquid.

2D Shapes: Perimeter and area

Shape	Diagram	Formula
Square	x above, x on each side, x below (square)	Perimeter: sum of all sides Perimeter $= x + x + x + x = 4x$ Area: length × breadth (or width) Area $= x \times x = x^2$ *Not in the *Formulae and Tables* booklet
Rectangle	y above, x on each side, y below (rectangle)	Perimeter: sum of all sides Perimeter $= x + y + x + y = 2x + 2y$ Area: length × breadth Area $= x \times y = xy$ *Not in the *Formulae and Tables* booklet

Shape	Diagram	Formula
Triangle		Perimeter: sum of all sides Perimeter $= a + b + c$ Area: Half the base by $\perp$ (perpendicular) height Area $= \dfrac{1}{2}bh$ *In the *Formulae and Tables* booklet
Parallelogram		Perimeter: sum of all sides Perimeter $= 2a + 2b$ Area: base by $\perp$ height Area $= bh$ *In the *Formulae and Tables* booklet
Circle (disc)		Circumference: the perimeter of a circle. Perimeter $= 2\pi r$ Area: the enclosed space inside a circle. Area $= \pi r^2$ *In the *Formulae and Tables* booklet

Points to note

Units of measurement

Length	Area
1 cm = 10 mm 1 m = 100 cm 1 km = 1000 m	$1 \text{ cm}^2 = 10 \text{ mm} \times 10 \text{ mm} = 100 \text{ mm}^2$ $1 \text{ m}^2 = 100 \text{ cm} \times 100 \text{ cm} = 10\,000 \text{ cm}^2$

Volume	Capacity
$1 \text{ cm}^3 = 10 \text{ mm} \times 10 \text{ mm} \times 10 \text{ mm} = 1000 \text{ mm}^3$ $1 \text{ m}^3 = 100 \text{ cm} \times 100 \text{ cm} \times 100 \text{ cm} = 1\,000\,000 \text{ cm}^3$	Capacity (Volume) of a 3D shape is the measure of the amount liquid which the 3D shape can carry. 1 litre = 1000 cm^3

Always remember to read the question carefully to ensure you are working in the correct units.

Example

The perimeter of a rectangular field is 280 m.
The length of the longer side is 100 m. Find:
 (a) the length of the shorter side; and
 (b) the area of the field.

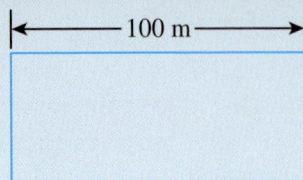

Solution

 (a) Let the shorter side $= x$. Then:

$x + 100 + x + 100 = 280$

$2x + 200 = 280 \Rightarrow 2x = 280 - 200 \Rightarrow 2x = 80$

$\dfrac{2x}{2} = \dfrac{80}{2} \Rightarrow x = 40$ m

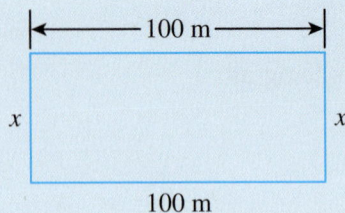

 (b) Area = length × breath = $100 \times 40 = 4000$ m^2

Example

Calculate the area of the figure in the diagram.

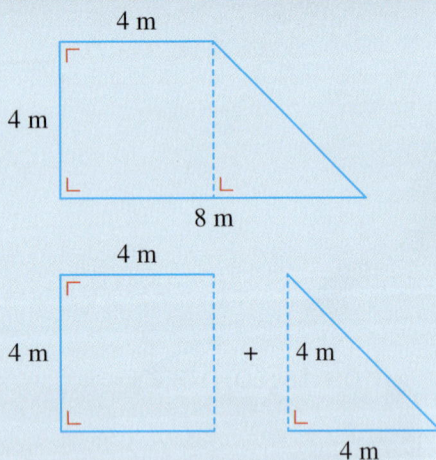

Solution

Always break up the given combined shaped
into standard shapes.
Area of square + Area of triangle

$= \text{side}^2 + \dfrac{1}{2}(\text{breadth} \times \text{height})$

$= (4)^2 + \dfrac{1}{2}(4)(4) = 16 + 8 = 24$ m^2

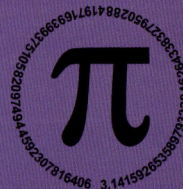

Points to note

- Pi represents the ratio of any circle's circumference to its diameter.
- $\text{Pi}(\pi) = \dfrac{\text{circumference}}{\text{diameter}} = 3 \cdot 14159\ldots$
- There is no repeatable pattern in the digits of Pi.
 Mathematicians have calculated Pi to billions of
 digits, and have never found any pattern to the digits.

- We generally take $\text{Pi}(\pi) = 3 \cdot 14$ or $\dfrac{22}{7}$ or use the π button on the calculator.

- If you are asked to leave your answer in terms of π, then do not substitute
 in for π. Leave your answer with π in it.

Example

A plastic disc has a diameter of 15 cm. A smaller disc of
radius 3·5 cm is removed from the larger disc as shown.
Find the area of the remaining plastic, correct to two
decimal places. Take $\pi = 3.14$.

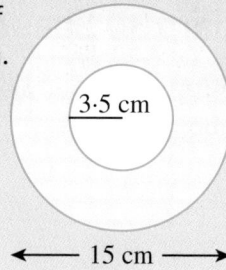

Solution

First find the area of the original disc of plastic.

$\text{Area} = \pi r^2 = 3.14 \left(\dfrac{15}{2}\right)^2 = 176.625 \text{ cm}^2$

Then find the area of the disc of plastic removed.

$\text{Area} = \pi r^2 = 3.14(3.5)^2 = 38.465 \text{ cm}^2$

So the remaining area of plastic =
area of large disc − area of small disc

$= 176.625 - 38.465 = 138.16 \text{ cm}^2$

$= 138.16 \text{ cm}^2$ to 2 d.p.

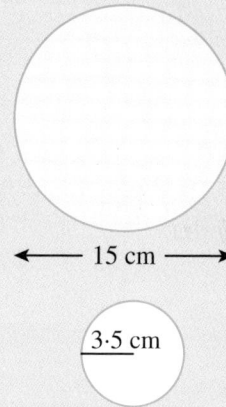

Example

A rectangular piece of metal has a width of
16π cm. Two circular pieces, each of radius 7 cm,
are cut from the rectangular piece, as shown.

(a) Find the length, l, of the rectangular
piece of metal.

(b) Calculate the area of the metal remaining
(i.e. the shaded section), giving your answer in terms of π.

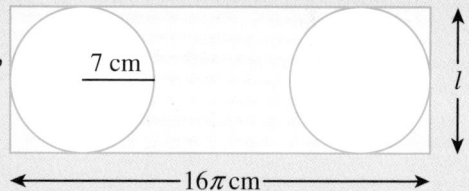

(SEC 2007)

Solution

(a) From the diagram we can see that l = diameter of each circle.

$\therefore l = 2(7) = 14$ cm

(b) Area of the rectangle $= 16\pi \times 14 = 224\pi \text{ cm}^2$

Area of the two circles $= 2\pi r^2 = 2\pi(7)^2 = 98\pi \text{ cm}^2$

Therefore, the area of the remaining metal $= 224\pi - 98\pi = 126\pi \text{ cm}^2$

3D Shapes: Volume and surface area

Standard 3D Shapes

Shape	Diagram	Formula
Cube		Volume: $x \times x \times x = x^3$ Surface area: $6x^2$ *Not in the *Formulae and Tables* booklet
Cuboid		Volume: $l \times w \times h$ Surface area: $2(l \times w) + 2(w \times h) + 2(l \times h)$ *Not in the *Formulae and Tables* booklet
Cylinder		Volume: $\pi r^2 h$ Curved surface area: $2\pi rh$ Total surface area: $2\pi rh + 2\pi r^2$ *In the *Formulae and Tables* booklet
Sphere		Volume: $\frac{4}{3}\pi r^3$ Surface area: $4\pi r^2$ *In the *Formulae and Tables* booklet
Hemisphere		Volume: $\frac{2}{3}\pi r^3$ Curved surface area: $2\pi r^2$ Total surface area: $3\pi r^2$ *Not in the *Formulae and Tables* booklet
Cone		Volume: $\frac{1}{3}\pi r^2 h$ Curved surface area: πlr *In the *Formulae and Tables* booklet

In general when solving questions based on volume and surface area we can follow these steps:

1 State the relevant formula.

2 Substitute the known variables.

3 Solve for the required value.

Example

A rectangular solid is shown.

(a) Find the volume of the rectangular solid.

(b) Find the total surface area of the rectangular solid.

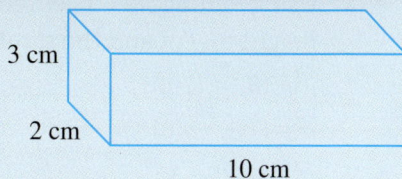

3 cm

2 cm

10 cm

Solution

(a) Volume: $l \times w \times h$ ... state the relevant formula

    $= 10 \times 2 \times 3$ ... substitute the known variables

    $= 60 \text{ cm}^3$ ... solve for the required value

(b) Surface area: $2(l \times w) + 2(w \times h) + 2(l \times h)$ ... state the relevant formula

    $= 2(10 \times 2) + 2(2 \times 3) + 2(10 \times 3)$ ... substitute the known variables

    $= 40 + 12 + 60 = 112 \text{ cm}^2$ ... solve for the required value

Example

Find the volume and total surface area of a cylinder of radius 7 cm and height 10 cm. Take $\pi = 3{\cdot}14$, and give your answer correct to two decimal places.

Solution

Volume of a cylinder: $\pi r^2 h$ ... state the relevant formula

$= (3{\cdot}14)(7)^2(10)$ ... substitute the known variables

$= 1538{\cdot}6 \text{ cm}^3$ ... solve for the required value

Total surface area: $2\pi rh + 2\pi r^2$ ... state the relevant formula

$= 2(3{\cdot}14)(7)(10) + 2(3{\cdot}14)(7)^2$ ... substitute the known variables

$= 439{\cdot}6 + 307{\cdot}72 = 747{\cdot}32 \text{ cm}^2$ ... solve for the required value

Example

A solid cone has a vertical height of 6 cm. The slant height is 7·5 cm.

(a) Find the radius of its base, correct to one decimal place.

(b) Find the total surface area in cm².

Give your answer correct to three significant figures. Let $\pi = 3\cdot14$

(SEC 2004)

Solution

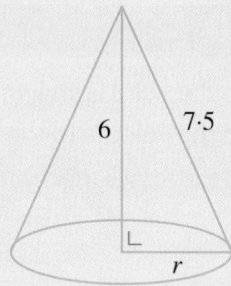

(a) Using Pythagoras' Theorem: since the vertical height = 6 cm and the slant height = 7·5 cm, then:

$r^2 + (6)^2 = (7\cdot5)^2$

$r^2 = (7\cdot5)^2 - (6)^2$

$r^2 = 56\cdot25 - 36$

$r^2 = 20\cdot25$

$r = \sqrt{20\cdot25} = 4\cdot5$ cm.

(b) Total surface area = $\pi r l + \pi r^2$ ... state the relevant formula

$= (3\cdot14)(4\cdot5)(7\cdot5) + (3\cdot14)(4\cdot5)^2$ ... substitute the known variables

$= 105\cdot975 + 63\cdot585$ ... solve for the required value

$= 169\cdot56$ cm² $= 170$ cm², correct to 3 s.f.

Example

Find **(a)** the volume and **(b)** the surface area of the given sphere; leave your answers in terms of π.

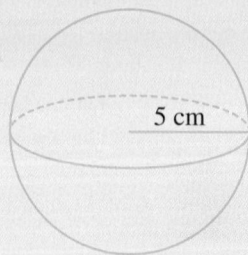

5 cm

Solution

(a) Volume $= \frac{4}{3}\pi r^3$ ... state the relevant formula

$= \frac{4}{3}\pi(5)^3$ ... substitute the known variable

$= \frac{4}{3}\pi(125) = \frac{500}{3}\pi = 166\cdot67\pi$ cm³ ... solve for the required value

(b) Surface area $= 4\pi r^2$ ... state the relevant formula

$= 4\pi(5)^2$ ... substitute the known variable

$= 4\pi(25) = 100\pi$ cm² ... solve for the required value

Prisms

A prism is any 3D object with the following properties:

- Opposite ends are identical.

- All sides or faces are flat.

- It has the same cross-sectional area along its entire length.

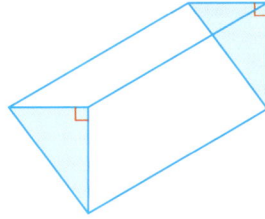

Points to note

Cross-section of a prism

If you cut through a prism along its length or depth, the 2D shape that you form is called the cross-section.

The area of this shape is called the cross-sectional area of the prism.

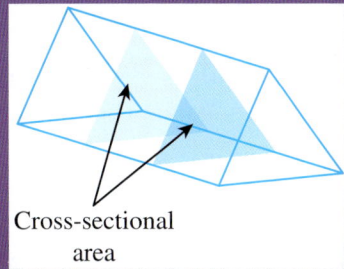

Cross-sectional area

Volume of a prism

The volume of any prism can be found by multiplying the cross-sectional area by the length or depth of the prism.

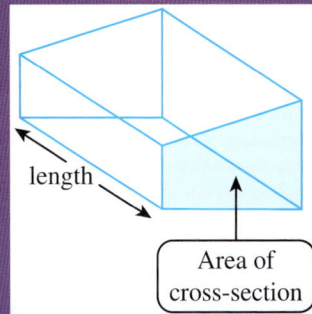

length

Area of cross-section

Total surface area of a prism

The total surface area of any prism is equal to the sum of the areas of each side.

Example

(a) Draw a sketch of the cross-section of the given prism and find its cross-sectional area.

(b) Hence, find the volume of the prism.

(c) Find the total surface area of the prism.

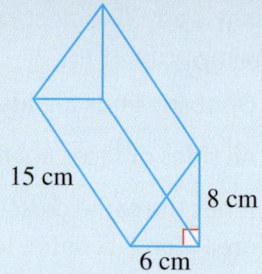

15 cm   8 cm   6 cm

Solution

(a) Cross-section of the prism:

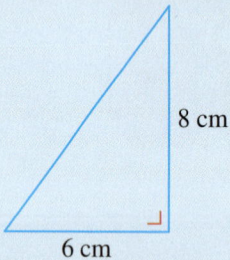

8 cm

6 cm

Cross-sectional area of the prism

= area of the triangle

= half the base times ⊥ height

$= \frac{1}{2}bh$

$= \frac{1}{2}(8)(6) = 24$ cm^2

(b) Volume of the prism = cross-sectional area times length = 24 × 15 = 360 cm^3

(c) The total surface area of any prism is equal to the sum of the areas of each side.

Using Pythagoras' Theorem to find the third side of the cross-section

$a^2 + b^2 = c^2$

$(8)^2 + (6)^2 = x^2$

$100 = x^2$

$\sqrt{100} = x = 10$ cm

So the total surface area is made up as shown in the diagram below.

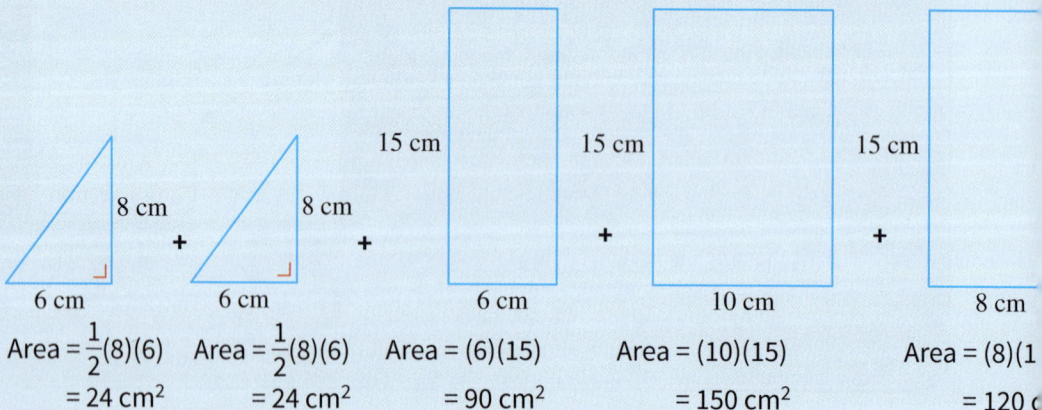

8 cm   8 cm   15 cm   15 cm   15 cm

6 cm   6 cm   6 cm   10 cm   8 cm

+   +   +   +

Area $= \frac{1}{2}(8)(6)$ Area $= \frac{1}{2}(8)(6)$ Area $= (6)(15)$ Area $= (10)(15)$ Area $= (8)(1$

= 24 cm^2 = 24 cm^2 = 90 cm^2 = 150 cm^2 = 120 c

Total surface area of the prism

= 24 cm^2 + 24 cm^2 + 90 cm^2 + 150 cm^2 + 120 cm^2 = 408 cm^2

Nets of 3D shapes

A net of a 3D shape is a 2D representation of the 3D shape. The 2D net can be folded up to form the 3D shape. There may be several possible nets for one 3D shape.

The following are some examples of nets of standard 3D shapes.

Shape	Diagram	Sample net
Cube		
Cuboid		
Cylinder		
Cone		

Shape	Diagram	Sample net
Triangular-based prism (right–angled)		
Triangular-based prism (isosceles)		
Equilateral triangular-based prism		

Example

Identify which of the following nets will form a cube.

A

B

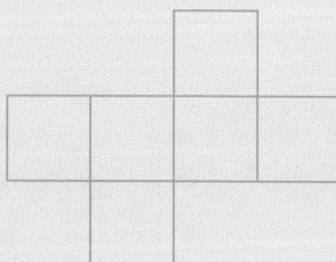

C

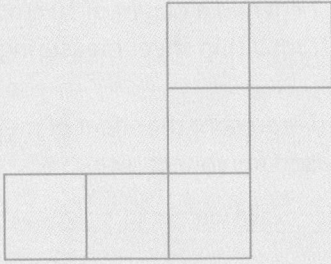

D

Solution

A

This is not a net of a cube as the two highlighted squares will overlap.

B

This is a net of a cube.

C

This is not a net of a cube as the two highlighted squares will overlap.

D

This is not a net of a cube as the two highlighted squares will overlap.

A soup tin in the form of a cylinder has a diameter of 7 cm and a height of 10 cm. The cylinder is constructed from pieces of metal cut from a thin sheet measuring 23 cm by 18 cm.

(a) Which one of the four diagrams A, B, C or D could represent the sheet of metal from which the cylinder has been cut? Give a reason for your choice.

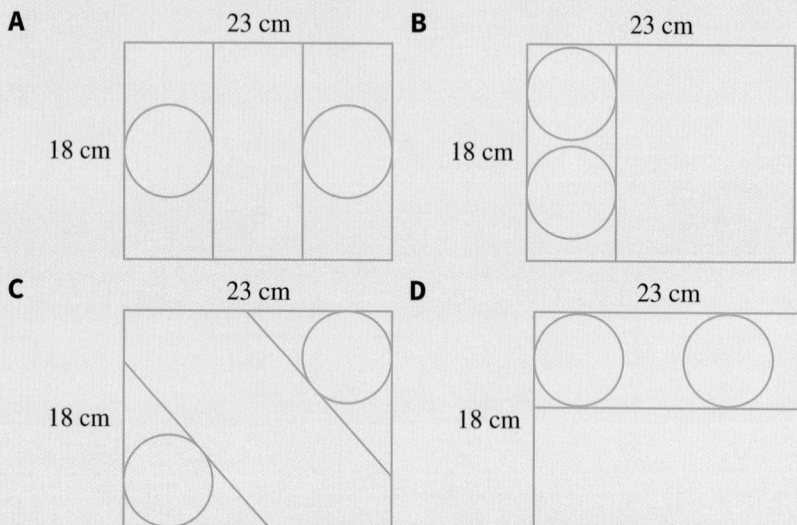

A
23 cm
18 cm

B
23 cm
18 cm

C
23 cm
18 cm

D
23 cm
18 cm

(b) Find the area of metal which remains after the pieces have been cut out.

(c) Find the capacity of the soup tin.

(SEC 2012)

Solution

(a) To construct the cylinder we need two circles of radius 3·5 cm and a rectangular piece $2\pi r \times h$ where h, height, is 10 cm.

$2\pi r = 2\pi(3\cdot5) = 7\pi = 21\cdot991 \simeq 22$ cm

Hence a rectangular piece 22 cm × 10 cm is required to make this cylinder, and only D has this.

(b) Area of the sheet of metal = 18 × 23 = 414 cm^2

Total surface area of the cylinder $= 2\pi rh + 2\pi r^2$ ... state the relevant formula

$= 2(3\cdot14)(3\cdot5)(10) + 2(3\cdot14)(3\cdot5)^2$ ... substitute the known variables

$= 219\cdot8 + 76\cdot93 = 296\cdot73$ cm^2 ... solve for the required value

Hence the metal remaining = 414 cm^2 − 296·73 cm^2 = 117·27 cm^2

(c) Volume of a cylinder: $\pi r^2 h$ ... state the relevant formula

$= (3\cdot14)(3\cdot5)^2(10)$ ... substitute the known variables

$= 384\cdot65$ cm^3 ... solve for the required value

(a) Draw a sketch of the net for the given prism, labelling all dimensions.

(b) Hence or otherwise find the total surface area of the prism. Give your answer correct to 2 decimal places.

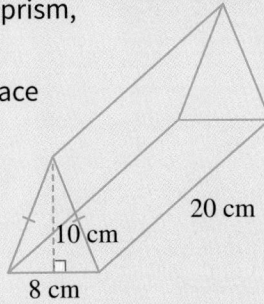

20 cm

10 cm

8 cm

Solution

(a) Net of the prism

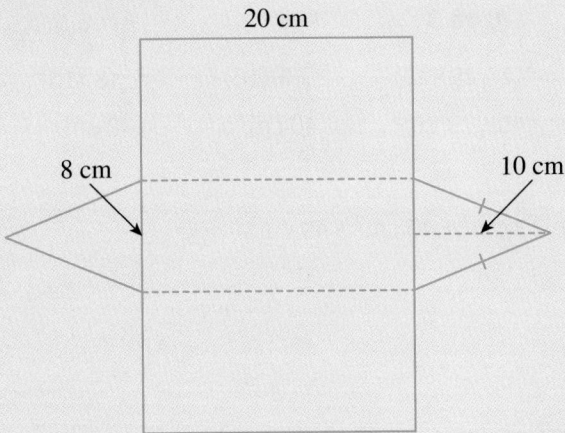

20 cm

8 cm

10 cm

(b) The total surface area of any prism is equal to the sum of the areas of each side. First use Pythagoras' Theorem to find the third side of the cross-section.

$$a^2 + b^2 = c^2$$
$$(4)^2 + (10)^2 = c^2$$
$$16 + 100 = c^2$$
$$\sqrt{116} = c = 2\sqrt{29} \text{ cm}$$

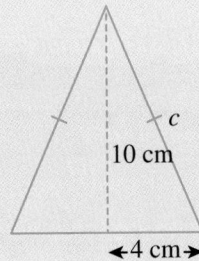

c

10 cm

4 cm

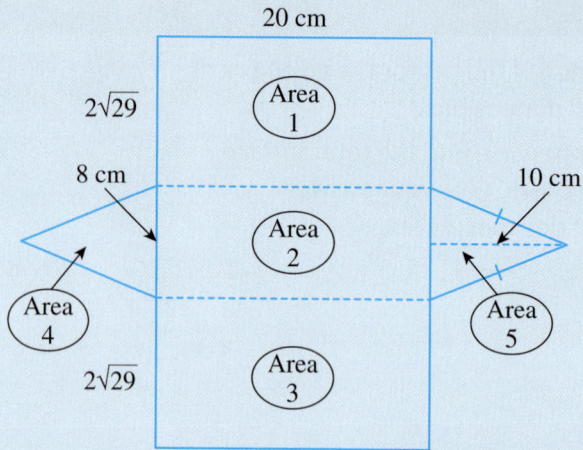

20 cm

$2\sqrt{29}$

Area 1

8 cm

Area 2

10 cm

Area 4

Area 5

$2\sqrt{29}$

Area 3

Area 1	Area 2	Area 3	Area 4	Area 5
$= (2\sqrt{29})(20)$	$= (8)(20)$	$= (2\sqrt{29})(20)$	$= \frac{1}{2}(8)(10)$	$= \frac{1}{2}(8)(10)$
$= 40\sqrt{29}$ cm²	$= 160$ cm²	$= 40\sqrt{29}$ cm²	$= 40$ cm²	$= 40$ cm²

Total surface area of the prism:

$= 40\sqrt{29}$ cm² $+ 160$ cm² $+ 40\sqrt{29}$ cm² $+ 40$ cm² $+ 40$ cm²

$= 670 \cdot 8131846$ cm²

$\approx 670 \cdot 81$ cm²

Solving for unknown measurements when given the volume or surface area of a shape

Points to note

In general when solving for unknown measurements when given the volume or surface area of a shape we follow these steps:

1 State the relevant formula and let it equal the given value.

2 Substitute the known variables.

3 Solve for the unknown value.

Problem solving – exponential functions

Example

The height of a cone is twice the radius. The volume of the cone is $\frac{16}{3}\pi\,cm^3$. Calculate the radius.

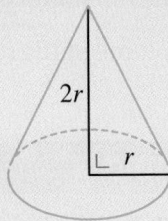

Solution

Volume of the cone

$\frac{1}{3}\pi r^2 h = \frac{16}{3}\pi$ ... state the relevant formula and let it equal $\frac{16}{3}\pi\ cm^3$

$\frac{1}{3}\pi r^2(2r) = \frac{16}{3}\pi$ ... substitute the known variables

$\frac{2}{3}\pi r^3 = \frac{16}{3}\pi$ ... solve for the unknown value

$\frac{2}{3}r^3 = \frac{16}{3}$ ... divide both sides by π

$2r^3 = 16$ ... multiply both sides by 3

$\Rightarrow r^3 = \frac{16}{2} = 8 \Rightarrow r = \sqrt[3]{8} = 2\ cm$

Example

The volume of a hemisphere is $486\pi\ cm^3$.

(a) Find the radius of the hemisphere.

(b) Find the volume of the smallest rectangular box that the hemisphere will fit into.

Solution

(a) Volume of a hemisphere $= \frac{2}{3}\pi r^3$

$\therefore \frac{2}{3}\pi r^3 = 486\pi$ ... state the relevant formula and let it equal $486\pi\ cm^3$

$\frac{2}{3}r^3 = 486$ ... solve for r

$r^3 = \left(\frac{3}{2}\right)486 = \left(\frac{1458}{2}\right) = 729$

$\Rightarrow r = \sqrt[3]{729} = 9\ cm$

(b) To find the smallest rectangular box needed:

- The minimum height of the box needs to be 9 cm.

- The minimum width and breadth each need to be 18 cm.

Volume of the rectangular box = (9)(18)(18) = 2916 cm³.

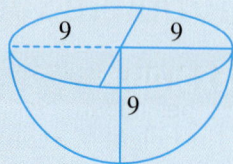

Example

A small sphere has a radius of 1·5 cm.

(a) Find the volume of the small sphere. Give your answer in cm³, in terms of π.

The volume of a large sphere is three times the volume of the small sphere.

(b) Find the radius of the large sphere. Give your answer in cm, in the form $\dfrac{a\sqrt[3]{a}}{b}$, where $a, b \in \mathbb{N}$.

(SEC 2015)

Solution

(a) Volume $= \dfrac{4}{3}\pi r^3$ ... state the relevant formula

$= \dfrac{4}{3}\pi(1·5)^3$ ... substitute the known variables

$= \dfrac{4}{3}\pi\left(\dfrac{27}{8}\right) = \dfrac{108}{24}\pi = \dfrac{9}{2}\pi$ cm³   ... solve for the required value

(b) Volume of the large sphere $= 3\left(\dfrac{9}{2}\pi\right) = \dfrac{27}{2}\pi$ cm³

$\dfrac{4}{3}\pi r^3 = \dfrac{27}{2}\pi$ ... state the relevant formula and let it equal the given value

$\dfrac{4}{3}r^3 = \dfrac{27}{2}$ ... solve for r

$r^3 = \left(\dfrac{3}{4}\right)\left(\dfrac{27}{2}\right) = \left(\dfrac{81}{8}\right)$

$\Rightarrow r = \sqrt[3]{\dfrac{81}{8}} = \dfrac{\sqrt[3]{81}}{\sqrt[3]{8}} = \dfrac{3\sqrt[3]{3}}{2}$ cm, as required.

Combined 3D shapes

Combined 3D shapes are shapes that are made up of two or more standard shapes added together or subtracted from one and other.

A shape that is made up by adding together two or more standard shapes.

A cone and cylinder combined

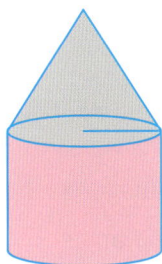

A shape that is made up by subtracting two or more standard shapes.

Two hemispheres removed from a cylinder

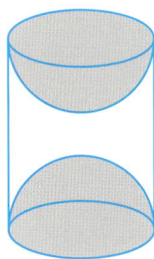

Points to note

In general when solving questions based on combined 3D shapes we follow these steps:

1 Separate the combined shape into standard 3D shapes.
2 State the relevant formula for each 3D shape in the question.
3 Substitute the known variables.
4 Solve for the required value.

Example

A capsule is made up of a cylindrical section and two hemispherical ends. The length of the cylindrical section is 170 cm and the diameter is 84 cm.

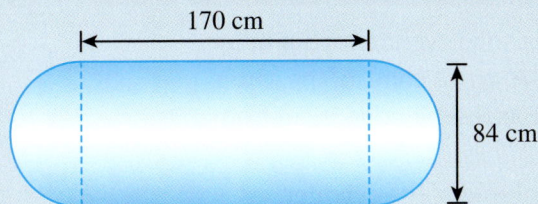

170 cm

84 cm

(a) Find the surface area of the capsule in cm². Give your answer correct to two significant figures.

(b) Find the volume of the capsule in m³. Give your answer correct to two decimal places.

(SEC 2003)

Solution

(a) Always separate the combined shape into standard 3D shapes, in this case a cylinder and sphere.

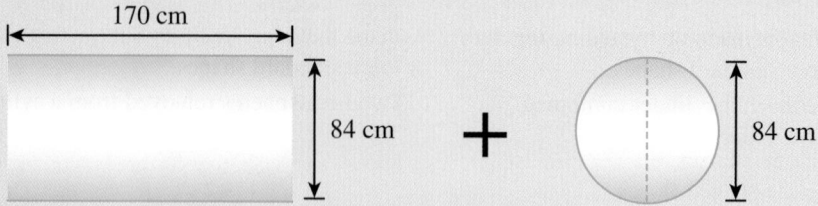

Total surface area = curved surface area of the cylinder + total surface area of the sphere

$= 2\pi rh + 4\pi r^2$ ... state the relevant formula for each 3D shape

$= 2\pi(42)(170) + 4\pi(42)^2$ ... substitute the known variables

$= 14\,280\pi + 7056\pi$ ... solve for the required value

$= 21\,336\pi = 21\,336(3\cdot14) = 66\,995\cdot04$ cm^2 = 67\,000 cm^2 to 2 sig. fig.

(b) Volume of the capsule = volume of the cylinder + volume of the sphere. Note that as the answer is required in m^3, all measurements need to be converted to metres.

Radius of 42 cm: Height of 170 cm:

$42 \text{ cm} = \dfrac{42}{100} = 0\cdot42 \text{ m}$ $170 \text{ cm} = \dfrac{170}{100} = 1\cdot70 \text{ m}$

So total volume $= \pi r^2 h + \dfrac{4}{3}\pi r^3$ ... state the relevant formula for each 3D shape

$= \pi(0\cdot42)^2(1\cdot70) + \dfrac{4}{3}\pi(0\cdot42)^3$ ... substitute the known variables

$= 0\cdot29988\pi + 0\cdot098784\pi$ ... solve for the required value

$= 0\cdot398664\pi = 0\cdot398664(3\cdot14) = 1\cdot25180496$ m^3 = 1\cdot25 m^3 to 2 d.p.

Example

The diagram shows a solid cylinder of diameter 54 cm and of height 70 cm. A cone, of the same diameter and height as the cylinder, is cut from inside the cylinder.

(a) Calculate the volume of the cylinder. Give your answer in terms of π.

(b) Calculate the volume of the cone. Give your answer in terms of π.

(c) What fraction of the cylinder remains after the cone is removed?   (SEC 2011)

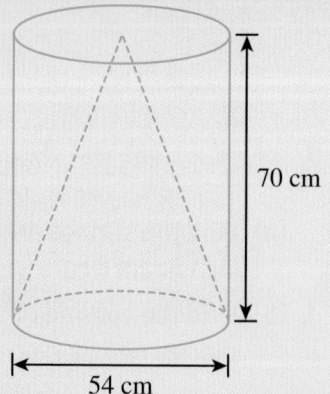

Solution

(a) Volume of a cylinder $= \pi r^2 h$ ... state the relevant formula

$= \pi (27)^2 (70)$ ... substitute the known variables

$= \pi (729)(70) = 51030\pi$ cm^3 ... solve for the required value

(b) Volume of a cone $= \frac{1}{3}\pi r^2 h$ ... state the relevant formula

$= \frac{1}{3}\pi (27)^2 (70)$ ... substitute the known variables

$= \frac{1}{3}(51030\pi) = 17010\pi$ cm^3 ... solve for the required value

(c) Remaining volume = volume of the cylinder – volume of the cone

$= 51030\pi - 17010\pi = 34020\pi$ cm^3

Hence fraction of volume remaining $= \dfrac{34020\,\pi}{51030\,\pi} = \dfrac{2}{3}.$

Example

A shape is made by placing a small cube
on top of a larger one, as shown. The cubes
have edges of length 1 unit and 2 units respectively.

(a) Find the total surface area of this shape.

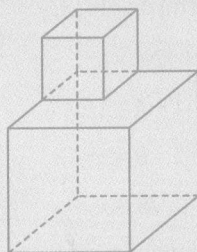

(b) The line segment [AB] is a diagonal
of the base of the shape, as shown.

  (i) Find |AB|. Give your answer in surd form.

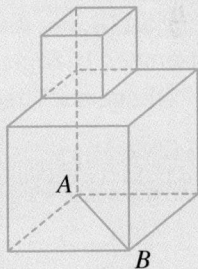

  (ii) The right-angled triangle ABC is constructed
inside this shape, as shown.
Find |BC|. Give your answer in surd form.

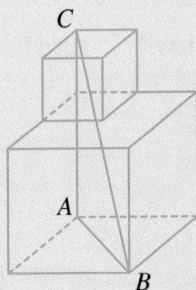

(SEC 2016)

Solution

(a) Total surface area is a combination of:

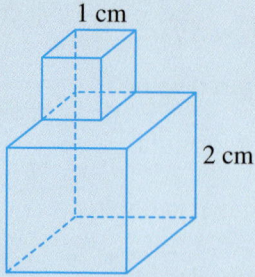

- a 1 cm cube with five sides visible and
- a 2 cm cube with six sides visible with a 1 cm² square removed.

Hence surface area $= 5(1)^2 + 6(2)^2 - (1)^2$

$$= 5 + 24 - 1 = 28 \text{ cm}^2$$

(b) (i) The diagram shows the constructed triangle is a right-angled triangle with the length of two of the sides known. Use Pythagoras' Theorem to solve for the third side, x.

$(2)^2 + (2)^2 = x^2$

$\quad 4 + 4 = x^2$

$\qquad 8 = x^2$

$\quad \sqrt{8} = x$

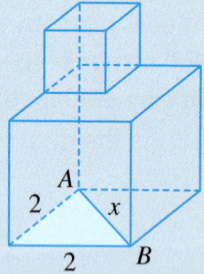

Answer in surd form: $|AB| = \sqrt{8} = 2\sqrt{2}$ cm.

(ii) As for part **(i)**, the diagram shows the constructed triangle is a right-angled triangle with the length of two of the sides known. Use Pythagoras' Theorem to solve for the third side, x.

$(3)^2 + (2\sqrt{2})^2 = x^2$

$\quad 9 + 8 = x^2$

$\qquad 17 = x^2$

$\quad \sqrt{17} = x$

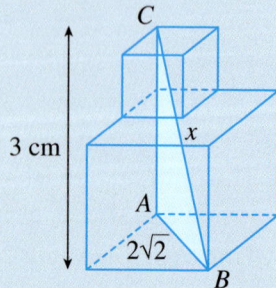

Answer in surd form: $|BC| = \sqrt{17}$ cm.

Displacement of liquid

Displacement of liquid refers to when an object is placed into liquid: this will cause the liquid to rise, and the rise in liquid is equal to the volume of the object.

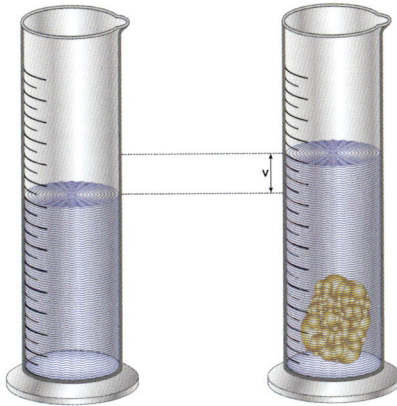

Example

A spherical golf ball has a diameter of 4 cm.

(a) Find the volume of the golf ball in terms of π.

A cylindrical hole on a golf course is 10 cm in diameter and 12 cm deep. The hole is half full of water.

(b) Calculate the volume of water in the hole, in terms of π.

The golf ball is dropped into the hole.

(c) Find the rise in the level of the water, correct to two decimal places.

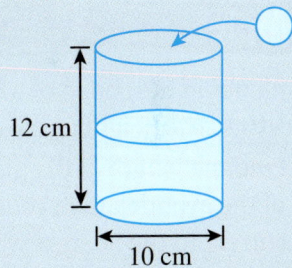

12 cm

10 cm

(SEC 2008)

Solution

(a) Volume of the golf ball (sphere) $= \dfrac{4}{3}\pi r^3$ ... state the relevant formula

$= \dfrac{4}{3}\pi(2)^3$ ... substitute the known variable

$= \dfrac{4}{3}\pi(8) = \dfrac{32}{3}\pi = 10{\cdot}67\,\pi \text{ cm}^3$ ... solve for the required value

(b) Volume of the water in the cylinder

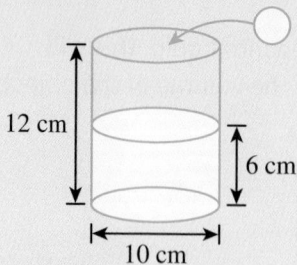

Volume : $\pi r^2 h$ ... state the relevant formula

$= \pi (5)^2 (6)$ ... substitute the known variables

$= \pi (25)(6) = 150\pi$ cm³ ... solve for the required value

(c) Let the rise of water in the cylinder $= h$. The volume of this part of the cylinder is therefore $\pi r^2 h$. So as the ball has a volume of $\frac{32}{3}\pi$ cm³:

$\pi r^2 h = \dfrac{32\pi}{3}$ ... state the relevant formula and let it equal the given value

$\pi (5)^2 h = \dfrac{32\pi}{3}$ ... substitute the known variables

$25h = \dfrac{32}{3}$ ... solve for the required value

$h = \dfrac{32}{3(25)} = \dfrac{32}{75} = 0.42666... = 0.43$ cm to 2 d.p.

Example

A container in the shape of a cylinder has a capacity of 50 litres. The height of the cylinder is 0·7 m.

(a) Find the length of the diameter of the cylinder. Give your answer correct to the nearest whole number.

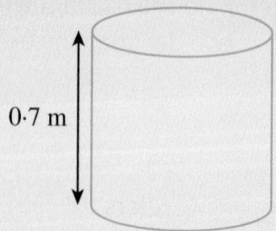

(b) A rectangular tank has a length of 0·6 m, a width of 0·35 m and its height measures 15 cm. Find the capacity of the rectangular tank.

(c) The rectangular tank is full of water. This water is then poured into the cylindrical container in **(a)** above. Find the depth of water in the cylinder. Give your answer correct to one decimal place.

(SEC 2012)

Solutions

(a) First change all measurements to the same unit. **Note: 1 litre = 1000 cm^3.**

50 litres = 50 000 cm^3 and 0·7 m = 70 cm

Volume of the cylinder = $\pi r^2 h$. Therefore:

$\pi r^2 h = 50\,000$ ... state the relevant formula and let it equal the given value

$\pi r^2 (70) = 50\,000$ ... substitute the known variables

$r^2 = \dfrac{50\,000}{\pi(70)} = 227 \cdot 36$ ... solve for the unknown value

$\Rightarrow r = \sqrt{227 \cdot 36} = 15 \cdot 08 = 15$ cm to the nearest whole number.

(b) Volume = $l \times w \times h$ ... state the relevant formula

         = $60 \times 35 \times 15$ ... substitute the known variables

         = 31 500 cm^3 ... solve for the required value

Hence capacity in litres = $\dfrac{31\,500 \text{ cm}^3}{1000} = 31 \cdot 5$ litres.

(c) Let the rise of water in the cylinder = h. The volume of this part of the cylinder is therefore $\pi r^2 h$. As the ball has a volume of 31 500 cm^3:

$\pi r^2 h = 31\,500$ ... state the relevant formula and let it equal the given value

$\pi (15)^2 h = 31\,500$ ... substitute the known variables

$\pi (225) h = 31\,500$ ... solve for the required value

$h = \dfrac{31\,500}{225\pi} = 44 \cdot 5634 = 44 \cdot 6$ cm, correct to 1 d.p.

Recasting

Recasting refers to melting down a given object and reforming it into another shape of the same volume.

A steelworks buys steel in the form of solid cylindrical rods of radius 10 centimetres and length 30 metres. The steel rods are melted to produce solid spherical ball-bearings. No steel is wasted in the process.

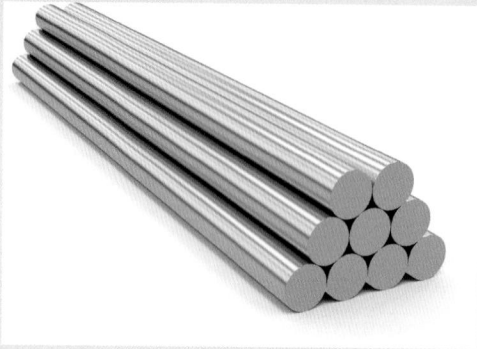

(a) Find the volume of steel in one cylindrical rod, in terms of π.

(b) If the radius of a ball-bearing is 2 centimetres, how many such ball-bearings can be made from one steel rod?

(c) Ball-bearings of a different size are also produced. One steel rod makes 225 000 of these new ball-bearings. Find the radius of the new ball-bearings.

Solution

(a) First, all measurements need to be converted to the same unit, cm or m. Here, we will convert all measurements to cm.

Length of 30 m: 30 m = 30(100) = 3000 cm

Volume of a cylinder: $\pi r^2 h$ ... state the relevant formula

$= \pi (10)^2 (3000)$ ... substitute the known variables

$= \pi (100)(3000) = 300\,000\pi \, cm^3$ ... solve for the required value

(b) Volume of a ball-bearing = volume of a sphere $= \dfrac{4}{3}\pi r^3$

$\dfrac{4}{3}\pi r^3$ ... state the relevant formula

$= \dfrac{4}{3}\pi (2)^3$ ... substitute the known variables

$= \dfrac{4}{3}\pi (8) = \dfrac{32}{3}\pi \, cm^2$ ... solve for the required value

Hence number of ball-bearings $= \dfrac{300\,000\,\pi}{\dfrac{32}{3}\pi} = 28\,125.$

(c) Total volume of 225 000 ball-bearings = $225\,000\left(\frac{4}{3}\pi r^3\right)$.

$225\,000\left(\frac{4}{3}\pi r^3\right) = 300\,000\,\pi$ ... state the relevant formula and let it equal the given value

$\Rightarrow \frac{4}{3}r^3 = \frac{4}{3}$ ... solve for the required value

$\Rightarrow r^3 = \left(\frac{3}{4}\right)\left(\frac{4}{3}\right) = 1$

Hence $r = \sqrt[3]{1} = 1$ cm.

Flow of liquid

This section shows how to solve problems in which liquid is flowing from one container into another container.

Points to note

The flow rate of a liquid is the measure of the volume of liquid that passes through a pipe or container per second.

Formula for the flow rate:

Flow rate through a pipe = cross-sectional area × the speed

$$= \pi r^2 \times speed$$

The unit of flow rate

Flow rate is measured in cm^3/s or m^3/s.

Example

Water flows through a cylindrical pipe with radius 2 cm at a speed of 20 cm/s into a rectangular tank with base 90 cm by 60 cm. What is the height of the water after 10 minutes? Take $\pi = 3.14$, and give your answer correct to one decimal place.

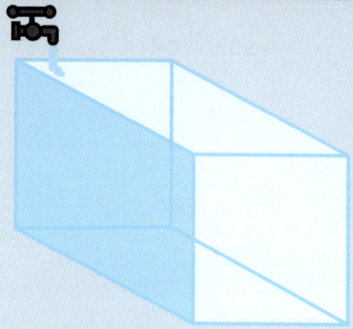

Solution

Flow rate through a pipe = cross-sectional area × speed

$$= \pi r^2 \times \text{speed}$$

$$= (3.14)(2)^2 \times 20$$

$$= 251.2 \text{ cm}^3/\text{s}$$

Length of time the water is flowing through the pipe = 10 minutes = 10(60) = 600 seconds.

Therefore total volume of water that has flown through the pipe in 10 minutes = $251.2 \times 600 = 150\,720 \text{ cm}^3$.

Let the rise of water in the tank = h. Then:

$l \times w \times h = 150\,720$ ... state the relevant formula and let it equal the given value

$90 \times 60 \times h = 150\,720$ ... substitute the known variables

$5400h = 150\,720$ ... solve for the required value

Hence $h = \dfrac{150\,720}{5400} = 27.9111 = 27.9$ cm, correct to 1 d.p.

Exercise

Q1 The perimeter of a rectangle is 200 cm. If length : breadth = 3 : 2, find the area of the rectangle.   *(SEC 2004)*

Q2 The perimeter of a square lawn is 96 m.

     (a) Find the area of the lawn in m².

     (b) A garden roller, in the shape of a cylinder, has a diameter of 75 cm and is 1 m wide, as shown in the diagram. Calculate the curved surface area of the roller in m² correct to one decimal place. Take $\pi = 3.14$.

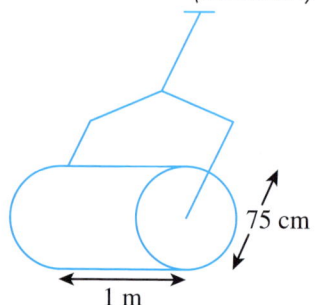

75 cm

1 m

(c) What percentage of the lawn will be
rolled when the roller has completed nine revolutions?　　*(SEC 2006)*

Q3 A solid cone has a vertical height of 4 cm. The radius of its base is 3 cm.

(a) Find, in terms of π, the volume of the cone.

(b) Find, in terms of π, the curved surface area of the cone.

Q4 A solid metal cylinder has height 20 cm and diameter 14 cm.

(a) Find its curved surface area in terms of π.

A hemisphere with diameter 14 cm is
removed from the top of this cylinder, as shown.

(b) Find the total surface area of the remaining
solid in terms of π.　　*(SEC 2005)*

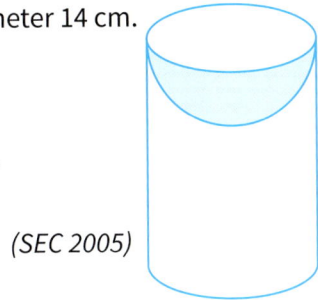

Q5 A hot water container is in the shape of a
hemisphere on top of a cylinder, as shown.
The hemisphere has a radius of 25 cm and
the container has a height of 90 cm. Find the
internal volume of the container in litres, giving
your answer correct to the nearest litre.

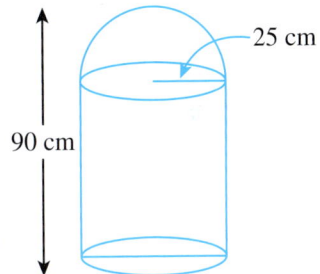

　　　　　　　　　　　　　　　(SEC 2007)

25 cm

90 cm

Q6 A packet of sweets is in the shape of a closed triangular-based prism. It has
a height of 8 cm and a triangular base with sides of length 4 cm, 4 cm, and
6 cm. Construct an accurate net of the prism. Show all of your construction
lines clearly.　　*(SEC 2016)*

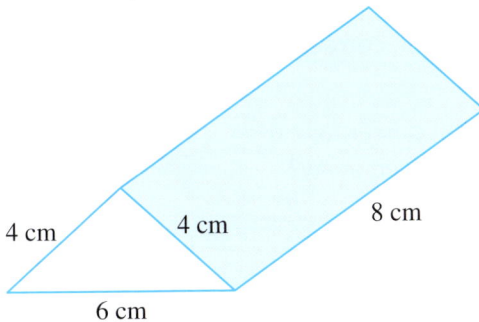

4 cm　　4 cm　　8 cm

6 cm

Q7 A solid rectangular metal block has length 12 cm and width 5 cm.
The volume of the block is 90 cm^3.

(a) Find the height of the block in cm.

(b) Find the total surface area of the block in cm^2.

(c) Each cm^3 of the metal has mass 8·4 g. The total mass of a number of
these metal blocks is 113·4 kg. How many blocks are there?

　　　　　　　　　　　　　　　　　(SEC 2003)

Q8 A solid metal hemisphere has a radius of 12 cm.

   (a) Calculate the volume of the hemisphere.
      Give your answer in terms of π.

   (b) A solid cone of radius 4 cm and
      height 12 cm is cut from the hemisphere.
      Calculate the volume of the cone. Give your answer in terms of π.

   (c) The remaining metal in the hemisphere is melted down and recast into
      cones of the same dimensions as the cone above. How many cones can
      be formed from the remaining metal?

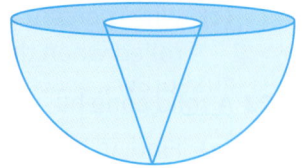

(SEC 2013)

Q9 (a) The volume of a sphere is 36π cm³. Find the
     radius of the sphere.

   (b) When the sphere is fully immersed in a
      cylinder of water, the level of the water
      rises by 2·25 cm. Find the radius of the cylinder.

Q10 An ornament is carved from a rectangular block of wood which has a
    square base and a height of 24 cm. The ornament
    consists of two identical spheres and two identical
    cubes as illustrated in the diagram. The diameter of
    each sphere is equal to the length of the side of
    each cube. The ornament has the same width as the
    original block.

   (a) Find the length of a side of one of the cubes.

   (b) Find the volume of the ornament, correct to
      one decimal place.

   (c) In making the ornament, what percentage of
      the original block of wood is carved away?

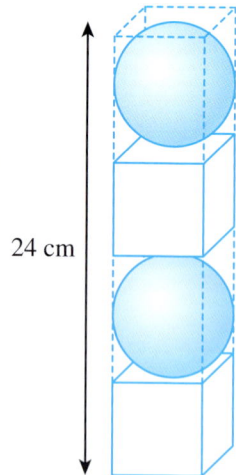

24 cm

(SEC 2012)

Q11 The diagram shows a rectangle of length 42 cm.
    The area of the rectangle is 966 cm².

   (a) Find the height of the rectangle.

   (b) Find the area of the shaded triangle.

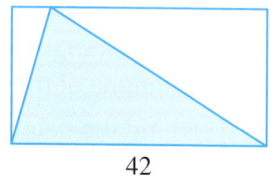

42

Solutions

Q1 First draw a sketch.

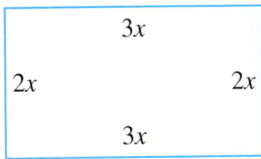

Given the perimeter of the rectangle is 200 cm:

$3x + 2x + 3x + 2x = 200$ ... state the relevant formula and let it equal the given value

$10x = 200$ ... substitute the known variables

$x = \dfrac{200}{10} = 20$ ... solve for the unknown value

Area of the rectangle = length × breadth

$= 2x \times 3x = 2(20) \times 3(20) = 40 \times 60 = 2400 \text{ cm}^2$

Q2 (a) Let the side of the square $= x$. Then

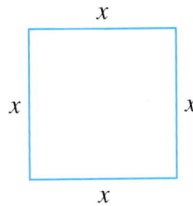

$4x = 96$

$\Rightarrow x = \dfrac{96}{4} = 24 \text{ m}$

So area of the lawn $= x^2 = (24)^2 = 576 \text{ m}^2$.

(b) As the answer is required in m^2, covert all measurements to metres.

Diameter = 75 cm

Therefore the cylinder has a radius of $= \dfrac{75}{2} \text{ cm} = 37\cdot5 \text{ cm}$

$= \dfrac{37\cdot5}{100} \text{ m} = 0\cdot375 \text{ m}.$

Curved surface area $= 2\pi r h$ ... state the relevant formula

$= 2\pi(0\cdot375)(1)$ ... substitute the known variables

$= 2(3\cdot14)(0\cdot375)(1) = 2\cdot355 \text{ m}^2$

$= 2\cdot4 \text{ m}^2$ to 1 d.p.   ... solve for the required value

(c) Area covered in nine revolutions $= 2\cdot4 \times 9 = 21\cdot6 \text{ m}^2$.

Hence % completed by nine revolutions $= \dfrac{21\cdot6}{576} \times 100 = 3\cdot75\%$

Q3 (a) Volume of a cone $= \dfrac{1}{3}\pi r^2 h$ ... state the relevant formula

$= \dfrac{1}{3}\pi(3)^2(4)$ ... substitute the known variables

$= \dfrac{1}{3}\pi(36) = 12\pi \text{ cm}^3$ ... solve for the required value

(b) Curved surface area: πrl. So first find l, using Pythagoras' Theorem.

$l^2 = (4)^2 + (3)^2 = 16 + 9 = 25$

$l = \sqrt{25} = 5$ cm

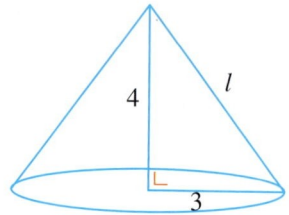

Total surface area $= \pi rl$	... state the relevant formula
$= \pi(3)(5)$	... substitute the known variables
$= 15\pi$ cm^2	... solve for the required value

Q4 (a)

Curved surface area $= 2\pi rh$	... state the relevant formula
$= 2\pi(7)(20)$	... substitute the known variables
$= 280\pi$ cm^2	... solve for the required value

(b) Let total surface area $= T$.

Then $T =$ curved surface area of the cylinder + area of circle + curved surface area of hemisphere.

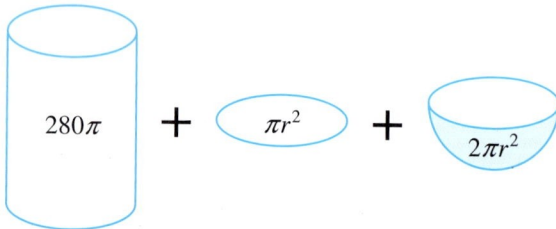

$T = 280\pi + \pi r^2 + 2\pi r^2$	... state the relevant formulae
$= 280\pi + \pi(7)^2 + 2\pi(7)^2$	... substitute the known variables
$= 280\pi + 49\pi + 98\pi = 427\pi$ cm^2	... solve for the required value

Q5 Total volume of the shape = cylinder + hemisphere.

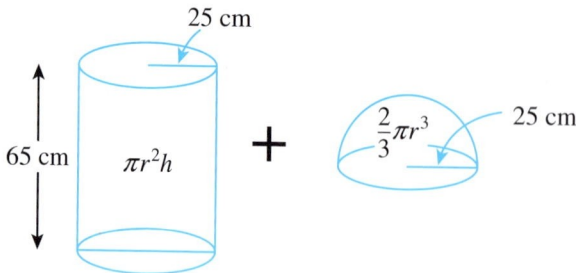

Total volume $= \pi r^2 h + \dfrac{2}{3}\pi r^3$	... state the relevant formulae
$= \pi(25)^2(65) + \dfrac{2}{3}\pi(25)^3$	... substitute the known variables
$= 40\,625\pi + 10\,416{\cdot}66667\pi$	... solve for the required value

$= 51041{\cdot}66667\pi = 160\,352{\cdot}125$ cm^3

Hence volume in litres $= \dfrac{160\,352{\cdot}125}{1000} = 160{\cdot}352125 = 160$ to the nearest litre.

Q6 Note: this diagram is not to scale.

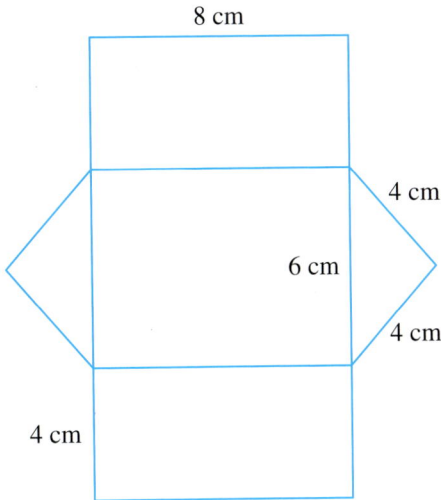

8 cm

4 cm

6 cm

4 cm

4 cm

Q7 (a) Volume $= l \times w \times h$ ... state the relevant formula

$(12)(5)h = 90$ ... substitute the known variables

$h = \dfrac{90}{60} = 1 \cdot 5$ cm   ... solve for the required value

(b) Surface area $= 2(l \times w) + 2(w \times h) + 2(l \times h)$ ... state the relevant formula

$= 2(5)(12) + 2(12)(1\cdot5) + 2(5)(1\cdot5)$ ... substitute the known variables

$= 120 + 36 + 15 = 171$ cm^2 ... solve for the required value

(c) First convert the total mass from kg to g. **Note: 1 kg = 1000 g.**

$113 \cdot 4$ kg $= 113\,400$ g

Mass of one block $= 90 \times 8 \cdot 4$ g $= 756$ g

Hence number of blocks $= \dfrac{113\,400 \text{ g}}{756 \text{ g}} = 150.$

Q8 (a) Volume of hemisphere $= \dfrac{2}{3}\pi r^3$ ... state the relevant formula

$= \dfrac{2}{3}\pi (12)^3$ ... substitute the known variables

$= \dfrac{2}{3}\pi (1728) = \dfrac{3456}{3}\pi = 1152\pi$ cm^3 ... solve for the required value

(b) Volume of cone $= \dfrac{1}{3}\pi r^2 h$ ... state the relevant formula

$= \dfrac{1}{3}\pi (4)^2 (12)$ ... substitute the known variables

$= \dfrac{1}{3}\pi (16)(12) = \dfrac{192}{3}\pi = 64\pi$ cm^3 ... solve for the required value

(c) The volume of the remaining metal

= volume of the hemisphere – volume of the cone

$= 1152\pi - 64\pi = 1088\pi$ cm^3

Hence number of cones that can be made $= \dfrac{1088\pi}{64\pi} = 17.$

Q9 (a) Volume of the sphere $= \dfrac{4}{3}\pi r^3$ ... state the relevant formula

$\dfrac{4}{3}\pi r^3 = 36\pi$ ... substitute the known variables

$\dfrac{4}{3}r^3 = 36$ ... solve for the required value

$r^3 = \left(\dfrac{3}{4}\right)36 = \left(\dfrac{108}{4}\right) = 27 \Rightarrow r = \sqrt[3]{27} = 3$ cm.

(b) Let the rise in height $= h$. The volume of this part of the cylinder is therefore $\pi r^2 h$. So as the ball has a volume of 36π cm^3:

$\pi r^2 h = 36\pi$ ... state the relevant formula and let it equal the given value

$\pi r^2 (2\cdot 25) = 36\pi$ ... substitute the known variables

$\pi r^2 (2\cdot 25) = 36\pi$ ... solve for the required value

$r^2 (2\cdot 25) = 36 \Rightarrow r^2 = \dfrac{36}{2\cdot 25} = 16$

Hence $r = \sqrt{16} = 4$ cm.

Q10 (a) From the diagram, the length of one side of the cube is $= \dfrac{24}{4} = 6$ cm.

(b) Total volume is made up of two cubes of side 6 cm and two spheres of diameter 6 cm.

$= 2(x)^3 + 2\left(\dfrac{4}{3}\pi r^3\right)$ ... state the relevant formula

$= 2(6)^3 + 2\left(\dfrac{4}{3}\pi (3)^3\right)$ ... substitute the known variables

$= 432 + 72\pi$ ... solve for the required value

$= 432 + 226\cdot 1946711$

$= 658\cdot 1945711$ cm$^3 = 658\cdot 2$ cm^3, correct to 1 d.p.

(c) The total volume of the block before carving $= 24 \times 6 \times 6 = 864$ cm^3

The volume of wood carved away $= 864$ cm$^3 - 658\cdot 2$ cm$^3 = 205\cdot 8$ cm^3

Hence, the percentage of the original block of wood that was carved away

$= \dfrac{205\cdot 8}{864} \times \dfrac{100}{1} = 23\cdot 82\%$

Q11 (a) Area of the rectangle $= 966$ cm^2.

So $l \times h = 966$ cm^2

$42 \times h = 966$

$\Rightarrow h = \dfrac{966}{42} = 23$ cm.

(b) Area of the triangle $= \dfrac{1}{2} \times l \times h = \dfrac{1}{2} \times 42 \times 23 = 483$ cm^2.